CW01072791

ISBN 978-90-04-22634-0

Full text of the lecture published in October 2011 in the *Recueil des cours*, Vol. 348 (2010).

Cover illustration : A photograph by Marie Bogdan, 2011.

HAGUE ACADEMY OF INTERNATIONAL LAW

*A collection of law lectures
in pocketbook form*

AIL-POCKET

2012

Private International Law
as Component of the Law
of the Forum

Private International Law as Component of the Law of the Forum

General Course

MICHAEL BOGDAN

TABLE OF CONTENTS

CHAPTER I

THE PURPOSE OF THIS GENERAL COURSE

According to the web-page of the Hague Academy of International Law, the purpose of the General Course on Private International Law, given each Summer within the framework of the Academy's programme, is to address in depth the trends and main features of private international law and offer students a comprehensive view of the subject. More than five years ago, in his letter inviting me on behalf of the Curatorium of the Academy to deliver the general course in 2010, the Secretary-General of the Academy, Professor Yves Daudet, informed me that the general course is designed to give the professor who is responsible for it the possibility to emphasize the aspects of private international law he is most interested in, leaving him entirely free as to the direction of the course.

In order to find out more about what is expected of me I have, therefore, taken a look at most of the previous general courses and I have became much impressed by their quality, both regarding contents and the manner of presentation. This has made me realize that it will be difficult to say something that has not been said before, often in a fashion much superior to that I am capable of. I have now a better understanding of what Professor Yvon Loussouarn had in mind when he called being invited to give the general course a *"redoutable privilège"*, a frightening privilege[1].

---

[1] Y. Loussouarn, *Recueil des cours*, Vol. 139 (1973), p. 275.

Reading the published general courses since their early volumes[2] takes the reader on an exciting journey through an ocean (or at least a lake) of multiple academic theories, some of them ephemeral and some of a more durable value; the cruise is almost comprehensive as there were relatively few internationally known scholars in the field who were not invited, sooner or later and some more than once, to present their ideas at the Academy. I have, therefore, decided to use, whenever possible, the *Recueil des cours* as the main source in the footnotes in the printed version of these lectures, rather than quoting the original works that made the various lecturer's ideas known in the global private international law community. The *Recueil* is readily available in many law libraries and it seems to me that the published courses are more pedagogical and often provide a more lucid picture of the author's theories than his earlier publications, probably because by the time of the lectures the ideas had matured and the lecturer has had the opportunity to test and polish them through scientific dialogues with critical colleagues[3].

I have noted that most of my learned predecessors had either focused on some of the current trends in the development of our field of law or critically revisited some of its traditional general problems. While some have produced a coherent and comprehensive treatise on private intenational law, others preferred to pick

---

[2] The first course devoted to private international law appears to have been A. Pillet's "Théorie continentale des conflits de lois", *Recueil des cours*, Vol. 2 (1924), pp. 447-483.

[3] It is also noticeable that the published, written versions of the recent general courses seem to differ substantially from the oral lectures they are supposed to reflect. In particular, the size of some of the published versions exceeds clearly what is humanly possible to cover during the time scheduled for the oral presentations.

cherries out of the cake and presented a set of lectures dealing with a number of selected issues. Another difference among the general courses is that some professors tried to deal with the subject in a truly general manner, which is sometimes reflected in the fact that they gave their course the simple title "General Course on Private International Law"[4], while others attempted to give their presentation a special, personal touch, mainly by discussing the issues from a special angle, often expressed in a more refined title or sub-title of their course[5]. In my opinion, all these approaches are fully legitimate.

I have chosen to devote my lectures to a critical review of most of the well-known — one might be tempted to say notorious — general problems of private international law as opposed to our subject's special part composed of specific conflict rules for marriage, succession, contracts, torts, etc. The review will be carried out with a special emphasis on the fact that private international law is basically a part of the legal system (in a wider sense) of the forum country. I am aware of the fact that some of my colleagues do not share my interest in our subject's general problems such as preliminary (incidental) issues, *renvoi* or classification and consider them to be parts of the disease

---

[4] See, for example, F. K. Juenger, *Recueil des cours*, Vol. 193 (1985), pp. 119-387; Y. Loussouarn, *Recueil des cours*, Vol. 139 (1973), pp. 271-385; A. Philip, *Recueil des cours*, Vol. 160 (1978), pp. 1-73; W. L. M. Reese, *Recueil des cours*, Vol. 150 (1976), pp. 1-193; F. Vischer, *Recueil des cours*, Vol. 232 (1992), pp. 9-255; E. Vitta, *Recueil des cours*, Vol. 162 (1979), pp. 9-243.

[5] See, for example, H. Gaudemet-Tallon, *Recueil des cours*, Vol. 312 (2005), pp. 1-489; J. D. González Campos, *Recueil des cours*, Vol. 287 (2000), pp. 9-438; T. C. Hartley, *Recueil des cours*, Vol. 319 (2006), pp. 11-324; E. Jayme, *Recueil des cours*, Vol. 251 (1995), pp. 9-367.

rather than parts of the cure[6]. A general course on private international law must, however, deal with the subject's general part rather than with specific rules on contracts, torts, marriages or successions. Furthermore, I shall attempt to demonstrate that far from being artificial inventions, the treatment of the general issues has highly practical consequences that cannot be ignored or avoided but have to be dealt with in one way or another.

What has just been said is related to an additional way of dividing the published general courses. It seems to me, with all due respect for my learned colleagues and predecessors, that some of them have decided to affirm and strengthen the common prejudice that private international law is a very difficult and complicated area of law, "inhabited by learned but excentric professors who theorize about mysterious matters in a strange and incomprehensible jargon"[7]. It has been asserted that judges, law students and practising lawyers fear problems of private international law nature like practically no other area of law. This preju-

---

[6] See, for example, F. K. Juenger, *Recueil des cours*, Vol. 193 (1985), p. 191, commenting on the "General Part" of Conflicts Law:

"The very nature of the problems that are the subject of this peculiar branch of our discipline ought to shake the belief in the power of conceptualism to resolve multistate problems. But instead of recognizing them as symptoms of an underlying malaise, traditionalists tend to be proud of the strange conundrums engendered by the system to which they are beholden. The 'discovery' of each of these self-inflicted embarrassments has been celebrated as a major intellectual breakthrough, even though what lurked in the dark should have been apparent from the outset."

[7] Dean Prosser, quoted from F. K. Juenger, *Recueil des cours*, Vol. 193 (1985), p. 131.

dice is not new; an American judge almost two centuries ago called our subject

> "the most intricate and perplexed of any that has occupied the attention of lawyers and courts: one on which scarcely any two writers are found to entirely agree, and on which it is rare to find one consistent with himself throughout"[8].

Private international law professors have even been accused of being "drunk on theories"[9] and of using the subject as "playground for their abstract activity". It has also been asked whether the intellectually fascinating nature of private international law and the intellectual satisfaction it gives are not in fact its main curse and a great evil[10].

It must be admitted that if legal writers and teachers can be divided into complicators and simplifiers, too many of the general courses at this Academy have perhaps been given by the former. It is also true that many legal scholars seem to consider it as their principal target to provide private international law with a theoretical framework of their own, trying almost desperately to invent new and esoteric terms and concepts, and stressing hair-splitting differences in relation to previous theories, while forgetting that the main purpose of the subject is to find reasonable solutions for everyday practical problems arising out of cross-border family relationships and commerce. Many of the published theories dealing with the general problems of private

---

[8] Judge Porter in a judgment delivered in 1827 by the Louisiana Supreme Court, as quoted by F. K. Juenger, *Recueil des cours*, Vol. 193 (1985), p. 166.

[9] See reference in F. K. Juenger, *Recueil des cours*, Vol. 193 (1985), p. 320.

[10] See O. Kahn-Freund, *Recueil des cours*, Vol. 143 (1974), pp. 446 and 466. See also P. Lalive, *Recueil des cours*, Vol. 155 (1977), pp. 84-85.

international law are too abstract and complicated for practical use[11]. Maybe at least some part of the explanation of this tradition lies in the high ambitions of the writers in this field, who aspire to construct logical and comprehensive approaches that foresee all possible situations and try to solve them in advance[12]. Another partial explanation of the more theoretical than practical value of many theories in this field may lie in the fact that problems of private international law nature used primarily to concern people belonging to high commercial and aristocratic circles and did not affect the everyday life of the common people, who had very little contact with foreigners and foreign countries. The situation has changed, however, with the advent of such phenomena as, for example, mass migration, cheap travel and the Internet. As it was put by one author, the international character of private-law relationships "est passé de l'extraordinaire à l'ordinaire" and this has made private international law to become commonplace ("banalisé")[13].

I am proud of belonging rather to the category of simplifiers, perhaps because of living and working under the everyday influence of Scandinavian legal pragmatism[14]. I am afraid that I cannot claim credit for any revolutionary discovery — or rather invention — of any brand-new principle or theory of private international law, and I cannot even pride myself on the cre-

---

[11] See T. C. Hartley, *International Commercial Litigation*, p. 512.

[12] See *ibid.*, p. 511.

[13] See C. P. Pamboukis, *Recueil des cours*, Vol. 330 (2007), p. 87.

[14] This pragmatism, combined with an aversion towards conceptualism, is one of the reasons why, in spite of their preference for statutory rather than judge-made law, the Nordic countries have not adopted systematic civil codes similar to the French code civil or the German BGB.

ation of any brand-new term or concept. Most of my opinions are within the mainstream thinking and they may even be accused of being traditional, which in certain quarters is a serious accusation indeed.

I hope that the relative simplicity of my theoretical approaches will not cause a disappointment to those who believe that there must be something wrong with a simple answer to a legal question. There is, of course, nothing wrong with a good theory and it seems to lie in the nature of private international law to attract the attention of legal theoreticians [15]. On the other hand, as it was put by Professor David McClean, who gave this General Course in 2000, "[l]awyers should not be afraid of simplicity" [16]. It is also worth noting that in spite of centuries of theoretical debates, many of the fundamental principles and methods of "that dark science called the conflict of laws" [17] remain controversial and that the few theories that seemed for a time to have won universal or almost universal acclaim became quickly challenged by the next generation of authors [18].

The approach used in the following is basically comparative, which has become usual in the last decades and contrasts with the early general courses presenting mostly the state of private international law in the country of the lecturer [19]. I have chosen to use, in addition to examples taken from international instru-

---

[15] See B. Oppetit, *Recueil des cours*, Vol. 234 (1992), pp. 331-433.

[16] See D. McClean, *Recueil des cours*, Vol. 282 (2000), p. 63.

[17] In the words of Professor John Dawson of Harvard Law School, as quoted by H. H. Kay, *Recueil des cours*, Vol. 215 (1989), p. 21.

[18] See F. Vischer, *Recueil des cours*, Vol. 232 (1992), p. 21.

[19] See references in E. Vitta, *Recueil des cours*, Vol. 162 (1979), p. 21.

ments and the large and important countries, even examples taken from Swedish private international law. Swedish conflict rules, whether statutory or judge-made, are as such neither more nor less suitable for this purpose than the corresponding rules of other countries, but they are of course the rules that I know best. Besides, I must confess that I find it difficult to resist the temptation to use this opportunity to make Swedish private international law better known among foreign colleagues.

Private international law (in English-speaking countries more often called "conflict of laws") in the narrowest sense is a field of law composed merely of conflict rules, i.e., rules designating the legal system governing the substance of a private-law [20] dispute having international character. In a wider sense it includes

---

[20] Legal relationships and disputes having international character exist also in public-law matters (administrative law, criminal law, etc.), and they may give rise to problems that are seemingly similar to those governed by private international law, such as the determination of geographical limits of application of national law, the jurisdiction of courts, and the recognition of foreign decisions. However, the issues and methods are different, in particular because normally it is only regarding private-law disputes that national courts consider applying foreign law or recognizing/enforcing foreign decisions. In some countries, the concept of private international law is much wider and includes, at least for pedagogical purposes, even some public-law issues (such as the acquisition and loss of citizenship, see B. Audit, *Droit international privé*, pp. 16-18; C. Kessedjian, *Recueil des cours*, Vol. 300 (2002), p. 122) and international criminal law (such as the jurisdiction of courts in penal proceedings), but these lectures limit themselves to civil matters and civil proceedings. The definition of the scope of private international law varies somewhat from country to country and is of purely academic or pedagogical importance, without direct relevance for the solution of concrete legal problems, see A. Philip, *Recueil des cours*, Vol. 160 (1978), p. 12.

also the rules concerning the special procedural issues arising in disputes having international implications, such as rules on the jurisdiction of courts and recognition and enforcement of foreign judgments[21]. All these rules are mutually connected. It is, for example, obvious that a restrictive approach to the recognition and enforcement of foreign judgments necessitates wider jurisdictional rules in order to avoid a legal vacuum and that wider jurisdictional rules will, in turn, lead to a more frequent application of foreign law, as the courts will have to deal with more cross-border situations[22]. Nevertheless, for practical reasons and in conformity with the traditions set by most of the previous general courses on private international law, this course will pay attention mainly — albeit not exclusively — to rules of conflict of laws and deal only to a lesser extent with jurisdictional rules and rules on the recognition and enforcement of judgments.

The fact that these lectures focus on conflict rules should not be understood as to mean that such rules are more important than the rules on jurisdiction or recognition/enforcement of judgments. The opposite may be closer to the truth. In fact, it can be argued that conflict rules are less important than the rules on jurisdiction, as the latter are decisive for the outcome of more disputes. It is not unusual that the same parties that have spent much time and incurred much cost on the jurisdictional issue give up or settle once that issue has been decided, simply because a final decision on the competent forum often determines whether a continued litigation is worthwhile or not[23]. To some extent this

---

[21] See A. V. M. Struycken, *Recueil des cours*, Vol. 311 (2004), pp. 189-190.

[22] See Chapter IV.3, *infra*.

[23] See, for example, T. C. Hartley, *International Commercial Litigation*, pp. 5-6.

depends on the almost universal principle that the court will apply the substantive rules designated by the conflict rules of the forum country, so that the determination of jurisdiction amounts, indirectly, also to the determination of the applicable law. At least as important, however, is that many aspects of procedure will be governed by the *lex fori*, for example the discovery and admissibility of evidence, the duty of the losing party to pay the winning party's costs or the availability of a jury trial. The prospects of having the future judgment enforced may also depend on the country where it has been rendered. The risk of high costs caused by judicial proceedings in a distant country, including exorbitant court or counsel fees, may suffice to discourage a potential plaintiff from bringing an action or compel the potential defendant to settle the case. The lack of confidence in the quality and impartiality of the courts in a particular country may have a similar effect.

A discussion about private international law as part of the law of the forum country might tend to see the conflict rules mainly from the viewpoint of a court or another official judicial or administrative authority[24] facing the task of making decisions according to the law and, consequently, occasionally facing the need to apply foreign legal rules. It is, however, important to keep in mind that private international law issues are frequently also encountered by practising lawyers, such as advocates and legal consultants, without there being any pending or forthcoming litigation. For example, while a court may have to decide whether a contract is valid under the legal system applicable to it, a legal consultant may have been asked to draft the contract so

---

[24] In the following, the terms "court", "judge" etc. are used to refer to any public authority making decisions according to the law.

that it fulfils the requirements imposed on it by the applicable law. As the purpose of the consultant's efforts is to anticipate and satisfy the law that would be applied by the courts in the case of a dispute, the fundamental questions discussed in these lectures are just as relevant for him as for a judge. However, the private international law problems facing a legal consultant are at times much more complicated and sophisticated than those confronting a judge. For example, while a judge can normally limit himself to applying the law determined by the conflict rules of the forum country and pronouncing a judgment on a contract's validity in that country, a legal consultant assisting in the making of a contract may be asked to make sure that the contract will be valid in several specified countries, and is thus compelled to take into account also the conflict rules of all of these countries as well as the substantive rules of the legal systems applicable under these conflict rules. Such and other similar efforts to prevent potential problems caused by the situation's connection with several countries, often denoted "conflict avoidance"[25], may have different forms depending, *inter alia*, on the availability of information. Sometimes it is simplest and most practical to satisfy the substantive-law requirements of all those legal systems that can conceivably be applicable. Thus, when drafting a will for a Nepalese citizen domiciled in Sweden, a Swedish lawyer asked to make a will which is to be used in both Sweden and Nepal may find it easier to comply with the substantive formal requirements of both countries than to find out which of the two legal systems would be used by Swedish and Nepalese courts when examining the will's validity as to form. It must also be remembered that the lawyers' time does not come free.

---

[25] See, for example, O. Kahn-Freund, *Recueil des cours*, Vol. 143 (1974), pp. 159-261.

If the value of the transaction at stake is limited, for example if the expected value of the estate of the person wishing to write a will does not exceed a few thousand euros, it is fully legitimate to refrain from expensive investigations into foreign substantive and conflict rules. In the example just given, this might mean that after informing the client and obtaining his informed consent the Swedish lawyer should draft the will in the local (Swedish) form, hoping — but not guaranteeing — that it will be recognized in Nepal as well.

In spite of the undoubtedly great and rising importance of the international legislative co-operation regarding private international law, it must be remembered that no successful unification or harmonization of conflict rules has ever taken place on the universal level, and that the conflict rules stemming from international legislative co-operation between a limited number of countries give rise to the same problems as non-harmonized rules, whenever they have to be used in relation to countries not participating in the legislative co-operation in question. These lectures will therefore focus on the last-mentioned problems and refrain from dealing with the particular issues arising from international legislative co-operation in the field of private international law. One of the principal aims of these lectures is to demonstrate the relationship between the national rules of private international law and the rest of the legal system of the forum country, in the first place its substantive private law and its law of civil procedure, as well as to illustrate the impact of the forum country's general ethical and other values on its private international law. A discussion about these issues sheds light on the very nature and fundamental features of private international law, including the very raison d'être of this branch of law.

CHAPTER II

HOW INTERNATIONAL IS PRIVATE INTERNATIONAL LAW?

1. Private International Law Is Part of the Lex Fori

In its 1929 judgment in the case concerning the *Payment of Various Serbian Loans Issued in France*, the Permanent Court of International Justice said the following[26]:

> "Any contract which is not a contract between States in their capacity as subjects of international law is based on the municipal law of some country. The question as to which this law is forms the subject of that branch of law which is at the present day usually described as private international law or the doctrine of the conflict of laws. The rules thereof may be common to several States and may even be established by international conventions or customs, and in the latter case may possess the character of true international law governing the relations between States. But apart from this, it has to be considered that these rules form part of municipal law."

This judicial statement is today hardly controversial[27]. In fact, the contents of one of the first pages in

---

[26] Judgment No. 14, PCIJ, Ser. A, No. 20, 1929, p. 41.

[27] See, however, A. Mills, *The Confluence of Public and Private International Law*, pp. 24 and 308, who rejects the whole dichotomy underlying the question of the international or national character of private international law, which in his view is a false distinction constructed by "international positivism", an "intellectual cage" in which international lawyers have imprisoned themselves, and a "conceptual wedge" that has been driven between public

practically all introductory textbooks on private international law and one of the first lessons taught to students in elementary courses on the subject is that private international law is not really international law
comparable to public international law (the law of
nations), but rather a part of the legal system, in a
wider sense, of the country of the forum[28]. The legal
system of the forum country (the *lex fori*) can in such
wider sense be said to comprise both the rules of
domestic (municipal) substantive private law[29] and the
rules of conflict of laws, even though the Latin term is
normally used to denote the first category only. The
word "international" in the name of this branch of law
is somewhat misleading, as it does not refer to the origin of the sources of the rules it consists of. The majority of important provisions of private international law
in most countries are of autonomous national origin
and consequently can be found in the same types of
sources as other rules of the *lex fori*, such as statutes

---

and private international law. In his view, the relationship
between public and private international is more complex
and dynamic than such a binary choice would allow, as
private international law is a blend of influences from
national and international norms, similar to the blend of
federal and state norms in the United States.

[28] See, for example, B. Audit, *Droit international privé*,
p. 3; M. Bogdan, *Svensk internationell privat- och
processrätt*, p. 23; C. M. V. Clarkson and J. Hill, *The
Conflict of Laws*, pp. 1-3; O. Kahn-Freund, *Recueil des
cours*, Vol. 143 (1974), p. 147; T. C. Hartley, *Recueil des
cours*, Vol. 319 (2006), pp. 25-26; J.-M. Jacquet, *Recueil
des cours*, Vol. 292 (2001), p. 159; G. Kegel and K.
Schurig, *Internationales Privatrecht*, p. 5; E. F. Scoles *et
al.*, *Conflict of Laws*, p. 2; F. Vischer, *Recueil des cours*,
Vol. 232 (1992), p. 22.

[29] The term "substantive law" is in these lectures
mainly used as the opposite of the conflict rules of private
international law. It follows from the context that sometimes it is used instead as the opposite of procedural law.

enacted by national parliaments, precedents made by national courts, national legislative preparatory materials *(travaux préparatoires)*, opinions of national legal writers, etc. During the last decades, many countries have in fact enacted their own codes of private international law[30]. This means also that the rules of private international law vary from country to country, so that, for example, Swedish private international law differs from, say, the private international law of Argentina. Some may regret this situation and strive to find uniform, international solutions, but such efforts have so far had a limited success on the universal level and it is far from certain that a general uniformity of conflict rules would always be desirable. On the other hand, the similarities between the private international law problems faced in different countries lead often automatically to similar solutions, even though the similarity is greater in some areas (such as contracts) than in other areas (such as family-law issues)[31].

The word "international" in "private international law" has thus a meaning that differs from what the same word means in "public international law". It does not have in mind the origin of the rules or the essential qualities of the parties[32], but refers rather to the cross-border character of the legal relationships involved. A typical dispute involving private international law may deal with almost any issue of private law, for example whether a delivery of goods has taken place in conformity with the contractual obligations of the seller, whether a person guilty of assault has to pay compen-

---

[30] See, for example, A. Bucher, *Recueil des cours*, Vol. 341 (2009), pp. 30-32.

[31] See, for example, A. Philip, *Recueil des cours*, Vol. 160 (1978), p. 10.

[32] The rules of public international law apply traditionally only among sovereign States and, to some extent, international organizations.

sation to the victim, whether a child is entitled to
financial support from its natural father or whether the
property of a deceased person is inherited by his surviving spouse. What makes these cases involving private international law different from other similar disputes is that the situation has an international character
due to the fact that the circumstances connect it with at
least one country[33] other than the country of the forum
— and thus with at least one legal system other than
the *lex fori*. The contract in dispute may have been
concluded between parties habitually residing in two
different countries, the assault may have taken place in
a country other than that of the habitual residence of
the wrongdoer or of the victim, the maintenance dispute may concern a child whose habitual residence
and/or nationality differ from those of the maintenance
debtor, the deceased whose estate is to be distributed
may have been a citizen of one country but habitually
resided in another and owned assets in a third one, etc.
One of the countries involved is usually the country of
the forum, but it need not always be the case. A situation may be international in the above sense even when
on its face it is related to a single country only, for
example a contractual dispute with all elements situated in the same country, provided that because of
some reason unrelated to the contract (such as the situation of some of the defendant's assets), the dispute is
adjudicated by a court in another country. It may also
happen that a legal relationship that was originally
purely domestic becomes truly internationalized by
supervening events, for example if a child moves

---

[33] The term "country" is here used to denote any territorial jurisdiction with a legal system of its own, irrespective of whether it is a sovereign State or merely a smaller
territorial unit within a larger State (for example, California within the United States or Scotland within the United
Kingdom).

abroad and demands that the father pay increased child support pursuant to the law of the country of its new habitual residence.

In theory, it could be possible to subject private-law disputes having international character to some kind of international courts applying some kind of substantive rules of international origin, but in reality such disputes are normally adjudicated by national courts, normally the same courts that handle corresponding cases of purely domestic nature, and these courts apply national substantive provisions. The international character of the legal relationship under scrutiny gives rise, however, to a number of special questions having no counterpart in purely domestic cases. One important question relates to the jurisdiction of the forum to deal with disputes having substantial connection(s) with a foreign country or countries. Of great importance are also rules on recognition and enforcement of foreign judgments.

As pointed out before, the core of private international law consists, however, of the rules on conflict of laws, that determine which of the national legal systems involved shall govern the disputed substantive-law issues.

Some authors point out that private international law of the forum must also be taken into account in purely domestic cases, mainly because by designating the relevant connecting factors it decides which cases are domestic and which are not[34]. This view, according to which the question of the applicable law has to be decided, at least unconsciously, in every case, is criticized by other authors, who suggest that the *lex fori* is

---

[34] See, for instance, G. Kegel and K. Schurig, *Internationales Privatrecht*, pp. 6-7; P. Lalive, *Recueil des cours*, Vol. 155 (1977), p. 23; M. Dogauchi, *Recueil des cours*, Vol. 315 (2005), pp. 28-35; E. Vitta, *Recueil des cours*, Vol. 162 (1979), p. 55.

applicable "par sa propre force" and not as a result of the private international law rules of the forum[35]. The practical importance of this scholastic discussion is normally limited; the opponents of the view that conflict rules govern even in purely domestic cases seem to fear, however, that it could lead to obligating the parties and/or the courts to waste their energy, in such cases, on the conflict issue in order to legitimate the application of the *lex fori* even if and when such application is self-evident due to the lack of any potentially relevant connection with any other legal system[36]. It seems to me that a dispute should be treated as an "international case" (i.e., a case deserving a reference to the conflict rules of the forum) if, due to its connections with more than one country, there is at least a slight possibility that a law other than the *lex fori* may be applicable. In some recent EU instruments, such cases are described as "situations involving a conflict of laws"[37]. A manifestly irrelevant connection, such as that the contract under scrutiny was written on paper manufactured abroad or that one of the parties has a grandmother of foreign origin[38], does not make the

---

[35] See, for example, Th. de Boer, *Recueil des cours*, Vol. 257 (1996), pp. 239-250; P. Picone, *Recueil des cours*, Vol. 276 (1999), pp. 29-30. This view seems to prevail in Anglo-American law, see P. Hay, *Recueil des cours*, Vol. 226 (1991), p. 291.

[36] See, for example, Th. de Boer, *Recueil des cours*, Vol. 257 (1996), p. 242.

[37] See Article 1, point 1, of the EC Regulation No. 593/2008 of 17 June 2008 on the Law Applicable to Contractual Obligations (Rome I), OJ 2008 L 177, p. 6, and Article 1, point 1, of the EC Regulation No. 864/2007 of 11 July 2007 on the Law Applicable to Non-Contractual Obligations (Rome II), OJ 2007 L 199, p. 40.

[38] See P. Lalive, *Recueil des cours*, Vol. 155 (1977), pp. 17-18; A. V. M. Struycken, *Recueil des cours*, Vol. 311 (2004), p. 182.

relationship subject to private international law, but the case can be "international" even if the examination of the existing potentially relevant connection(s) leads ultimately to the conclusion that the matter is after all governed by the *lex fori*. Consequently, the concept of international cases is much wider than the cases governed by foreign law, but much narrower than all disputes arising in the forum[39]. Of course, even the drawing of the line between the manifestly purely domestic cases and those cases where it is conceivable that foreign law may potentially play some role involves a certain, albeit summary, evaluation of the connecting factors *in casu* and this evaluation can be said to amount to a certain application of private international law of the forum.

In spite of their undeniable special characteristics, the rules of private international law of the forum country are in principle integral parts of its legal system and are thus subject to its hierarchy of legal sources. For example, it is for the law (normally the constitutional law) of the forum country to decide whether statutory conflict rules, rules on jurisdiction and rules on the recognition and enforcement of foreign decisions must be enacted by the parliament or can be issued by lower legislating bodies, such as in the form of government or ministerial decrees. The law of the country of the forum also decides whether judicial decisions on private international law issues create precedents binding on the courts in future cases. It normally also follows from the forum country's hierarchy of sources of law that the contents of the rules of private international law, whether statutory or judgemade, must be in conformity with the forum country's Constitution, for example regarding gender equality or

---

[39] Cf. the similar view of Th. de Boer, *Recueil des cours*, Vol. 257 (1996), pp. 250-253.

the prohibition of discrimination on the grounds of race or religion[40]. It is worth mentioning in this context that the German Federal Constitutional Court held on 22 February 1983[41] and 8 January 1985[42] that the application, regarding the matrimonial property regime and the divorce, of the law of the country of the nationality of the husband had to be abandoned due to its incompatibility with the German Federal Constitution's rule on the equality of the sexes[43]. With regard to jurisdiction, it is well established in the United States that the requirement of "due process of law" in the 5th and 14th Amendments to the US Constitution limits the extent of the exercise of long-arm jurisdiction by requiring that the defendant have certain minimum contacts with the forum such that the maintenance of the suit does not offend traditional notions of "fair play and substantial justice"[44].

The fact that private international law is basically of national origin should not conceal the fact that international co-operation is of particularly great importance in this field, due to the international nature of the disputes and legal problems involved. Such co-operation has a long tradition and there is even a special international body created for that purpose, The Hague Conference on Private International Law *(Conférence*

---

[40] See, for example, H. Gaudemet-Tallon, *Recueil des cours*, Vol. 312 (2005), pp. 133-137, 191 and 402-407.

[41] See *IPRax*, 1983, p. 223, with a comment by D. Henrich on pp. 208-210.

[42] See *IPRax*, 1985, p. 290, with a comment by G. Beitzke on pp. 268-272.

[43] See also the two similar decisions made on 26 February and 25 November 1987 by the Constitutional Court of Italy, *Revue critique de droit international privé*, 1987, p. 563, and 1988, p. 710, both with notes by B. Ancel.

[44] See the well-known leading case of *International Shoe Co*. v. *State of Washington*, 326 US 310 (US Supreme Court, 1945).

de La Haye de droit international privé[45]. In spite of
its name, this is not a mere conference or meeting
place but a properly constituted intergovernmental
organization, with a long history starting far back in
the nineteenth century. There are today almost 40
"Hague conventions", dealing with a variety of private
international law issues and having very varying num-
bers of ratifications.

However, an obligation to apply foreign law or to
recognize a foreign decision does not necessarily have
to follow from an international instrument dealing primarily with private international law. For example, the
recognition of the family status created or changed
abroad may conceivably, at least under certain circumstances, have to be respected pursuant to Article 8 (1)
of the European Convention for the Protection of
Human Rights and Fundamental Freedoms of 1950
("Everyone has the right to respect for his private and
family life, his home and his correspondence")[46].

Very important legislation on private international
law has also been enacted or is under preparation
within the framework of European integration[47]. The

---

[45] See the Conference's home page on the Internet,
<www.hcch.net>. Excellent concise presentations of the
Conference and its activities are found in, for example,
H. van Loon, *Svensk Juristtidning*, 1993, pp. 293-307;
A. Bucher, *Recueil des cours*, Vol. 341 (2009), pp. 32-35
and 506-523; A. V. M. Struycken, *Recueil des cours*,
Vol. 311 (2004), pp. 202-215. An interesting insight into
the Conference's work is provided by P. R. Beaumont,
Recueil des cours, Vol. 340 (2009), pp. 9-61.

[46] Cf. the judgment rendered on 28 June 2007 by the
European Court of Human Rights in the matter of *Wagner*
v. *Luxemburg*, application no. 76240/01.

[47] See, for example, K. Boele-Woelki and R. H. van
Ooik, *Yearbook of Private International Law*, Vol. IV
(2002), pp. 1-36; M. Bogdan, *Concise Introduction to EU
Private International Law*; A. Borrás, *Recueil des cours*,
Vol. 317 (2005), pp. 313-536.

large-scale involvement of private international law in that integration process is of a relatively recent date and is not unproblematic[48]. When the European Economic Community (EEC) was founded in 1957, the original Rome Treaty focused on the creation of a common market based on the freedom of movement for goods, persons, services and capital, and the rules intended to achieve this result were almost exclusively rules of administrative and other public law, such as rules regarding customs duties, qualitative and quantitative import restrictions, residence and labour permits, prohibition of anti-competitive behaviour, etc.

An important exception was the undertaking in Article 220 by the Member States to enter, "so far as is necessary", into negotiations with each other with a view to securing, *inter alia*, the simplification of formalities governing the reciprocal recognition and enforcement of judgments, resulting in the 1968 Brussels Convention on Jurisdiction and the Enforcement of Judgments in Civil and Commercial Matters. A true revolution took place in 1999, when the EC Treaty was amended by the Treaty of Amsterdam, introducing a new Article 65 empowering the Community to legislate in the field of judicial co-operation in civil matters having cross-border implications, "insofar as necessary for the proper functioning of the internal market". The measures foreseen in Article 65 included, *inter alia,* improving and simplifying the recognition and enforcement of decisions in civil and commercial cases and promoting the compatibility of the rules applicable in the Member States concerning the conflict of laws and of jurisdiction. Article 65 gave rise to a substantial number of EC statutes in the field of private interna-

---

[48] See, for example, C. Kohler, *Festschrift für Erik Jayme*, Munich, 2004, pp. 445-459.

tional law[49]. Upon the entry into force, in 2009, of
the so-called Lisbon treaty, Article 65 the EC Treaty
was replaced with Article 81 of the new Treaty on the

---

[49] Among the most important existing EU statutes in
the private international law field, one must mention, in
chronological order, the Regulation No. 1346/2000 of
29 May 2000 on Insolvency Proceedings, OJ 2000 L 160,
p. 1; Regulation No. 1348/2000 of 29 May 2000 on the
Service in the Member States of Judicial and Extrajudicial
Documents in Civil or Commercial Matters, OJ 2000 L 160,
p. 37; Regulation No. 44/2001 of 22 December 2000 on
Jurisdiction and the Recognition and Enforcement of Judgments in Civil and Commercial Matters, OJ 2001 L 12,
p. 1 (the Brussels I Regulation); Regulation No. 1206/
2001 of 28 May 2001 on Cooperation between the Courts
of the Member States in the Taking of Evidence in Civil or
Commercial Matters, OJ 2001 L 174, p. 1; Directive
No. 2003/8 of 27 January 2003 to Improve Access to
Justice in Cross-border Disputes by Establishing Minimum
Common Rules Relating to Legal Aid for Such Disputes,
OJ 2003 L 26, p. 41; Regulation No. 2201/2003 of 27 No-
vember 2003 concerning Jurisdiction and the Recognition
and Enforcement of Judgments in Matrimonial Matters
and the Matters of Parental Responsibility, Repealing
Regulation No. 1347/2000, OJ 2003 L 338, p. 1 (the
Brussels II Regulation); Regulation No. 805/2004 of 21
April 2004 Creating a European Enforcement Order for
Uncontested Claims, OJ 2004 L 143, p. 15; Regulation
No. 1896/2006 of 12 December 2006 Creating a European
Order for Payment Procedure, OJ 2006 L 399, p. 1; Regu-
lation No. 861/2007 of 11 July 2007 Establishing a Euro-
pean Small Claims Procedure, OJ 2007 L 199, p. 1; Regu-
lation No. 864/2007 of 11 July 2007 on the Law Applicable
to Non-Contractual Obligations (the Rome II Regulation),
OJ 2007 L 199, p. 40; Directive No. 2008/52 of 21 May
2008 on Certain Aspects of Mediation in Civil and
Commercial Matters, OJ 2008 L 136, p. 3; Regulation
No. 593/2008 of 17 June 2008 on the Law Applicable to
Contractual Obligations (the Rome I Regulation), OJ 2008
L 177, p. 6; Regulation No. 4/2009 of 18 December 2008
on Jurisdiction, Applicable Law, Recognition and Enforce-
ment of Decisions and Cooperation in Matters Relating to
Maintenance Obligations, OJ 2009 L 7, p. 1.

Functioning of the European Union, which further increased the legislative powers of the Union as compared to those of the former Community by replacing the condition "insofar as necessary for the proper functioning of the internal market" with the more generous formula "particularly when necessary for the proper functioning of the internal market". Within the foreseeable future, the EU is expected to enact rules on the applicable law regarding divorce[50], property rights of married couples[51], successions and wills[52], etc. In addition to statutes enacted on the basis of Article 65 of the EC Treaty and devoted wholly to private international law matters, EU law comprises many provisions of private international law relevance scattered in statutes dealing mainly with the approximation of laws for the purpose of the establishment of the internal market, for example in directives on unfair terms in consumer contracts[53], on the posting of workers[54], or on electronic commerce[55]. It has also happened that the European

---

[50] See the the European Commission's proposal of 30 March 2010 for a Regulation Implementing Enhanced Cooperation in the Area of the Law Applicable to Divorce and Legal Separation, COM(2010)105 final/2.

[51] See the EC Commission's Green Paper of 17 July 2006 on Conflict of Laws in Matters concerning Matrimonial Property Regimes, including the Question of Jurisdiction and Mutual Recognition, COM(2006)400 final.

[52] See the EC Commission's proposal of 14 October 2009 for a Regulation on Jurisdiction, Applicable Law, Recognition and Enforcement of Decisions and Authentic Instruments in Matters of Succession and the Creation of a European Certificate of Succession, COM(2009)154 final.

[53] See Article 6 (2) of Directive No. 93/13 of 5 April 1993 on Unfair Terms in Consumer Contracts, OJ 1993 L 95, p. 29.

[54] See Article 3 of Directive No. 96/71 of 16 December 1996 concerning the Posting of Workers in the Framework of the Provision of Services, OJ 1997 L 18, p. 1.

[55] See Article 3 of Directive No. 2000/31 of 8 June 2000 on Certain Legal Aspects of Information Society

Court of Justice discovered that a statute harmonizing substantive private law comprised an implied, silent conflict rule[56]. Last but not least, some of the general provisions of the Treaty on the Functioning of the European Union, such as the prohibition of discrimination on grounds of nationality in Article 18, the free movement of EU citizens in Article 45, and the right of establishment stipulated in Article 49 (formerly Articles 12, 18 and 43 of the EC Treaty) also have direct effect on the private international law of the Member States[57].

It must not be forgotten, however, that the existing international instruments are usually sectorial and territorially limited rather than comprehensive and universal. Furthermore, a closer look reveals that in practice even the seemingly unified and identical rules of private international law often function in different ways depending on varying national approaches to such general problems as classification, *renvoi*, the public policy reservation or whether foreign law is applied ex officio or not[58]. Most of these general problems will be discussed later in these lectures.

Services, in Particular Electronic Commerce, in the Internal Market, OJ 2000 L 178, p. 1.

[56] See *Ingmar* v. *Eaton*, case C-381/98, decided on 9 November 2000.

[57] See, for example, M. Bogdan, *Concise Introduction to EU Private International Law*, pp. 21-29; M. Fallon and J. Meeusen, *Yearbook of Private International Law*, Vol. IV (2002), pp. 37-66; judgments of the ECJ in *Boukhalfa* v. *Germany* (case C-214/94, decided on 30 April 1996), *Avello* v. *Belgium* (case C-148/02, decided on 2 October 2003), *Grunkin-Paul* (case C-353/06, decided on 14 October 2008) and *Überseering* v. *NCC* (case C-208/00, decided on 5 November 2002).

[58] The European Union will within the foreseeable future make an attempt to unify or harmonize the approach of the Member States to some of these general problems,

The unification of private international law is sometimes seen as a makeshift, temporary substitute to the more ambitious and much more difficult project of the unification or harmonization of substantive law[59]. It could be argued that private international law will no longer be needed if and to the extent the substantive private law becomes unified on the international level. It is certainly true that the question of applicable law loses much of its practical relevance whenever the choice is between rules of identical contents, but experience shows that even the most successful projects regarding the unification of substantive law, such as the 1980 United Nations Convention on Contracts for the International Sale of Goods (CISG) or the EC Regulation on the Statute of a European Company (SE)[60], leave many questions to be answered by national law, and thus do not make private international law superfluous. For example, Article 7, point 2, of CISG stipulates that questions concerning matters not expressly regulated therein are to be settled in conformity with the general principles on which CISG is based or, in the absence of such principles, "in con-

---

see Article 30, point 1, of Regulation No. 864/2007 of 11 July 2007 on the Law Applicable to Non-Contractual Obligations (Rome II), OJ 2007 L 199, p. 40, with the attached Commission Statement on the Treatment of Foreign Law, OJ 2007 L 199, p. 49. In this statement, the Commission promises to publish at the latest in August 2011 a study on the application of foreign law in civil and commercial matters and "to take appropriate measures if necessary". The Commission has commissioned the Swiss Institute of Comparative Law (Institut suisse de droit comparé) in Lausanne to prepare the report. See U. P. Gruber and I. Bach, *Yearbook of Private International Law*, Vol. XI (2009), pp. 157-169.

[59] See, for example, E. Jayme, *Recueil des cours*, Vol. 251 (1995), p. 57.

[60] Regulation No. 2157/2001 of 8 October 2001, OJ 2001 L 294, p. 1.

formity with the law applicable by virtue of the rules of private international law". Pursuant to a conflict rule in Articles 9 and 10 of the EC Regulation on the Statute for a European Company, matters not regulated by the Regulation itself are in principle governed by the law of the Member State where the SE has its registered office. Furthermore, the very application of the uniform rules of substantive law often presupposes that a conflict rule of the forum leads to the application of a legal system containing such uniform rules; thus, Article 1, point 1 *(b)*, of CISG states that its uniform rules apply to contracts of sale of goods between parties whose places of business are in different States "when the rules of private international law lead to the application of the law of a Contracting State"[61]. It is, besides, far from certain that the unification of substantive private law is always desirable. In the words of Erik Jayme, the characteristic feature of contemporary private international law is the "conflict of cultures"[62]. Karl Kreuzer uses a more dramatic metaphor, calling private international law "the battlefield for heterogeneous legal cultures"[63]. Substantive law is one of the expressions of culture and just as it would be misguided and in fact impossible to achieve a universal cultural unification concerning food or music, it would be wrong and futile to strive to create a universal private law[64], except where unified rules of more-or-less

---

[61] Cf., however, Article 1, point 1 *(a)*, of CISG, prescribing its application also to contracts between parties whose places of business are in different contracting States.

[62] See E. Jayme, *Recueil des cours*, Vol. 251 (1995), p. 52: "En fait, ce qui vraiment caractérise le droit international privé actuel, ce sont les conflits de cultures."

[63] See K. Kreuzer, *Revue hellénique de droit international*, 2009, p. 631.

[64] Cf., for example, P. Legrand, "European Legal Systems Are Not Converging", 45 *International and Comparative Law Quarterly* 52-81 (1996).

technical nature are really necessary for increasing the efficiency of crossborder commercial transactions.

2. Is There an International Obligation to Apply Foreign Law?

The fact that private international law is basically a part of the legal system of the forum country does not, *per se*, necessarily mean that in the absence of relevant treaties or other similarly assumed international obligations (such as the requirements of EU law), the forum country has completely free hands to form its conflict rules as it pleases. In the course of the history of private international law it has sometimes been argued that national courts have to apply foreign law because even in the absence of conventions or other international instruments, they are obliged to do so by customary (general) public international law[65]. A somewhat "softer" claim is that even though public international law does not impose any duty to apply a particular foreign legal system, such as the *lex patriae* or the *lex domicilii* in family matters, it forbids the application of the substantive rules of the *lex fori* when the situation under scrutiny has no significant connection

---

[65] See, for example, F. A. Mann, *Foreign Affairs*, p. 135, who writes that the true explanation of why courts apply foreign law or recognize foreign acts is that a refusal to do so would be contrary to public international law. For instance, a strongly Catholic country considering all marriages in the world not celebrated pursuant to the rituals of the Catholic church to be invalid would in his view act *ultra vires* and commit an international wrong, see F. A. Mann, *Recueil des cours*, Vol. 186 (1984), p. 21. See also G. S. Maridakis, *Recueil des cours*, Vol. 105 (1962), p. 390. It is, of course, possible that today the conclusion given by Mann in his example is correct due to the forum country's other international commitments, such as those regarding human rights.

at all with the forum country[66]. For example, F. Vischer asserts that applying the *lex fori* to situations which lack any relevant connection to the forum State would be an offence against international law[67], even though he concedes that there is no established rule of public international law clarifying which connections are "relevant". A more prudent author has asserted that an absolute refusal to pay attention to or to consider the application of foreign law is all over the world looked upon as "close to a breach of the law of nations"[68], and a US Supreme Court judgment from 1895 indicates that private international law was considered "neither a matter of absolute obligation, on the one hand, nor a mere courtesy and good will, upon the other"[69].

However, today the prevailing opinion seems to be that in the absence of international instruments stipulating the contrary, each State is in principle free to formulate its conflict rules as it fits its national views of justice and local interests[70], including the right to subject certain issues exclusively to its own substantive law, i.e., to refuse to let certain issues to be governed by a legal system other than the *lex fori*[71]. Restraints

---

[66] See F. A. Mann, *Recueil des cours*, Vol. 186 (1984), p. 31; G. van Hecke, *Recueil des cours*, Vol. 126 (1969), p. 418.

[67] See F. Vischer, *Recueil des cours*, Vol. 232 (1992), p. 26.

[68] See H. Eek, *Recueil des cours*, Vol. 139 (1973), p. 39.

[69] See *Hilton* v. *Guyot*, 159 US 113 (1895) at 163-164.

[70] See, for example, K. Lipstein, *Recueil des cours*, Vol. 135 (1972), pp. 167-173 and 192; A. Philip, *Recueil des cours*, Vol. 160 (1978), p. 10; A. V. M. Struycken, *Recueil des cours*, Vol. 311 (2004), p. 180.

[71] In the words of Hans Kelsen, as formulated in a letter published in *Annuaire de l'Institut de droit international,* Vol. 47 II, 1957, pp. 115-125 (on p. 119),

"[p]uisque le droit international général n'impose aux Etats aucune obligation concernant les normes du droit

imposed by international law, if any, are thus very mild[72].

It is possible that the intense search by some authors for international roots of conflict rules has to some extent psychological reasons. As it was put by Trevor Hartley,

> "[i]t was somehow felt that a set of rules that determine how far the legal system of a State can extend internationally must derive its authority from something more elevated that that legal system itself"[73].

To use my own country as an example, it is submitted that in the absence of pertinent international obligations imposed by treaties or EU law, Sweden does not violate any rules of customary international law by deciding unilaterally that the capacity to marry, an application for a divorce or an adoption shall in Swedish courts in principle always be decided by applying Swedish family law[74]. The country or countries where the persons involved are domiciled or of

---

national que l'on appelle le droit international privé, et lorsqu'il n'y a pas de droit international particulier, c'est-à-dire conventionnel, qui oblige les Etats dans ce domaine, les organes législateurs des Etats sont complètement libres de donner aux normes du droit international privé n'importe quel contenu. Il n'y a même pas de nécessité juridique d'établir dans le cadre d'un droit national des normes de droit international privé ..."

[72] See, for example, D. J. L. Davies, *Recueil des cours*, Vol. 62 (1937), pp. 450-452; G. Kegel and K. Schurig, *Internationales Privatrecht*, pp. 15-17; A. Philip, *Recueil des cours*, Vol. 160 (1978), p. 10; E. F. Scoles *et al.*, *Conflict of Laws*, p. 2.

[73] See T. C. Hartley, *Recueil des cours*, Vol. 319 (2006), pp. 25-26.

[74] See the present wording of Chapter 1, Section 1, para. 1, and Chapter 3, Section 4, para. 1, of the Swedish Act (1904:26) on Some International Marriage and Guardianship Relationships, and Section 2, para. 1, of the Swedish Act (1971:796) on International Adoption Relationships.

which they are citizens cannot, relying on customary international law, demand that Swedish courts apply their laws (these countries are, on the other hand, free to deny recognition of the resulting Swedish decision, unless of course there is some international instrument obliging them to recognize it).

The situation is somewhat different with regard to jurisdiction of courts, because denying access to justice to foreigners, just like the maltreatment of foreigners in other procedural respects, may under certain circumstances amount to a violation of customary international law *(déni de justice)*.

It is true that a survey of all systems of private international law in the world probably would allow the conclusion that most conflict rules of most countries designate a legal system having a reasonably close connection with the relationship it is supposed to govern. Even some of the more specific conflict rules are so widely recognized and used that they are almost universal, for example the principle of *locus regit actum*, the application of the *lex rei sitae* with regard to rights *in rem* in immovable property and recognition of the freedom of the parties to an international commercial contract to agree on the applicable law (party autonomy)[75]. This practice is, however, not a conclusive evidence of the existence of a binding customary rule of general public international law, as it cannot be shown that the States perceive the practice as binding (there is no *opinio juris et necessitatis* required for the existence of such binding customary rules)[76]. Legally

[75] See E. Hambro, *Recueil des cours*, Vol. 105 (1962), pp. 46-63; G. S. Maridakis, *Recueil des cours*, Vol. 105 (1962), p. 393.

[76] See, for example, R. Ago, *Recueil des cours*, Vol. 58 (1936), p. 289; E. Hambro, *Recueil des cours*, Vol. 105 (1962), p. 47; J. Maury, 57 *Recueil des cours*, Vol. 57 (1936), pp. 354-357; M. F. Yasseen, *Recueil des cours*,

binding international custom must be distinguished
from State practices not reflecting a legal obligation.
To my knowledge, there is no decision of any international court or tribunal where a State was found guilty
of violating the customary law of nations by not applying foreign private law and there are practically no
reported cases where an official diplomatic protest has
been lodged by a State alleging that another country
has violated customary public international law by not
applying, in a private dispute, the law of the complain-
ing State or by an excessive application of the *lex
fori*[77]. On the contrary, there is some support for the
view that international law permits the forum country
to *refuse* to apply foreign law on the grounds of
public policy even in those cases where the application
of that foreign law is stipulated by an internatio-

Vol. 116 (1965), pp. 395-396. Article 38 of the Statute of
the International Court of Justice, listing the sources of
international law, includes international custom, as evidence of a general practice "accepted as law".

    [77] See R. Ago, *Recueil des cours*, Vol. 58 (1936),
pp. 288-289; O. Kahn-Freund, *Recueil des cours*, Vol. 143
(1974), p. 176, with a few references. Similarly, there
seem to have been no official protests against the exorbitant jurisdictional rules of some countries, such as Article
14 of the French Civil Code giving French courts jurisdiction on the mere ground of the French citizenship of the
plaintiff, or Chapter 10, Section 3, of the Swedish Code of
Judicial Procedure giving Swedish courts jurisdiction on
the mere ground of the presence of the defendant's assets,
see G. van Hecke, *Recueil des cours*, Vol. 126 (1969),
p. 425. J. Maury, *Recueil des cours*, Vol. 57 (1936),
pp. 355 and 428-431, who believed that there is an obligation under public international law to apply foreign law
(even though not specified in detail), explained the lack
of diplomatic complaints etc. partly by the fact that the
States in general respected that obligation and partly by
the small importance attached by them to private international law questions which from their point of view
are mere "bagatelles".

nal treaty comprising no explicit *ordre public* reservation[78].

The conclusion that customary international law imposes no or only very weak requirements on the conflict rules of individual countries is supported also by the fact that the national conflict rules are far from identical and vary substantially from country to country[79]. In fact, it happens that a Swedish court applies the law of a foreign country even in a situation where the private international law of the foreign country in question does not consider its own legal system applicable and prefers to apply another — for example Swedish — law[80]. Under such circumstances it would be manifestly incorrect to assert that the Swedish conflict rule orders the application of the foreign law because of some duty that Sweden owes to the foreign State in question.

As mentioned above, according to some older theories the application of foreign law is required, if not by international law, then at least by some kind of established comity or courtesy vis-à-vis foreign countries and the desire not to offend them by showing disrespect. Thus, the so-called Dutch School, as represented by Ulrich Huber (1635-1694) and others, formulated a theory pursuant to which the application of foreign law was required by comity of nations, which was not merely an expression of a benevolent attitude towards other States but was rather based on reciprocity and self-interest[81]. The Dutch School exercised substantial

---

[78] See Chapter X.2, *infra*.

[79] See, for example, O. Kahn-Freund, *Recueil des cours*, Vol. 143 (1974), pp. 170-171.

[80] See the discussion about *renvoi* in Chapter IX, *infra*.

[81] See, for example, D. J. L. Davies, *Recueil des cours*, Vol. 62 (1937), pp. 453-460; M. Jänterä-Jareborg, *Recueil des cours*, Vol. 304 (2003), pp. 203-206; G. Kegel and K. Schurig, *Internationales Privatrecht*, pp. 175-176; E. F. Scoles *et al.*, *Conflict of Laws*, pp. 14-15.

influence in many countries, in particular in the early United States, as is demonstrated by Joseph Story's famous *Commentaries on the Conflict of Laws, Foreign and Domestic*, published in 1834[82]. Among modern authors, Frank Vischer suggested that the notion of comity seems to express, more accurately than public international law, the duties which States owe each other in the question of the choice of law, as it "underlines the obligation of the State to co-operate internationally and to give due regard to the justified interests of other States and their subjects"[83]. It seems that the proponents of comity find it difficult to draw the line between an obligation under public international law and pure courtesy. It cannot, in any case, be asserted that the foreign country whose law is declared applicable has reasons to perceive this to be a benefit to which it is legally entitled or that a foreign country whose law is not applied has reasons to feel offended. As will be shown later[84], rules of private international law serve in principle the interests of the forum country rather than the interests of other countries.

---

[82] See, for example, G. Kegel and K. Schurig, *Internationales Privatrecht*, p. 180; E. F. Scoles *et al.*, *Conflict of Laws*, pp. 18-19.

[83] See F. Vischer, *Recueil des cours*, Vol. 232 (1992), p. 27.

[84] See Chapter III.4, *infra*.

CHAPTER III

WHY AND IN WHOSE INTEREST DO COURTS APPLY FOREIGN LAW?

1. The Problem

Experience gained from many years of teaching gives me reason to believe that many undergraduate law students, when confronted for the first time with private international law, react with bewilderment. They are puzzled and confused, because private international law differs in several respects radically from the other subjects they have encountered during their previous legal studies.

The most fundamental question many beginners raise is, however, fully rational and legitimate: if, as shown above, there is no international obligation to apply foreign law, why do we need private international law at all, why can the courts not always apply their own law (the *lex fori*)? After all, the fact that the forum has jurisdiction to deal with the dispute indicates normally in itself that the dispute has some kind of connection with the forum country. Besides, the application of foreign law requires time-consuming and expensive investigations about the contents of the foreign rules and increases dramatically the risk of misunderstanding and wrong decisions. Occasionally I even meet the argument that the substantive provisions of the *lex fori* must, by definition, be considered by the court to be better than foreign rules. The substantive law of the forum country normally reflects what the legislator of that country considers to be most just, fair, suitable and appropriate, and the replacement of the *lex fori* with rules of foreign law, based on foreign perceptions of justice and fairness, is thus by some seen as necessarily amounting to a change for the worse. For example, if in the Dutch substantive private (civil) law the Dutch legislator has regulated the extent of the liability of the tortfeasor to compensate the injured person, it must reasonably mean that the Dutch legislator is of the opinion that these rules reflect what is most appropriate, just and fair. Why should these values in some cases be disregarded by applying foreign law, based on different perceptions of justice? Besides, if a foreign rule is deemed preferable to that of the *lex fori*, would it not be better to amend the *lex fori* using the foreign rule as a model rather than apply the foreign rule?

It is true that, at first glance, the practical and theoretical reasons speaking in favour of applying the *lex fori* in all situations might seem to prevail. It is an undeniable fact that from a strictly practical viewpoint the application of foreign law is always less convenient for the court than applying the *lex fori*[85]. Another undeniable fact is that foreign law is frequently misunderstood or applied wrongly. The judges and other members of the legal profession have undergone extensive theoretical and practical training, usually consisting of many years of hard work, just to prepare them for working within their own legal system. Very few of them have expert knowledge of foreign law and it is in any case beyond what is humanly possible to master all of the hundreds of legal systems existing on this planet. To obtain reliable information about the contents of relevant rules in a foreign legal system, which one has never studied, is time-consuming, difficult and sometimes even impossible. The language of the foreign legal system may be a problem and there is a substantial risk that the foreign rules will be misunder-

[85] See, for example, M. Jänterä-Jareborg, *Recueil des cours*, Vol. 304 (2003), p. 220.

stood when interpreted by someone lacking insight into their natural context. A well-known German legal writer has stated that a judge applying foreign law is always a worse judge than a judge applying his own law, because with regard to foreign law he is no more than a mere dilettante acting in an uneasy and amateurish way, while when applying his own law he can act courageously as a supreme expert[86]. Even though the empirical investigations concerning this problem that have been carried out are few, rather old and deal only with a limited number of cases, they make it very clear that in too many — perhaps even most — of the examined decisions the foreign rules had not been applied correctly[87]! In view of this, would it not be preferable to apply always the *lex fori*?

2. *Legitimacy of the Application of Foreign Law*

The idea of resolving disputes in accordance with foreign law gives rise, furthermore, to the question of legitimacy of the legal system as such. If the forum country is a democracy, the rules of the *lex fori* can normally be assumed to emanate directly or indirectly (depending on the legislative mechanism of the forum country) from the will of the people of that country, whereas the substantive contents of foreign law has its roots in the will of a foreign people that may embrace very different values. The law of many totalitarian countries does not have any democratic legitimacy at all, as it reflects merely the will of some hereditary monarch, a military dictator or a political or religious

---

[86] See K. Zweigert, *Rabels Zeitschrift*, 1973, p. 445. Cf. also Th. de Boer, *Recueil des cours*, Vol. 257 (1996), pp. 317-328; P. M. M. Mostermans, *Netherlands International Law Review*, 2004, p. 400.

[87] See M. Jänterä-Jareborg, *Recueil des cours*, Vol. 304 (2003), pp. 312-313.

group with no mandate derived from free elections. On the other hand, if the forum country considers the whole or parts of its law to be of a divine origin, as is the case in some Islamic countries[88], the forum may find it highly problematic to disregard these rules in favour of some foreign rules of secular origin, irrespective of their reasonable content and undeniable democratic roots.

As to the objections regarding the low degree of democratic legitimacy of the application of foreign law, the answer must be that the conflict rules of the forum are integral parts of the legitimately created *lex fori* in a wider sense, and that this legitimizes also the application of the foreign law which these conflict rules may in turn designate in individual cases. Theoretically, it is possible to argue that the forum does not apply foreign law at all but merely applies its own conflict rule[89] which in one way or another incorporates the applicable foreign law into the *lex fori*. According to this view, the forum does not, therefore, apply or enforce foreign law but rather creates and applies *ad hoc* a special *lex fori* rule whenever the case has relevant foreign elements[90]. This so-called "local law theory" seems to be related to Hans Kelsen's general theory of law based on the existence in each legal system of a "fundamental rule" *(Grundnorm)*, normally its constitution, from which all other rules of that system must be

---

[88] See, for example, M. Charfi, *Recueil des cours,* Vol. 203 (1987), pp. 321-454 ; K. Kreuzer, *Revue hellénique der droit international* 2009, pp. 636-637.

[89] See, for example, C. M. V. Clarkson and J. Hill, *The Conflict of Laws*, pp. 8-9 and 13-14.

[90] See T. Gihl, *Den internationella privaträttens historia och allmänna principer*, pp. 11 and 324-334 ; T. C. Hartley, *International Commercial Litigation*, p. 528 ; E. F. Scoles *et al.*, *Conflict of Laws*, pp. 22-23 with further references.

derived[91]. Some authors distinguish in this context between the substantive content of the foreign rule and its binding force; while the former is derived from a foreign legislator, the latter is derived from the legislator of the forum country[92].

3. Do Conflict Rules Serve the Interests of Foreign Countries?

Accepting that in the absence of a binding treaty or other international instrument the forum country is under no legal or moral obligation to make its courts apply foreign law does not necessarily mean that the interests of foreign countries to have their laws applied have to be ignored.

There are, in fact, theories advocating the application of the legal system which has the greatest or most

---

[91] See H. Kelsen's letter published in *Annuaire de l'Institut de droit international,* Vol. 47 II, 1957, pp. 115-125 (on pp. 119-120):

"D'ailleurs, je ne crois pas qu'il soit correct de caractériser le droit international privé comme une règle stipulant dans un certain Etat que certains rapports sociaux doivent être régis par le droit établi dans un autre Etat, ou comme une norme du droit d'un Etat selon laquelle le droit d'un autre Etat doive être appliqué. En effet, l'Etat ne peut appliquer que son propre droit, ou, formulé d'une manière plus exacte : l'organe d'un Etat ne peut appliquer que les normes de son propre droit national . . . Quand un juge, autorisé par une loi de son Etat, applique — comme on dit — la norme tirée du droit d'un autre Etat, la raison de validité de la norme appliquée par le juge n'est pas la Constitution de cet autre Etat, mais la Constitution de l'Etat dont il est l'organe. Par conséquent, le juge applique, dans ce cas aussi, une norme de son propre Etat."

Cf. E. Vitta, *Recueil des cours*, Vol. 162 (1979), pp. 32-33.
[92] See, for example, A. V. M. Struycken, *Recueil des cours*, Vol. 311 (2004), p. 68.

significant legitimate interest to have its substantive rules applied in the particular case. The common ground of these theories is that they start with the analysis of the established or presumed policies underlying the relevant substantive rules of all those legal systems that in some way are related to the case and therefore could conceivably be applicable. These policies indicate whether the various national legislators have a legitimate interest to have their laws applied in the case under scrutiny, i.e. to have their policies advanced in the particular case. For example, a country whose law protects manufacturers by imposing a maximum limit on product liability may be considered to have a substantial interest in having this limit applied if the manufacturer is its resident but not if he resides elsewhere, and a country protecting its courts from complicated calculations by introducing simplified rules for the assessment of damages has no real interest in having these simplified rules applied by courts in other jurisdictions (an obvious complication is that the same rule of substantive law may be intended to serve several policies at the same time, for example both to protect manufacturers and to simplify the assessment of the damages).

Approaches based on this kind of reasoning are fundamentally unilateralist[93], because they start from the assumption that in principle it depends on the attitude of each country whether its law should be applied or not. They can be traced back to the Statutist school in the Middle Ages but have relatively recently gained considerable influence in the United States[94] as parts of the so-called American "choice-of-law revolu-

---

[93] See Chapter IV.1, *infra*.

[94] Similar views can sometimes be found also among European writers, see for example A. Bucher, *Recueil des cours*, Vol. 239 (1993), pp. 71-74.

tion"[95], in particular the "governmental interest theory" originally developed by Brainerd Currie (1912-

---

[95] For a closer presentation and discussion of this "revolution", see S. C. Symeonides, *Recueil des cours*, Vol. 298 (2002), pp. 9-448. A more concise critical description is found in a large number of courses given at this Academy, for example, R. De Nova, *Recueil des cours*, Vol. 118 (1966), pp. 591-610; D. J. Evrigenis, *Recueil des cours*, Vol. 118 (1966), pp. 332-394; F. K. Juenger, *Recueil des cours*, Vol. 193 (1985), pp. 207-252; D. F. Cavers, *Recueil des cours*, Vol. 131 (1970), pp. 73-171; G. Kegel, *Recueil des cours*, Vol. 112 (1964), pp. 91-236; P. Lalive, *Recueil des cours*, Vol. 155 (1977), pp. 326-370; G. Parra-Aranguren, *Recueil des cours*, Vol. 210 (1988), pp. 159-182; W. Reese, *Recueil des cours*, Vol. 111 (1964), pp. 301-417; F. Vischer, *Recueil des cours*, Vol. 232 (1992), pp. 44-73; E. Vitta, *Recueil des cours*, Vol. 162 (1979), pp. 163-187; A. Bucher, *Recueil des cours*, Vol. 341 (2009), pp. 54-61. The "revolution" was a reaction to the previous, conceptualistic and rigid state of private international law in the United States, symbolized by the first Restatement and characterized by "broad, all-embracing, inflexible, monolithic rules, based on a single connecting factor chosen on metaphysical grounds" (S. C. Symeonides, *Recueil des cours*, Vol. 298 (2002), p. 422; see also W. L. M. Reese, *Recueil des cours*, Vol. 150 (1976), pp. 37-42). Today the attitude towards the "revolutionary" theories is far less positive, even in the United States, than it used to be: "The U.S. conflict revolution has aged, and it has not aged well", see R. Michaels, *Yearbook of Private International Law*, Vol. XI (2009), p. 12. In the words of L. Brilmayer, *Recueil des cours*, Vol. 252 (1995), p. 20,

"[t]he so-called modern approaches have been around for decades, and can no longer attract adherents through the simple fact of looking fresh and labelling themselves progressive. Their practical problems are becoming clearer."

Brilmayer criticizes, for example, that the weight given to substantive policies in the choice-of-law process has gone too far at the expense of choice-of-law policies: "the pendulum has swung a bit too far" (p. 111).

1965)[96]. Currie opposed openly the very usefulness of
having established conflict rules as such and stated
explicitly that "[w]e would be better off without
choice-of-law rules"[97]. His original theory, focusing on
the task of the forum to promote the substantive policies embodied in the substantive rules of the *lex fori*,
was that the forum should apply its own law if the
issue was within the scope of the forum State's governmental concern, that is, if the forum country was not
indifferent to the application of its law (for example if
the interests of at least one of its domiciliaries were at
stake). The interests of other States, however legitimate, were to be disregarded in this situation. Currie
meant, furthermore, that the *lex fori* should also apply
if the forum country had no interest in the matter but
the issue was within the scope of legitimate interest of
more than one foreign State, or if there was no interested State at all. In Currie's theory, at least in its original form, there is thus no place for any real balancing
or weighing of the governmental interests of different
States. Currie's theory was, in addition, extremely oriented towards the application of the *lex fori*, as he was
willing to accept the application of foreign law only in
a relatively small group of cases, namely in those situations where the forum State had no interest at all in the
application of its law and there was only one single
other State having such interest.

---

[96] See, for example, B. Currie, *Selected Essays*. Cf.
also B. Audit, *Recueil des cours*, Vol. 305 (2003), pp. 247-
250 and 295-301; P. Hay, *Recueil des cours*, Vol. 226
(1991), pp. 350-355; H. H. Kay, *Recueil des cours*,
Vol. 215 (1989), pp. 9-204; G. Kegel, *Recueil des cours*,
Vol. 112 (1964), pp. 97-207; G. Kegel and K. Schurig,
Internationales Privatrecht, p. 199; E. F. Scoles *et al.*,
Conflict of Laws, pp. 25-38; S. C. Symeonides, *Recueil
des cours*, Vol. 298 (2002), pp. 38-50; S. Vrellis, *Recueil
des cours*, Vol. 328 (2007), pp. 279-289.
[97] See B. Currie, *Selected Essays*, p. 183.

Currie's theory might seem attractive in those situations where there is only one interested country (the so-called "false conflict"), but it has the weakness of unpredictability, as the ascertainment of the interest of the various countries in the application of their laws is often based on pure guesswork and can be manipulated to achieve a certain result, in particular in order to enable the court to apply its own law.

Less extreme is the American Restatement (Second) of the Conflict of Laws from 1971[98], which appears to express the most accepted and most judicially followed of the various "modern American theories"[99]. It lists seven factors that should influence the choice of the applicable law by reflecting the "most significant relationship" to the occurrence and the parties. Among these seven factors are the relevant policies of the forum State, the relevant policies of other interested States and the relative interest of those States in the determination of the particular issue[100]. In contrast to Currie, the Restatement recommends the counterbalancing of the *relative* interests of the States involved and does not automatically revert to the *lex fori* whenever the forum country has some interest in the issue or

---

[98] The privately published but highly authoritative restatements have the ambition to provide, in the form of fictitious codified and commented provisions, an accurate and concise text which restates the currently valid American law in a particular field. See, for example, P. Hay, *Recueil des cours*, Vol. 226 (1991), pp. 358-385; E. F. Scoles *et al.*, *Conflict of Laws*, pp. 58-68; S. C. Symeonides, *Recueil des cours*, Vol. 298 (2002), pp. 58-63.

[99] See E. F. Scoles *et al.*, *Conflict of Laws*, p. 68.

[100] The other factors are the needs of the interstate and international systems, the protection of party expectations, the basic policies underlying the particular field of law, the objectives of certainty, predictability, and uniformity of result, and the ease of determining and applying the law identified as applicable.

whenever there are several foreign States having such interest.

Such judicial weighing of State interests constitutes the basis also of the "comparative impairment theory" which weighs and compares the negative impact the non-application of the law of a particular State would have on that State's interests[101]. An early proponent of this kind of approach was the French author Antoine Pillet (1857-1926), who was of the view that one should apply the law of the country whose interests would suffer most if its law were not applied ("le principe du moindre sacrifice")[102].

It is important to realize that within a typical governmental interest analysis there is usually no or very little place for comparisons between the national legislative policies in the sense of determining which law represents a better qualitative policy. The analysis is based rather on a mere weighing of the strength of each interested State's commitment, under the circumstances *in casu*, to the policies advanced by its own law. An example of this kind of reasoning is *Griffith* v. *United Air Lines, Inc.*, decided by the Supreme Court of Pennsylvania in 1964[103]. In this case, a Pennsylvania domiciliary flying from Pennsylvania to Arizona was killed in a crash in Colorado. The defendant airline was a Delaware corporation with its principal place of business in Illinois. The estate of the decedent could recover very little compensation under Colorado law, which limited damages to loss of earnings and expenses sustained or incurred prior to death, but

---

[101] See E. F. Scoles *et al.*, *Conflict of Laws*, pp. 31-32.

[102] See A. Pillet, *Recueil des cours*, Vol. 2 (1924), pp. 467-471. See also B. Audit, *Droit international privé*, p. 69; G. Kegel and K. Schurig, *Internationales Privatrecht*, p. 190.

[103] 203 A. 2d 796 (Supreme Court of Pennsylvania, 1964).

might recover a substantial amount under the law of Pennsylvania, which permitted recovery for the decedent's likely earnings during the period of his whole life expectancy. The Court decided to abandon the previous strict *lex loci delicti* rule in favour of a more flexible approach based on the analysis of the policies and interests underlying the particular disputed issue. As far as Colorado was concerned, the Court found indications that the limitation imposed by Colorado law was intended to prevent Colorado courts from engaging in speculative computation of expected earnings and that it could therefore be based on procedural considerations of purely local concern; this meant that Colorado would be unconcerned if a Pennsylvania court was willing to engage in such computations. Or, the limitation might have been intended to protect Colorado defendants from large verdicts against them, but the defendant airline was not domiciled in Colorado although doing some business there. On the other hand, the Court found Pennsylvania's interest in the amount of recovery to be great, *inter alia*, because it was the domicile of the decedent and his family and thus vitally concerned with the well-being of the surviving dependents. The law of Pennsylvania, therefore, was applied.

Of great interest in this connection is also the case *In re Paris Air Crash of March 3, 1974*[104], concerning an air crash in France of an American-manufactured aircraft owned and operated by a Turkish airline, killing a large number of people from a large number of different countries and states. The United States District Court for the Central District of California decided to follow the governmental interest approach. For reasons of justice, it rejected the idea of making

---

[104] 399 F. Supp. 732 (United States District Court for the Central District of California, 1975).

the applicable law depend on the domicile of the individual claimant and went on to say that California was interested in protecting resident defendants and would not allow enhanced recovery to plaintiffs because of the fortuitous place of the crash or residence of the litigants. *A fortiori* California would not allow non-residents a greater recovery than the law of California allowed its own resident plaintiffs. As for those countries or states whose laws would have resulted in less of a recovery than would be obtained by applying California law, the Court was confident that they had no interest in limiting recovery of their resident plaintiffs as against a non-resident. California, as the state of residence of designers and manufacturers, had a most significant interest in applying its measure of damages to a product distributed throughout the world for the sake of uniformity of decisions. Furthermore, there was the interest of ensuring the integrity of American products on the very competitive world market. The Court concluded that the United States and the State of California clearly had governmental interests in applying California law, which interests were significantly greater than the interest of the other countries involved. Surprisingly enough, this conclusion was applied not only as to the liability of the aircraft manufacturer but even regarding the liability of the Turkish air carrier.

A somewhat more flexible governmental interest analysis, taking into account also the values embraced by the forum, is advocated by Weintraub, who summarized his "consequences-based approach" in the following way [105]:

> "First, the court must determine whether the states that have a contact with the parties or with the

---

[105] See R. J. Weintraub, 43 *Texas International Law Journal* 407 (2008).

transaction have conflicting laws. Second, if there are conflicting laws, the court must determine the policies underlying those laws. Third, the court must decide whether, if a state's law is not applied, that state is likely to experience a consequence that its policy seeks to avoid. Fourth, application of the law of a state that will experience consequences must be fair to the parties in the light of their contacts with that state.

Ideally, the court should choose the law that will advance the policies of the chosen state and not cause consequences in any other state that the other state's laws are intended to avoid. If this is not possible, the court should explain the result in terms of consequences. Why has the court decided to avoid consequences in the chosen state and impose consequences on other states? Reasonable persons may disagree with the court, but at least the opinion will deal directly with the issues that are at the core of sensible choice of law."

The nature of the governmental interests analysis may often lead to a situation where different legal systems are found applicable to the same claim, depending on the issue that is disputed *(dépeçage)*[106]. In a tort case, it can, for example, be argued that the country where the wrongful act was committed has a great interest in the regulation of behaviour in its territory and is therefore interested in the application of its law with regard to such issues as the definition of negligence, the imposition of strict liability for certain acts or the imposition of punitive damages, whereas it has no interest in the determination of the amount of compensatory damages if the parties are foreign[107]. Thus,

---

[106] See, for example, P. Hay, *Recueil des cours*, Vol. 226 (1991), pp. 374-377.

[107] See, for example, S. C. Symeonides, 82 *Tulane Law Review* 1782-1784 (2008),

in the case of *Kiehn* v. *Elkem-Spigerverket A/S Kemi Metal*[108], concerning an action brought against a Norwegian corporation because of the death in Norway of the plaintiff's relative who was a resident of Pennsylvania, the United States Court for the Middle District of Pennsylvania held that although Norwegian law governed the issue of liability, the issue of damages was governed by Pennsylvanian law in view of the strong interests and policies of Pennsylvania at stake in the damage aspect of the litigation. A similar *dépeçage* of issues was made in 1980 by the United States District Court for the Northern District of California in the case of *Browne* v. *McDonnell Douglas Corporation*[109]. The case arose out of a midair collision in 1976 between two aircraft near Zagreb in what then was Yugoslavia. The defendant was the American manufacturer of one of the planes, and the plaintiffs were the heirs of the various victims coming from England, Germany, Australia and Turkey. The plaintiffs contended that the law of California governed both the issue of liability and the issue of damages, including the California rule imposing joint and several liability on tortfeasors, whereas the defendant argued that the law of Yugoslavia governed both the strict liability and the joint and several liability issues and that the law of the domiciles of the various plaintiffs governed the issue of damages. The Court pointed out that it would follow California's conflict rule based on the government interest analysis and that the governmental interests which might be implicated had to be analysed separately with respect to each of the three separate issues involved: product liability, wrongful death recovery and the imposition of

---

[108] 585 F. Supp. 413 (United States District Court for the Middle District of Pennsylvania, 1984).

[109] 504 F. Supp. 514 (United States District Court for the Northern District of California, 1980).

joint and several liability. No jurisdiction other than California had been shown to have any interest which would be impaired if its law were not applied to the first two issues. In particular, the States of domicile of the various plaintiffs had no interest in applying their more restrictive rules and thus limiting recovery of their resident plaintiffs as against a non-resident defendant. The situation was different, however, concerning the issue of joint and several liability. Under California law, the manufacturer could be held liable for the full amount of damages, notwithstanding the existence of co-tortfeasors. Yugoslavia, on the other hand, followed the principle of proportionate liability under which a defendant is only held to pay that portion of the damage for which he is held responsible. In the opinion of the Court, California's interest in providing full recovery was not implicated in the present case because none of the plaintiffs were California residents. The application of California law would, besides, impair Yugoslavia's interest in deterring the tortuous conduct of its residents within its borders. Therefore, the Court applied Yugoslavia's rule of proportionate liability, whereas California law was applied to the issues of strict liability and wrongful death recovery.

One of the main weaknesses of the government interest theory, as it is advocated by some American scholars and courts, is that it permits the court to arrive at virtually any solution it happens to prefer in the particular case. This is a weakness the government interest theory shares with the other "modern" and "revolutionary" approaches, including the "most significant relationship approach" of the Restatement (Second) of the Conflict of Laws (see *supra*).

The reported judgments create the impression that they do not give the real reasons behind the court's decision. The rise of these American non-rule

approaches[110], by some European scholars disparag-
ingly called *"l'impressionnisme juridique"* and
equalled to the bursting of a bulldozer into a well-kept
garden[111], may have something to do with the recruit-
ment and status of American judges, who normally are
elder lawyers appointed from the ranks of practising
attorneys with substantial experience. Such judges can
perhaps be expected to possess an amount of "judicial
intuition" that will lead them to reasonable conclusions
even when the rule in a particular case is that there is
no fixed rule. In the countries of continental Europe,
the judges, at least in trial courts, are sometimes quite
young lawyers in their early thirties or perhaps even
late twenties who have joined the judiciary directly
after graduation from law school and who need more
guidance than their American colleagues. The legislators in most European countries, as well as the EU law-
makers, therefore prefer clear-cut statutory conflict
rules, while the "revolutionary" American approaches,
characterized by an anti-rule syndrome, presuppose
that the judges have free hands. Another reason why
the flexible American approaches have not been
embraced in Europe is that they have been formed primarily for the solution of conflicts between the laws of
the closely related sister states within the United
States, where the courts of one sister state can be
expected to understand and to respect and support the

---

[110] The difference between an approach and a legal rule
has been described so that the former does not prescribe a
solution in advance, but simply enumerates the factors that
should be taken into account in the judicial fashioning of
an *ad hoc* solution. See, for example, J. D. González
Campos, *Recueil des cours*, Vol. 287 (2000), p. 280 (quoting S. C. Symeonides); W. M. L. Reese, *Recueil des cours*,
Vol. 150 (1976), pp. 44-65 and 186.

[111] See, for example, Y. Loussouarn, *Recueil des cours*,
Vol. 139 (1973), pp. 338-339.

interests and policies of the other sister states[112].
Besides, much (albeit not all) of the American case law
based on the government interest theory has been created by federal courts, which do not feel and are not
even expected to feel any particular allegiance towards
any of the mutually competing policies and interests of
the various states within the Union: for the federal
courts it may be less problematic to put the interests of
the state where they sit and the interests of the other
involved sister states on the same footing. Thus, even
if the governmental interest analysis could be regarded
as suitable for conflicts of law within the United States
(which, however, is very doubtful), it can hardly be
transplanted into conflicts between the legal systems of
completely independent countries with substantial differences not only in the contents of their substantive
legal rules but also in their social structure and socially
accepted values[113]. The practical difficulties encountered by the courts in guessing the policies and meas-
uring the interests of foreign States are obvious, starting with the question which States should have their
governmental interests considered at all. In our globalized world it is not inconceivable, for example, that an
environmentally conscious country with strict rules on
liability for environmental damage is interested in having these strict rules applied to any emission contribut-
ing to the global warming, regardless of where on our

---

[112] See, for example, E. Vitta, 30 *American Journal of
Comparative Law* 6-7 (1982).

[113] See, for example, S. Strömholm, *Torts in the Conflict of Laws*, p. 25. In the words of D. McClean, *Recueil
des cours*, Vol. 282 (2000), pp. 66-67, the American
choice-of-law theories such as government interest analysis and comparative impairment are products of an intellectual history which the rest of the world does not share,
and are largely home-grown products, searching for answers for what are largely home-grown problems.

planet the emission takes place and who is responsible for it, but the fact that a foreign country considers itself to be interested is by itself hardly a reason for the application of its law by the courts of other countries. It appears that the application of the governmental interest theory presupposes the existence of an implied, tacit conflict rule of the forum State listing the jurisdictions whose connection with the dispute is so close that their interests are legitimate and relevant. All this makes the outcome of the conflict-of-law process unpredictable[114]. It also seems that the position of the various governmental interest theories, after they have dominated the choice-of-law thinking in the United States for almost 30 years, has in recent years become considerably weaker[115].

4. The Interest of the Forum Country in Functioning Cross-Border Family Relations and Commerce

It is submitted that the conflict rules, just like any other autonomous rules of the forum country, are normally enacted and applied in the forum country's own

---

[114] Such unforeseeability of results seems to be a common feature of most American approaches, for example the "principles of preference" proposed by D. F. Cavers, *Recueil des cours*, Vol. 131 (1970), pp. 151-162, the "*lex fori* by non-choice" approach of A. A. Ehrenzweig, *Recueil des cours*, Vol. 124 (1968), pp. 181-272, the "principle of reasonableness" recommended by A. F. Lowenfeld, *Recueil des cours*, Vol. 245 (1994), pp. 292-295 etc.

[115] See E. F. Scoles *et al.*, *Conflict of Laws*, pp. 34 and 102-103. The governmental interest theory and some of the other "revolutionary" American approaches have deservedly been called the "Desperanto of conflicts law", see A. A. Ehrenzweig, *Recueil des cours*, Vol. 124 (1968), p. 254, and a "crisis of conflict of laws", see G. Kegel, *Recueil des cours*, Vol. 112 (1964), pp. 91-236.

interest and have the task of advancing its policies[116]. This might, at a superficial glance, seem somewhat strange. How can it lie in the interest of the forum country to apply foreign law? The answer is, in fact, quite simple and not new: Joseph Story, the great classic of American private international law, expressed it very well some 150 years ago, when he saw the foundation of the subject in "mutual interest and utility", "the inconveniences which would result from a contrary doctrine" and "a sort of moral necessity to do justice"[117]. Sir Hersch Lauterpacht, one of the most respected judges at the International Court of Justice, expressed in his votum in the *Boll* case the view that the application of the laws of foreign States pursuant to private international law is dictated by considerations of "justice, convenience, the necessities of international intercourse between individuals"[118]. These formulations refer obviously to the interests of the forum country to ensure rational, appropriate and just solutions in cases containing foreign elements[119]. Just like in purely domestic situations, the forum country is even in cases containing foreign elements interested in creating a legal framework conducive to stable and functional families, confidence in contracts, well-functioning markets, reasonable compensation for tort victims, etc.[120].

It is submitted that the arguments of utility, and the inconveniences and injustices that would result from a

---

[116] See, for example, A. Bucher, *Recueil des cours*, Vol. 341 (2009), p. 170: "L'Etat du for, auteur de la règle de conflit, s'inspire de son propre intérêt de régulation quant à la loi applicable aux situations internationales."

[117] See J. Story, *Commentaries*, p. 32.

[118] *ICJ Reports 1958*, p. 94.

[119] See H. Eek, *Recueil des cours*, Vol. 139 (1973), p. 17.

[120] See A. V. M. Struycken, *Recueil des cours*, Vol. 311 (2004), pp. 30-31.

general refusal to apply foreign law, are the decisive factors behind the forum country's rules on conflict of laws. International legal intercourse would simply be greatly impeded if foreign laws were generally ignored by the forum [121].

It is important to realize that the application of a foreign legal rule does not suggest that this rule is, as such, more "just" or otherwise of a better quality than the *lex fori*. The foreign rule is applied rather because it is deemed, by the legislator of the forum country, to be better suited (better placed, *mieux placé*) for regulating a situation whose connections with a foreign country or foreign countries are closer and more relevant than its connections with the country (and law) of the forum. It is true that the dispute is almost always somehow connected with the forum country, as the courts there would otherwise have no jurisdiction to deal with it, but this connection, for example the present habitual residence of the defendant, may be sufficient and suitable for founding jurisdiction while being irrelevant from the point of view of the substance of the dispute, for example regarding the validity of a contract made abroad many years before the defendant decided to move to the country of the forum. What is a "just" outcome in an individual case may thus vary depending on the geographical context of the situation. This phenomenon has been referred to by one author as "justice pluralism" [122].

There are several reasons why a certain connection with a foreign country makes it natural to apply that country's law. It is not difficult to construct and present examples showing that sometimes foreign law must be

---

[121] See, for example, Th. de Boer, *Recueil des cours*, Vol. 257 (1996), p. 274.
[122] See A. Mills, *The Confluence of Public and Private International Law*, p. 5.

applied in order to avoid results that would be totally absurd. Imagine, for instance, that the Swedish legislator enacts a conflict rule saying that the validity of a marriage ceremony in respect of the authority of the celebrating official is always governed by Swedish substantive family law. One of the consequences of such a rule would be that perhaps 98 per cent of all marriages on this planet would be refused recognition in Sweden, because they had not been celebrated by a person authorized by Swedish law to perform marriage ceremonies. This could have very grave negative consequences, not merely for the spouses themselves but also for other persons, such as their children or heirs. Practically all married immigrants, and even all married persons merely visiting Sweden as tourists, would have to go through a new, Swedish marriage ceremony at the border, if they wished to be considered married in the eyes of the Swedish authorities. It is hardly necessary to explain why such a system would be absurd and contrary to common sense not only in the eyes of lawyers but even, and in the first place, in the opinion of the members of the legally untrained public, who certainly assume that their marriages are recognized even beyond the country where the wedding ceremony was performed. It is, therefore, hardly surprising that the private international law of almost all countries contains a rule stipulating that a marriage concluded abroad pursuant to foreign law shall in principle be considered to fulfil the formal requirements if it is formally valid under the law of the place where it was concluded (the *lex loci celebrationis*)[123]. This example

---

[123] See, for example, M. Bogdan, *Svensk internationell privat- och processrätt*, pp. 182-183; C. M. V. Clarkson and J. Hill, *The Conflict of Laws*, pp. 270-272; G. Kegel and K. Schurig, *Internationales Privatrecht*, pp. 808-810; E. F. Scoles *et al.*, *Conflict of Laws*, pp. 564-570.

shows also that the relevant connecting factor making certain foreign law applicable does not have to reflect a particularly strong connection with the foreign country in question; the couple may have married in a country they were visiting temporarily as tourists, without being its citizens or habitual residents.

Similarly, international trade in goods presupposes that a person, who purchased or otherwise acquired ownership right to an object pursuant to the law of the country where that object was situated at that time, can normally transfer the acquired object to another country without losing his title at the border. This may seem to be something self-evident and elementary, but it presupposes that the country to which the object has been moved has a conflict rule prescribing that the acquisition of rights *in rem* shall be governed by the law of the place where the object was situated at the time when the right was acquired (the *lex rei sitae*)[124]. Both this example and the previous example concerning marriage can be considered to relate to the need to protect "duly acquired rights" (vested rights, *droits acquis*)[125].

Foreign law is, however, often applied also in situations where it is difficult to speak of the protection of rights duly acquired under the laws of another country. It is, for example, quite common in the private interna-

---

[124] See, for example, M. Bogdan, *Svensk internationell privat- och processrätt*, pp. 297-299; C. M. V. Clarkson and J. Hill, *The Conflict of Laws*, pp. 419-427; G. Kegel and K. Schurig, *Internationales Privatrecht*, pp. 765-773; E. F. Scoles *et al.*, *Conflict of Laws*, pp. 1053-1101.

[125] See, for example, D. J. L. Davies, *Recueil des cours*, Vol. 62 (1937), pp. 461-475; G. Parra-Aranguren, *Recueil des cours*, Vol. 210 (1988), pp. 143-158; F. Rigaux, *Recueil des cours*, Vol. 213 (1989), pp. 152-165; A. V. M. Struycken, *Recueil des cours*, Vol. 311 (2004), pp. 448-452.

tional law of many countries that non-contractual liability is subjected to the law of the country where the
damage occurred (the *lex loci damni*), that inheritance
rights are governed by the personal law (*lex patriae* or
lex domicilii) of the deceased or that contracts of sale
are in the absence of a choice-of-law clause governed
by the law of the country of the seller. Behind these
and many other similar conflict rules, which may lead
to the application of foreign law, there are varying
practical and theoretical considerations. The idea they
usually have in common seems to be that each private-law relationship should preferably be governed by
the law of the country with which it has the closest
(strongest, most significant, etc.) natural connection,
i.e. where it has its natural centre of gravity[126]. The
main reason why the law having the closest connection
to a legal relationship is usually considered particularly
suitable to govern it is that the parties tend to adapt
their behaviour to that law, which in turn is assumed to
be best adapted to the circumstances and the human,
cultural and socio-economic environment of the situation. A consistent designation and application of the
law of the country of the closest connection has also
the advantage of not being biased or discriminatory.

In certain parts of private international law, for
example regarding the law applicable to contractual
obligations, the conflict rules of some countries refer
simply in general terms to the law having the closest
connection with the legal relationship in question and
leave it to the court to evaluate and compare the contacts in each individual case, but the principle of closest connection is of importance also because it serves
as the basis for legislative considerations when more
specific conflict rules, whether fixed ones or mere pre-

---

[126] See A. V. M. Struycken, *Recueil des cours*, Vol. 311
(2004), pp. 233-235.

sumptions [127], are formulated and enacted (i.e., the specific conflict rules are supposed to lead normally to the application of the law of the country with closest connection with the legal relationships in question). The principle of closest connection is, furthermore, sometimes used to fill gaps in those situations where there are no established statutory or judge-made conflict rules al all.

The need to promote economic efficiency also speaks in favour of applying foreign law, because insisting under all circumstances on the application of the *lex fori* may lead to economic isolation and constitute an obstacle to the freedom of establishment and the free movement of persons, goods, services and capital. This is the raison d'être of the so-called country-of-origin principle (also called the principle of mutual recognition) existing in the law of the European Union [128].

Furthermore, the application of the legal system with which the legal relationship is most closely con-

---

[127] The borderline between fixed conflict rules and mere presumptions is not always easy to draw. For example, Article 4, point 1, of the EC Regulation No. 593/2008 of 17 June 2009 on the Law Applicable to Contractual Obligations (Rome I), OJ 2008 L 177, p. 6, contains a list of seemingly fixed conflict rules, but point 3 of the same Article provides that where it is clear from all the circumstances of the case that the contract is manifestly more closely connected with a country other than that indicated by these rules, then the law of that other country will apply. Such general escape clauses *(clauses échappatoires)* can in practice turn the seemingly fixed conflict rules into mere presumptions, albeit very strong ones, but they have significant advantages as well, see e.g. K. Siehr, *Yearbook of Private International Law*, Vol. VII (2005), pp. 28-29.

[128] See Chapter II.1, *supra*, and, for example, M. Bogdan, *Concise Introduction to EU Private International Law*, pp. 26-30; H. Muir Watt, *Recueil des cours*, Vol. 307 (2004), pp. 177-218.

nected can, at least in theory, contribute to achieving a
certain degree of uniformity, and thereby indirectly
also predictability[129], of judicial decisions in various
countries[130]. Foreseeability is of particular weight in
cases involving private international law, where the
difficulty to predict the applicable law comes in addition to the usual interpretation problems concerning the
substantive legal rules[131]. If each court applies exclusively the *lex fori*, the outcome will naturally vary
from country to country and there will be a huge incen-
tive for plaintiffs to devote their time and energy to
tactical forum shopping. If the private international law
of all countries directly or indirectly (through specific
conflict rules) designates the law which is most closely
connected with the legal relationship under scrutiny,
this will, at least in theory, lead to the application of
the same legal system and, therefore, hopefully to the
same outcome (the so-called decisional harmony), thus
making forum shopping much less attractive[132]. This
would greatly contribute to legal security and foreseeability, because for the parties it is often impossible or
very difficult to predict which country's courts will be
seised of potential future disputes. It must be admitted,
however, that such uniformity of result is not easy to
achieve, primarily because the opinions about which
connection is closest are often divided among national
legislators. For example, while the private international
law of some countries adheres to the idea that a natural
person is in family-law matters most closely connected

---

[129] See, for example, A. Philip, *Recueil des cours*,
Vol. 160 (1978), pp. 31-32.
[130] See, for example, C. M. V. Clarkson and J. Hill, *The
Conflict of Laws*, p. 8.
[131] See, for example, P. Hay, *Recueil des cours*,
Vol. 226 (1991), pp. 292-293.
[132] See, for example, A. V. M. Struycken, *Recueil des
cours*, Vol. 311 (2004), pp. 231-232.

with the country of which he or she is a citizen, other countries prefer to subject such matters to the law of the country where he or she habitually resides or is domiciled.

Such and other similar differences between the rules of private international law of various countries often give rise to legal relationships that are "limping", i.e. are valid in some countries while being considered invalid in other jurisdictions. Limping marriages, contracts, wills, etc. can cause serious practical inconveniences, even though they may occasionally be advantageous from the point of view of the individual concerned, for example when a remarried widow can continue to collect a pension after her first husband because her new marriage is not recognized in the country from where the pension originates. Even if the creation of limping relationships is probably impossible to avoid totally, their number would certainly rise dramatically if the courts in each country insisted on the exclusive application of the *lex fori*.

On the basis of these considerations, Paul Lagarde has formulated a "principle of proximity" *(le principe de proximité)*, as one of the fundamental general principles of private international law, summarized by the statement that a legal relationship is to be governed by the law of the country with which it is most closely connected[133]. This principle is particularly conspicuous when the conflict rule does not use any specific connecting factor but rather explicitly refers to the law of the country with which the relationship is most closely connected[134]. However, many — probably most —

---

[133] See P. Lagarde, *Recueil des cours*, Vol. 196 (1986), p. 29: "Un rapport de droit est régi par la loi du pays avec lequel il présente les liens les plus étroits." See also A. Bucher, *Recueil des cours*, Vol. 341 (2009), pp. 75-78.

[134] See, for example, Article 4 (1) of the Rome Convention on the Law Applicable to Contractual Obligations

countries base some of their conflict rules on other, competing principles. One such principle is called by Lagarde "the principle of sovereignty" *(le principe de souveraineté)*, making a certain connection with the forum country sufficient for the application of the *lex fori* regardless of the fact that the connection in question does not normally amount to the relationship's strongest connection[135]. An extreme example of such conflict rules are the unilateral rules prescribing the application in all situations of the *lex fori*, even though such rules may to some extent be counterbalanced by restrictive jurisdictional rules permitting adjudication only when the dispute is very closely connected with the forum country[136]. Another competing general principle of private international law often referred to by authors is the principle of party autonomy, permitting the parties in respect of some types of legal relationships (such as contracts) to reach a binding agreement on the law to be applied to their mutual rights and obligations[137]. The principle of party autonomy leads sometimes to the application of the law of a country without a close natural connection with the relationship but has other advantages, for example that the parties can agree on the application on a legal system whose

---

from 1980, even though complemented by certain presumptions in Article 4 (2)-(4).

[135] See P. Lagarde, *Recueil des cours*, Vol. 196 (1986), pp. 49-56.

[136] See, for example, Section 2 of the Swedish International Adoption Act (1971:796), which stipulates that adoption applications are always decided in accordance with Swedish law, while Section 1 of the same Act provides that adoption petitions may be filed in the Swedish courts only if the adopter(s) is/are citizens of or domiciled in Sweden or if a special permission has been granted by the Swedish authorities in the individual case.

[137] See, for example, P. Lagarde, *Recueil des cours*, Vol. 196 (1986), pp. 61-65.

contents they both are familiar with or which is particularly developed in a special field (such as English law regarding contracts of maritime insurance). By their choice, the parties can also achieve a high degree of predictability, regardless of whether they choose the *lex fori* or some foreign law.

Regardless of which of the above-mentioned principles prevails in a particular case, it is submitted that foreign law is applied in the interest of the forum country, even though this interest (mainly the interest in the good functioning of private-law relationships regarding family, contracts, etc.) is usually shared by foreign countries as well. Foreign law is normally not applied as a kind of service, courtesy or assistance given to a foreign country, but rather because the application of foreign law in certain situations is conducive to the smooth functioning of international commercial and family relations and such smooth functioning lies in the interest of the forum country. The fact that a particular dispute is to be decided by applying foreign law does not render the forum country into a mere indifferent "observateur détaché"[138]. It is an elementary fact that the whole machinery of the law in the forum country, ranging from the parliament making laws to courts implementing them and bailiffs enforcing them, is an integral part of the State apparatus financed by the forum country's taxpayers, and there is usually no reason to spend their tax money unless there is something in it for them. The forum "borrows" foreign law to the extent required by the forum's conflict rules, which reflect the forum country's own interests and policies. This is evidenced, *inter alia*, by the refusal of many countries, including Sweden, to accept *renvoi* and their

---

[138] See J.-M. Jacquet, *Recueil des cours*, Vol. 292 (2001), p. 195; A. Bucher, *Recueil des cours*, Vol. 341 (2009), pp. 99-105.

readiness to apply of foreign law even when the country of origin of that law is of the opinion that a completely different legal system should govern the issue [139].

The suggestion that foreign law is applied in the interest of the forum country does not mean that the interests of the litigating natural and legal persons are disregarded, but their collective interests coincide generally with those of the forum. This is illustrated very well by the American Second Restatement's list of relevant choice-of-law principles [140], which mentions not only the needs of the interstate and international systems, the relevant policies of the forum, the relevant policies and relative interests of other interested States and the basic policies underlying the particular field of law, but also the protection of justified expectations of the parties, certainty, predictability and uniformity of result and ease in the determination and application of the law to be applied. The latter factors, especially the protection of justified expectations of the parties and the certainty, predictability and uniformity of result, may seem to focus mainly on private interests, but this is not quite true because the forum country as such is at least as much interested in the justice being done. In fact, it can be argued that the forum country has a keener interest in these matters than the parties in an individual dispute. For the litigants, the prospect of winning is probably more important than the certainty, predictability and uniformity of result, at least if we have in mind their interests at the time of the litigation.

The governmental interest approach and other similar theories are wrong in assuming that, for example, a country whose policy and law restrict the liability of

---

[139] See Chapter IX, *infra*.
[140] See § 6 of *Restatement 2nd of the Law of Conflict of Laws*, Vol. 1, p. 10.

sellers or wrongdoers is only interested in having these
restrictions implemented when the seller or wrongdoer
is its resident, while having no interest in the application of its law when the seller or wrongdoer resides
abroad (especially if the buyer or victim is a local resident) [141]. It certainly does not lie in the long-term interest of the forum country to make its courts protect its
residents against legitimate claims raised by foreign
plaintiffs; such parochial discrimination would be
extremely short-sighted and it would in the long run
cause the forum country enormous damage, not merely
in the form of a loss of face but also economically
through the loss or increased price of foreign invest-
ments and trade. It is submitted that all countries can
be presumed to share a common interest in finding an
appropriate and reasonable solution to private disputes
having an international character. Such solution must,
of course, be based on reasonable and just rules of substantive law, but the ideas of substantive justice vary
from country to country and it is, therefore, necessary
to use private international law to designate the legal
system which is connected with the dispute and with
the legal relationship concerned in such a way that it
can be assumed to lead to an appropriate result corresponding to the legitimate intentions and reasonable
expectations of the parties.

In order to avoid misunderstandings, it must be
stressed that the weight given here to the interests of
the forum country is in no way a pleading in favour
of the exclusive application of the *lex fori*. On the
contrary, it is submitted that the forum country's interest in finding reasonable solutions for disputes having
international implications will very often require and
necessitate the application of foreign substantive law,

---

[141] Cf. C. M. V. Clarkson and J. Hill, *The Conflict of
Laws*, p. 499.

probably more often than would follow from the American government interest theories described above (it should be recalled how extremely *lex fori-*oriented Currie's original theory of governmental interest really was).

What has been said applies in principle also to conflict rules found in international treaties and other binding international instruments. It is certainly true that the application of such conflict rules and of the substantive law designated by them serves also the interest of the foreign countries that are parties to the instrument in question, as otherwise they would hardly have found it meaningful to accede to it. This is true even when such conflict rules are not based on the principle of reciprocity and designate the law of a third country [142]; the interest in achieving predictability and uniformity of decisions may, for example, carry a greater weight than the parochial interest of having one's own legal system applied. It must not be forgotten that it is the interest of the forum country that has led to the adoption of or accession to the instrument in question.

The fact that this interest is shared by other countries does not imply any fundamental departure from the main principle that private international law, just like any other part of the legal system, is basically an expression of the interests (in the widest sense) of the country of the forum.

The realization of the fact that private international law is a part of the legal system of the forum country and, consequently, serves in the first place the interests

---

[142] See, for example, Article 2 of the EC Regulation No. 593/2008 of 17 June 2008 on the Law Applicable to Contractual Obligations (Regulation Rome I), OJ 2008 L 177, p. 6, which stipulates that "[a]ny law specified by this Regulation shall be applied whether or not it is the law of a Member State".

of the forum country, is very important for the understanding of most of the general private international law issues that will be discussed in the following. That is also the reason why this fact is highlighted in the subtitle of this general course.

CHAPTER IV

SOME CHARACTERISTIC FEATURES
OF CONFLICT RULES

1. Bilateral and Unilateral Conflict Rules

Typical conflict rules are mainly of a technical and formal nature, as they do not themselves deal with the substance of the dispute but merely point out the legal system to be applied. For example, Article 3 of the Hague Convention of 4 May 1971 on the Law Applicable to Traffic Accidents stipulates, as a main rule, that "[t]he applicable law is the law of the State where the accident occurred". Conflict rules are therefore "law about applicable law" or "rules about applicable rules" rather than rules offering directly a substantive solution for the dispute.

The use of the term "conflict rules" (*règles de conflit*, *Kollisionsregeln*, etc.) is firmly established, but it is at least as misleading as "private international law rules", because the determination of the applicable legal system does not normally concern conflicting interests, animosity or disagreement between the legislators in different countries. It rather reflects the simple fact that the relationship or dispute is connected with more than one legal system and it must be decided which of them will be applied in order to resolve the dispute at hand.

It is thus a conflict which is "purement virtuel"[143]. It takes place in the head of the judge rather than between different legal systems.

---

[143] See B. Audit, *Droit international privé*, p. 7.

In some situations, it would be theoretically possible to replace this virtual conflict with a compromise
between the substantive-law solutions of the legal systems having a close connection with the relationship or
dispute concerned. For example, if there are two such
legal systems and one of them would give the plaintiff
100,000 while the other would give him zero, a seemingly reasonable compromise would be to entitle the
plaintiff to 50,000. Nevertheless, this kind of compromising is for several reasons normally not used in private international law. It would, first of all, lead to a
result which is incompatible with both legal systems.
The principal objection is, however, that the connections between the disputed issue and the different legal
systems involved vary usually in intensity and relevance and that a reasonable compromise would require
going beyond the mechanical ascertainment of a simple
arithmetical average.

The weighing and counter-balancing of the existing
connections would have to be carried out with some
kind of a mathematical precision, which would be very
difficult to achieve. It is, of course, possible to construct examples where such compromising appears
attractive, but these concern practically always rather
unusual situations where the relationship's connections
with the two countries involved carry exactly the same
weight, such as the property division between spouses
who are and have always been of different nationality
and have always habitually resided in their respective
countries of citizenship (i.e., never resided in the same
country).

The spiritual father of the prevailing design of typical conflict rules, at least on the European Continent,
was the great German jurist Friedrich Carl von Savigny
(1779-1861), who advocated the idea, influenced by
natural-law thinking, that foreign law should be given
effect by the forum whenever the legal relationship

under scrutiny had its natural centre of gravity (seat, *Sitz*[144]) in a foreign country[145].

The most important contribution of Savigny, which helped to create the fundamental paradigm of the private international law of most European countries up to the present day, was also the idea that foreign law and the *lex fori* are in principle equal and entitled to be treated in the same way by means of bilateral conflict rules, preferably using the same connecting factor or factors (for example the nationality or habitual residence of the person concerned) irrespective of whether in a particular case this leads to the application of foreign law or of the *lex fori*. An extension of this approach is that the national legislator should enact such conflict rules as he can reasonably wish to see introduced by the lawgivers of other countries.

Despite the advent of many modern theories and the attempts of some modern writers to replace Savigny's model with inventions of their own[146], it appears that Savigny's heritage survives and remains strong[147]. In

---

[144] Such seat of a legal relationship is naturally always a mere fiction or metaphor, as legal relationships are not tangible and cannot be situated anywhere in a physical sense. See, for example, J. D. González Campos, *Recueil des cours*, Vol. 287 (2000), pp. 51 and 57.

[145] See, for example, J. D. González Campos, *Recueil des cours*, Vol. 287 (2000), pp. 34-66; M. Jänterä-Jareborg, *Recueil des cours*, Vol. 304 (2003), pp. 206-210; A. Bucher, *Recueil des cours*, Vol. 341 (2009), pp. 43-54; G. Kegel and K. Schurig, *Internationales Privatrecht*, pp. 183-184; A. Mills, *The Confluence of Public and Private International Law*, pp. 56-60.

[146] See, for example, P. H. Neuhaus, *Rabels Zeitschrift*, 1982, pp. 4-25; P. Picone, *Recueil des cours*, Vol. 276 (1999), pp. 9-296; G. P. Romano, *Revue critique de droit international privé*, 2006, pp. 496-519.

[147] See, for example, A. V. M. Struycken, *Recueil des cours*, Vol. 311 (2004), p. 319: "legislators and drafters of international conventions have not substituted a better

most countries, the ideal conflict rule is even today considered to be bilateral, unbiased in favour of the *lex fori* and neutral in the sense that it designates the applicable law on the basis of a connecting factor rather than having regard to its substantive contents[148], even though not even such ideal conflict rules can guarantee that foreign law and the *lex fori* are in fact treated in the same way (for example, foreign law can be avoided by means of the exception of *ordre public*, a procedural characterization of the disputed issue or the requirement that the applicable foreign rule, in contrast to the *lex fori*, must be pleaded and proved by a party). The traditional Savignian approach prevails also in the recent codifications of private international law within the framework of European integration[149] and traditionally also enjoy the support of a prevailing part of private international law scholars, who sometimes consider it to reflect the equality of States pursuant to public international law. In its resolution of 12 September 1989, the Institute of International Law *(Institut de droit international)* pointed out that one of the objec-

---

method"; J. D. González Campos, *Recueil des cours*, Vol. 287 (2000), p. 65: "si l'ancien paradigme n'est déjà plus généralement admis, aucun autre n'a encore trouvé une acceptation générale par la doctrine". Similarly, P. H. Neuhaus, *Rabels Zeitschrift*, 1982, p. 25, writes that a number of modern problems certainly escape solution under Savigny's principles, but adequate substitutes, resignation aside, have yet to be found.

[148] See, for example, H. Gaudemet-Tallon, *Recueil des cours*, Vol. 312 (2005), p. 183; F. K. Juenger, *Recueil des cours*, Vol. 193 (1985), pp. 159-163.

[149] See, for example, the EC Regulation No. 864/2007 of 11 July 2007 on the Law Applicable to Non-Contractual Obligations (Rome II), whose main general rule in Article 4 (1) prescribes the application of the law of the country in which the direct damage occurs. It makes no difference whether that country is the country of the forum or not.

tives of choice-of-law rules is international harmonization and that the adoption of bilateral choice-of-law rules tends to favour this objective. Therefore, the resolution recommended the adoption of choice-of-law rules based on connecting factors which lead to the application of foreign law under the same conditions as lead to the application of the law of the forum, and called upon States to refrain from adopting choice-of-law rules which broaden the scope of application of the law of the forum as against that of foreign law [150].

In contrast to bilateral conflict rules, unilateral conflict rules designate normally merely the scope of application of the *lex fori*. Some unilateral conflict rules are comprehensive in the sense that they leave no space at all for foreign law, for example Section 2, paragraph 1, of the Swedish Act (1971:796) on International Adoption Relationships stipulates that adoption applications are in Sweden always examined and adjudicated in accordance with Swedish substantive law. Other unilateral conflict rules may leave some space for foreign law, for example Chapter 3, Section 6, of the Swedish Act (1904:26) on Some International Marriage and Guardianship Relationships stipulates that questions of custody and maintenance, arising in Swedish divorce proceedings and regarding children sojourning in Sweden, are governed by Swedish law. This rule, as such, does not provide an answer to the question about the law to be applied to custody and maintenance in other situations, in particular when the child does not sojourn in Sweden. Bilateral conflict rules are usually (albeit not necessarily always) more comprehensive [151].

---

[150] See *Annuaire de l'Institut de droit international*, session de Saint-Jacques-de-Compostelle, Vol. 63 II, 1989, pp. 333-337.

[151] See G. A. L. Droz, *Recueil des cours*, Vol. 229 (1991), p. 33.

The filling of the "gap" left by a non-comprehensive unilateral conflict rule depends on whether the private international law of the forum prefers a bilateralist or unilateralist approach. The use of a unilateral conflict rule may very well be combined with the use of a bilateralist approach to the gap-filling, which may even lead, through interpretation or judicial creativity, to a complete bilateralization of the unilateral rule by applying foreign law when the case is connected with a foreign country in such a way that a corresponding connection with the forum country would lead to the application of the *lex fori*. The demarcation between bilateral and unilateral conflict rules thus does not necessarily coincide with the line between the conflict rules treating foreign law as equal to the *lex fori* and conflict rules favouring, in one way or another, the application of the latter. Unilateral conflict rules, referring to the *lex fori* only, usually give the *lex fori* a privileged position, but this does not always have to be the case, as a unilateral conflict rule may simply restrict itself to those situations where the *lex fori* is to govern while leaving the question of applicable law regarding the same legal issue open as far as other situations are concerned [152].

The unilateralist approach to the gap-filling does not reject the idea of filling the gap by applying foreign law, but would only apply the foreign law that aspires itself to be applied [153]. Consistently implemented, the unilateralist approach means that the private international law of the forum should only delimit the scope of application of the *lex fori* and abstain from deciding

---

[152] See, for example, B. Audit, *Droit international privé*, p. 94.

[153] See G. A. L. Droz, *Recueil des cours*, Vol. 229 (1991), p. 31; F. Rigaux, *Recueil des cours*, Vol. 213 (1989), pp. 128-136; E. Vitta, *Recueil des cours*, Vol. 162 (1979), p. 159.

which legal system should govern in situations falling beyond that scope. The latter issue should depend on the existence of foreign legal system(s) claiming application.

This may obviously cause complications when application is claimed by more than one foreign law (positive conflict) or when there is no foreign law claiming application (negative conflict). A simple but basically correct description of the difference between the unilateralist and the bilateralist approach is that the former starts from the legal rule and its aims, while the latter departs from the legal relationship and its nature [154].

The unilateralist-bilateralist dichotomy must be distinguished from the distantly related problem of the so-called "spacially conditioned internal rules" or "rules with a localizing limitation" within the applicable foreign legal system [155]. It is, for example, conceivable that certain substantive provisions of the *lex causae* are intended to be applied only when the situation, in addition to the connection making the *lex causae* applicable in the eyes of the forum, has additional ties with the country of the *lex causae*. Imagine, for example, that the Kingdom of Ruritania passes a law stipulating that the freedom of disposing of one's estate by the means of a testament (will) is limited by compulsory shares of minor children habitually residing in Ruritania, while no corresponding protection is afforded to children habitually residing abroad. Such geographical "auto-

---

[154] For a concise description of unilaterism as opposed to bilateralism, see for example Y. Loussouarn, *Recueil des cours*, Vol. 139 (1973), pp. 376-379; F. Vischer, *Recueil des cours*, Vol. 232 (1992), pp. 32-43.

[155] See, for example, D. F. Cavers, *Recueil des cours*, Vol. 131 (1970), pp. 133-135; P. Lalive, *Recueil des cours*, Vol. 155 (1977), pp. 311-319; K. Lipstein, *Recueil des cours*, Vol. 135 (1972), pp. 204-206.

limitation" of a particular Ruritanian provision is clearly not a rule of conflict of laws but merely a rule of substantive Ruritanian law, which normally should be respected also by the courts in other countries, for example when due to the deceased's Ruritanian nationality those courts apply Ruritanian succession law.

The private international law of most countries consists today of both bilateral and unilateral conflict rules, and hybrid rules can be found as well. It deserves to be repeated that the bilateral nature of a conflict rule does not guarantee that the rule treats foreign law and the *lex fori* alike, even though such equality of treatment is normally considered desirable as a matter of principle. A bilateral conflict rule may expressly require more for the application of foreign law than for the application of the *lex fori*[156] and, as pointed out above, it may also discriminate against foreign law in a covert way, for example by excluding many issues by classifying them as being of procedural nature and therefore automatically governed by the *lex fori*[157]. In particular, conflict rules taking into account the content of the potentially applicable legal system tend tacitly and indirectly to give preference to the *lex fori*. It is possible to mention Robert A. Leflar's "better-law approach"[158], pursuant to which the attractive-

---

[156] See, for example, Section 2 of the Swedish Act (1985:367) on International Questions concerning Paternity, according to which a man who is or has been married to a child's mother is presumed to be the father if such a presumption exists under the law of the State in which the child was domiciled at birth. If under that law no one is considered the father, the law of the State where the child was a citizen at birth is applied, but only if the child's domicile at birth was not in Sweden.

[157] See, for example, C. M. V. Clarkson and J. Hill, *The Conflict of Laws*, pp. 466 and 485.

[158] See, for example, R. A. Leflar, *American Conflicts Law*, pp. 243-265, and cf. C. M. V. Clarkson and J. Hill,

ness, from the point of view of the forum, of the substantive contents of the potentially applicable legal systems should be one of the five "choice-influencing
considerations" to be taken into account at the determination, in individual cases, of the law to be applied
(the other four considerations being predictability of
results, maintenance of interstate and international
order, simplification of the judicial task and the advancement of the forum's governmental interests). The
content-oriented "better law approach" is used by some
American courts[159], and it will hardly come as a surprise that the forum usually considers its own law to
be "better", i.e. to be most compatible with its own
values[160]. In addition to this bias, the "better-law
theory" undermines certainty and predictability; a conflict rule, which instructs the court to apply the substantive law it likes most, is hardly any rule at all.
Taking into account of the contents of the substantive
rules can be done legitimately in many other ways,
for example using alternative or cumulative conflict
rules[161].

2. Are Conflict Rules Value-Neutral?

The "technical" character of conflict rules is sometimes considered to make them necessarily void of ethical and other social values, in contrast to the rules of

---

The Conflict of Laws, pp. 494-495; P. Hay, *Recueil des
cours*, Vol. 226 (1991), pp. 355-357; E. F. Scoles *et al.*,
Conflict of Laws, pp. 52-58; S. C. Symeonides, *Recueil
des cours*, Vol. 298 (2002), pp. 51-55.

[159] See, for example, E. F. Scoles *et al.*, *Conflict of
Laws*, p. 53.

[160] See, for example, E. F. Scoles *et al.*, *Conflict of
Laws*, p. 54.

[161] See Chapter IV.2, *infra*, and, for example, B. Audit,
Recueil des cours, Vol. 305 (2003), pp. 336-343.

substantive law which are normally based on value
judgments [162]. A typical conflict rule is certainly more
space-oriented than value-oriented; it does not say who
is right and who is wrong as far as the substance of the
dispute is concerned, but designates merely the legal
system that will decide the issue. In most cases, typical
conflict rules are intended to function without regard to
the contents of the national legal systems involved, and
it is therefore usually quite difficult to accuse a particular conflict rule to be generally more favourable
to men than to women, to old people than to young
people, to rich people than to poor people, etc. Some
critics have, consequently, criticized traditional rules of
conflict of laws for being "blindfolded" or mechanical; in the words of D. F. Cavers they operate as a doc-
trinal slot machine, which upon the insertion of a
coin produces automatically the appropriate law [163].

This rather disparaging description is not always
well founded, and today it seems to be generally
admitted that conflict rules are not necessarily quite
detached from the values of substantive law and blind
as far as the achievement of substantive justice is concerned [164]. In reality, the conflict rules can usually be
expected to be based on the same political, ethical,
religious and other values that are embraced by the
same legislator [165] when enacting domestic substantive
rules (Erik Jayme speaks about a "cohérence des

---

[162] See, for example, K. Zweigert, *Rabels Zeitschrift*,
1973, pp. 443-445.
[163] See D. F. Cavers, 47 *Harvard Law Review* 191-192
(1933-1934).
[164] See, for example, A. E. von Overbeck, *Recueil des
cours*, Vol. 176 (1982), p. 48.
[165] The legislator is here defined as the person or persons having influence on the making of the conflict rules,
such as politicians in respect of statutory conflict rules and
judges in respect of judge-made conflict rules.

valeurs")[166]. Even though conflict rules can hardly be reduced to shadow projections of the forum country's substantive law, it is reasonable to expect that they will take into account the basic substantive policies underlying the particular field of substantive *lex fori*[167]. For example, a national legislator believing in gender equality and implementing it consistently in substantive legal fields such as family law will hardly use the citizenship or habitual residence of the husband or of the father as connecting factors in private international law; a firm belief in the equal rights of children irrespective of whether born in or out of wedlock will lead to the use of the same conflict rule for all children regarding maintenance; the treatment under substantive family law of *de facto* cohabitation as a legitimate stable family form with important legal effects will probably lead to the adoption of a conflict rule on its legal effects that is similar to the conflict rule regarding the legal effects of marriage; the view that immigrants should as soon as possible be assimilated will probably lead to the application of the family law of the country of their new habitual residence, while the opposite view giving more weight to the right of immigrants to preserve their traditional family values will probably result in the application of the family law of the country of their "roots" (normally the country of their citizenship), etc.

On the other hand, the aims and functioning of the

---

[166] See E. Jayme, *Recueil des cours*, Vol. 251 (1995), pp. 129-130. See also H. Gaudemet-Tallon, *Recueil des cours*, Vol. 312 (2005), pp. 191-193 and 395-405; J. D. González Campos, *Recueil des cours*, Vol. 287 (2000), p. 314, and F. Pocar, *Recueil des cours*, Vol. 188 (1984), p. 355.

[167] See, for example, Section 6 of the Restatement (2nd), which mentions such policies among the factors relevant to the choice of the applicable law.

conflict rules are undeniably on a level which differs
from that of the substantive rules, and this may be one
of the reasons why the conflict rules can survive even
very fundamental changes in the society (it can be
noted, as an example, that the Czechoslovak Act on
Private International Law, adopted under the commu-
nist regime in 1963[168], remains in force today, both in
the Czech Republic and in Slovakia, even though with
some amendments).

Many authors differentiate, in fact, between "substantive-law justice" and "private-international-law
justice" (even though it might be more correct to speak
about "substantive-law values" and "private-international-law values")[169]. A typical, traditional conflict

---

[168] Act No. 97/1963 concerning Private International
Law and the Rules of Procedure relating Thereto.

[169] See, for example, G. Kegel and K. Schurig, *Internationales Privatrecht*, p. 131, who differentiate between
"materiellprivatrechtliche Gerechtigkeit" and "internationalprivatrechtliche Gerechtigkeit", even though they point
out that justice is indivisible. See also B. Audit, *Droit
international privé*, p. 83, who writes that conflict rules
are intended to achieve "la justice de droit international
privé" rather than "la justice matérielle", even though he
admits that the separation between these two types of justice has become less clear due to the increasingly frequent
taking into account of the contents of substantive rules at
the designation of the applicable law. E. Jayme, *Recueil
des cours*, Vol. 251 (1995), pp. 94-95, speaks about "justice conflictuelle", J. D. González Campos, *Recueil des
cours*, Vol. 287 (2000), p. 310 differentiates between "conflict justice" and "substantive justice", and S. C. Symeonides, *Recueil des cours*, Vol. 298 (2002), pp. 397-405,
uses the terms "conflicts justice" and "material justice". In
a similar way, it seems reasonable to differentiate between
the justice of the dispute's outcome (which results from a
combination of a conflict rule and the applicable substantive rule) and the jurisdictional justice concerning the
plaintiff's access to courts and the protection of the defendant against burdensome or inconvenient fora *(Zuständig-*

rule does not aspire to achieve substantive "justice" between a husband and his wife or between a seller and a buyer in a particular case, and it is of course possible that the final result the designated substantive rule leads to is sometimes perceived as less than fair in this respect. The "justice" pursued by the conflict rule is of a different kind: "La justice de droit international privé n'est pas la justice du droit matériel." [170] The private international law justice requires, for example, that the applicable substantive legal system be so closely connected with the legal relationship under scrutiny that it can be presumed to be particularly well adapted and suited for that relationship's social context. Further, the application of this legal system should not come as a surprise to the parties [171], the applicable legal system should be the law with which the parties can be presumed to be particularly familiar, the rules of conflict of laws should promote the stability of legal relations and avoid the creation of "limping" legal relationships, the conflict rules should not without good reasons systematically give privileged treatment to a party of a certain race or gender (for example the husband) by designating the law that is

---

keitsgerechtigkeit). On the other hand, S. Vrellis, *Recueil des cours*, Vol. 328 (2007), pp. 311-332, denies the existence of any particular conflicts justice different from the concept of justice in substantive law, as in his view there can be only one just (or most just or least unjust) solution: "il n'y a qu'une solution juste". See also A. Bucher, *Recueil des cours*, Vol. 341 (2009), pp. 52-53.

[170] See C. Kessedjian, *Recueil des cours*, Vol. 300 (2002), p. 221.

[171] According to Th. de Boer, *Recueil des cours*, Vol. 257 (1996), pp. 297-299, the predictability of the applicable law should not carry great weight, because average persons lacking previous experience in dealing with multistate legal problems are anyway not aware of the possibility that the court may apply foreign law.

normally more accessible to this party than to his counterpart, etc. The private international law justice may also be denoted "systemic justice", as it concerns the appropriate allocation of regulatory authority between legal systems rather than the regulation of private rights themselves[172].

The various considerations of justice in the sense of private international law collide at times, and a suitable compromise must be found. For example, while there are good reasons to subject the legal capacity of a natural person to the law of the country to which he has a stable connection (normally his *lex patriae* or his *lex domicilii*) rather than to the law of the country where he happens to be at each particular moment, the interests of his local co-contractants require that they be protected against the effects of an unforeseeable foreign legal system[173]. Or, imagine a Swedish businessman or a Swedish author directing his Internet site to the Swedish market or Swedish readers. His site is, however, accessible to Internet surfers all over the world and he ends up being sued for trademark infringement or defamation allegedly causing damage in a distant country pursuant to that country's law. A similar problem arises if the businessman advertises or the author publishes an article in a Swedish newspaper and a few copies thereof are sold in a foreign country.

---

[172] See A. Mills, *The Confluence of Public and Priavte International Law*, pp. 16-20.

[173] Thus, Article 13 of the EC Regulation No. 593/2008 of 17 June 2008 on the Law Applicable to Contractual Obligations (Rome I), OJ 2008 L 177, p. 6, provides that in a contract concluded between persons who are in the same country, a natural person who would have capacity under the law of that country may invoke his incapacity resulting from the law of another country, only if the other party to the contract was aware of that incapacity at the time of the conclusion of the contract or was not aware thereof as a result of negligence.

Regardless of how fair and just the substantive contents of the law of that country may be, it is not obvious that the application of its law (the *lex loci damni*) would be fair and just in view of the circumstances.

It follows from the above that the various aspects of conflict justice may coincide in particular cases, but may as frequently collide. Similar collisions are conceivable also betwen conflict justice and substantive justice, so that the application of the law which is most fair in substance can be unfair from the viewpoint of private international law or vice versa[174]. For example, the old-fashioned conflict rule designating the law of the country of the husband as the law governing the matrimonial property regime may be conceived as unfair and discriminatory by many women even though there are no reasons to believe that the application of this legal system will generally lead to substantive results that are less advantageous to the wives than the application of their own law; the contrary may, in fact, be true in many cases[175]. The application of the law of the country of the husband may, nevertheless, be unfair to the wives in other respects than concerning the contents of the substantive legal rules; it can, for example, be assumed that it is an advantage for the husband that the applicable law is the law he is more familiar with, or has better chances to procure information about, than his wife. In modern family law, where the mutual rights and duties of both spouses are in principle the same, there is of course no reason to apply the law of the country of the husband, thus giving him the advantage of an easier access to information about the contents of the applicable rules. Such privileged treatment

---

[174] See, for example, H. Gaudemet-Tallon, *Recueil des cours*, Vol. 312 (2005), pp. 173-174.
[175] See, for example, H. Gaudemet-Tallon, *Recueil des cours*, Vol. 312 (2005), p. 404.

of one of the parties may, on the other hand, sometimes be fully legitimate in other areas, such as when
the conflict rules regarding contractual obligations designate as applicable the law of the party who is to
effect the performance which is characteristic of the
contract[176], for example the law of the seller in respect
of contracts for the sale of goods[177], because the characteristic performance (normally meaning the specific
performance to be effected in kind) is usually more
complicated from the legal point of view than the relatively simple monetary obligation of the other party.

What has been said does not mean that the conflict
rules are always interested merely in achieving "justice
conflictuelle" and are indifferent to the ultimate substantive outcome of the dispute. In fact, a conflict rule
may be formed having regard to both substantive and
choice-of-law policies, even though sometimes there
can be different views about which of them should prevail in the cases where the two policies pull in different
directions[178]. The conflict rule can attempt to influence
the substantive outcome in a certain direction by several means, the most extreme example being an open
call on the judge to apply the "better law". As has
already been mentioned, the application of the better
rule of substantive law has been proposed by the
American author Robert Leflar within the framework

---

[176] See, for example, Article 4, point 2, of the 1980 EC
Convention on the Law Applicable to Contractual
Obligations (the Rome Convention), OJ 1998 C 27, p. 36.

[177] See, for example, Article 8, point 1, of the Hague
Convention of 22 December 1986 on the Law Applicable
to Contracts for the International Sale of Goods and
Article 4, point 1 *(a)*, of the EC Regulation No. 593/2008
of 17 June 2008 on the Law Applicable to Contractual
Obligations (Rome I), OJ 2008 L 177, p. 6.

[178] See, for example, L. Brilmayer, *Recueil des cours*,
Vol. 252 (1995), pp. 9-111.

of his theory of "choice-influencing considerations"[179]. Related to the "better law approach" is the teleological approach proposed by Friedrich K. Juenger, that would make judges apply substantive rules that in their opinion are of superior quality and most appropriate[180]. The same can be said about the "consequences-based approach" of R. J. Weintraub[181]. In Europe, the use of "the better law approach" has received some support from Konrad Zweigert regarding those cases where the private international law of the forum does not give a clear reference to a particular legal system[182]. He suggests that in such situations, usually arising when there is a gap in the system of specific conflict rules of the forum country, private international law ceases to ensure its principal values such as protection of reasonable expectations of the parties and international equality of decisions, and the judge should resort to applying the better rule after having compared the laws of the jurisdictions concerned in the case at issue. This residual use of "the better law approach" would, in his view, give a rich social dimension to private international law. The use of the better substantive law has, on the other hand, received much criticism, *inter alia* because it would run a serious risk of becoming arbitrary and give a *de facto* preferential treatment to the *lex fori*[183].

---

[179] See R. A. Leflar, *American Conflicts Law*, pp. 243-265. Cf. S. C. Symeonides, *Recueil des cours*, Vol. 298 (2002), pp. 51-55; F. Vischer, *Recueil des cours*, Vol. 232 (1992), pp. 112-114.

[180] See F. K. Juenger, *Recueil des cours*, Vol. 193 (1985), pp. 286-299.

[181] See Chapter III.3, *supra*.

[182] See K. Zweigert, *Rabels Zeitschrift*, 1973, pp. 447-448 and 452.

[183] See, for example, J. D. González Campos, *Recueil des cours*, Vol. 287 (2000), pp. 339-345.

A more subtle preference *(préférence cachée)* for or
against a certain substantive solution may be reflected,
for example, in the use of alternative or cumulative
connecting factors[184]. In particular, the alternative conflict rules may often presuppose an examination and
taking into account of the substantive contents of
several potentially relevant legal systems before the
applicable law is finally designated.

Thus, Article 18 of the EC Rome II Regulation
No. 864/2007 of 11 July 2007 on the Law Applicable to
Non-Contractual Obligations[185] stipulates that the person having suffered non-contractual damage may bring
his claim directly against the insurer of the person
liable if the law applicable to the non-contractual obligation *or* the law applicable to the insurance contract
so provides. This alternative conflict rule discloses that
the legislator is sympathetic to such direct action and
wants to promote it. An even more salient example is
the Hague Convention of 1961 on the Conflicts of
Laws Relating to the Form of Testamentary Dispositions, which obviously wishes to minimize the risk
that a will, which is valid in other respects, is denied
validity due to some purely formal flaws. Pursuant to
the alternative conflict rule in Article 1 of this Convention, a will is therefore valid as regards form if its form

[184] See, for example, A. Bucher, *Recueil des cours*,
Vol. 283 (2000), pp. 72-75; G. Cansacchi, *Recueil des
cours*, Vol. 83 (1953), pp. 95-106; H. Gaudemet-Tallon,
Recueil des cours, Vol. 312 (2005), p. 232; J. D. González
Campos, *Recueil des cours*, Vol. 287 (2000), pp. 360-368;
J.-M. Jacquet, *Recueil des cours*, Vol. 292 (2001), p. 204;
P. Lalive, *Recueil des cours*, Vol. 155 (1977), pp. 105 and
342-343; A. E. von Overbeck, *Recueil des cours*, Vol. 176
(1982), pp. 81-84; P. Picone, *Recueil des cours*, Vol. 276
(1999), pp. 84-118; F. Vischer, *Recueil des cours*, Vol. 232
(1992), pp. 83 and 116-119; E. Vitta, *Recueil des cours*,
Vol. 162 (1979), p. 40.
[185] OJ 2007 L 199, p. 40.

complies with the internal law of the place where the testator made it, *or* the internal law of a country where the testator had his domicile *or* habitual residence at the time when he made the will *or* at the time of his death, *or* the internal law of a country of the testator's nationality at the time when he made the will *or* at the time of his death, *or* — as far as immovable assets are concerned — the internal law of the country where the assets are situated. While this conflict rule does not give preference to any of the alternative connecting factors, there can also be alternative conflict rules which designate connecting factors in a certain order of precedence *(la cascade)* [186]. For example, Section 2 of the Swedish Act (1985:367) on International Questions concerning Paternity provides that the husband or former husband of the mother of a child will be deemed to be the child's father if this follows from the law of the country where the child acquired habitual residence at birth; however, if that law does not designate any father, the law of the country where the child acquired citizenship at birth will be applied instead (unless the child acquired at birth habitual residence in Sweden). The "cascade" is necessary in this case, because a parallel application of two legal systems could otherwise result in two different men being considered the father of the same child.

The preference for certain substantive results is particularly prominent in elective conflict rules, giving one of the parties the right to choose the applicable law, for example Article 7 of the above-mentioned EC Regulation Rome II, providing for the application to environmental damage of the law of the country in which the direct damage occurs "unless the person

---

[186] See A. E. von Overbeck, *Recueil des cours*, Vol. 176 (1982), pp. 84-86, who speaks about "les rattachements subsidiaires en fonction du résultat".

seeking compensation for damage chooses to base his or her claim on the law of the country in which the event giving rise to the damage occurred". Such elective conflict rules, without saying so explicitly, are intended to lead to the application of the law most favourable to the claimant. An example of an alternative conflict rule making no secret of promoting the interests of one of the parties at the expense of the other is Section 24 of the above-mentioned Czech (originally Czechoslovak) Act No. 97/1963 concerning Private International Law and the Rules of Procedure Relating Thereto, providing that relations between parents and children, including upbringing and maintenance, are governed by the law of the State whose citizen the child is, but if the child lives in the Czech Republic, such relations may be considered under Czech law "if it is in the interest of the child". Such references to the interest of one of the parties is not unproblematic, as one legal system may be more favourable to that party in some respects but not in other respects [187].

A cumulative — as opposed to alternative — use of several connecting factors may, on the other hand, reflect a desire to avoid a certain result or to make it more difficult to achieve, for example if the conflict rule requires for the granting of a divorce that divorce requirements pursuant to the *lex fori* as well as pursuant to the personal laws of both spouses are fulfilled. The difference between the alternative and the cumulative use of connecting factors is, however, largely a matter of style rather than substance; the contents of the above-mentioned alternative conflict rule on the form of testamentary dispositions can, for example, be easily re-written in the form of a cumulative conflict

---

[187] See, for instance, A. E. von Overbeck, *Recueil des cours*, Vol. 176 (1982), p. 87.

rule stipulating that a will is *invalid* as to form if —
and only if — it is invalid pursuant to *all* the legal systems mentioned therein. Some combinations of legal
systems, intended to achieve or avoid certain substantive results, are difficult to classify as alternative or
cumulative, for example Article 6, point 2, of the EC
Regulation No. 593/2008 of 17 June 2008 on the Law
Applicable to Contractual Obligations (Rome I)[188],
which deals with certain consumer contracts and stipulates that the choice of law made by the parties may
not have the result of depriving the consumer of the
protection afforded to him by the mandatory rules of
the otherwise applicable legal system (normally the
law of the country in which the consumer has his
habitual residence).

3. The Relationship between Conflict Rules, Jurisdictional Rules and Rules on Recognition and Enforcement of Foreign Judgments

The rules on the jurisdiction of courts and on the
recognition and enforcement of foreign judgments are
of a nature which is fundamentally different from that
of the rules about applicable law (conflict rules). In
some countries, for example Germany, rules about the
jurisdiction of courts and recognition/enforcement of
foreign judgments are considered to be constituent
parts of "international procedural law" *(Internationales
Zivilprozessrecht)* of the forum country, separate from
that country's private international law *stricto sensu*. In
many countries, for example Sweden, the terminology
is not used consistently, but this does not create any
real problems as such demarcations are of no legal relevance.

In contrast to conflict rules, the jurisdictional rules,

---

[188] OJ 2008 L 177, p. 6.

as well as recognition and enforcement rules, do not
lead to the application of foreign law[189]. These and
other procedural matters are practically always governed by the *lex fori*. Nevertheless, it has already been
mentioned that conflict rules, jurisdictional rules and
the rules on recognition/enforcement of foreign judgments are mutually intertwined[190]. A country with a
very restrictive attitude towards the recognition and
enforcement of foreign judgments may be compelled to
extend the jurisdiction of its courts even to cases with
relatively weak connection with the forum, in order to
avoid the risk of creating a legal vacuum where the
forum country has no jurisdiction while foreign judgments are not accepted. The extension of jurisdiction
to such cases leads, in turn, to a more frequent application of foreign law, as the forum will more frequently
face situations with a dominant connection with a foreign country (and consequently with a foreign legal system).

Despite this interconnection, the philosophy behind
conflict rules and jurisdictional rules is not the same,
due to the differences between their respective purposes. While the rules about applicable law should
preferably be based mainly on the close connection of
the legal relationship in dispute with the country of the
substantive provisions to be applied, jurisdictional
rules should instead mainly consider the possibilities of
the forum country to organize and carry out a fair, con-

---

[189] Among other procedural issues having international
implications, it is possible to mention the service of documents or taking of evidence in one country upon the
request from a court conducting civil proceedings in
another country, and the duty of plaintiffs who are foreign
nationals and/or habitual residents to deposit a security for
costs *(cautio judicatum solvi)*.
[190] See, for example, F. K. Juenger, *Recueil des cours*,
Vol. 193 (1985), p. 133.

venient and efficient judicial procedure, which may frequently presuppose, *inter alia*, a certain degree of physical control and power of the forum country over the parties and/or the object of the dispute[191]. Therefore, jurisdictional rules are mainly influenced by procedural considerations, such as the need to make evidence easily available, the wish to improve the access to justice for the weaker party (for instance a consumer of employee), the effort to secure the enforcement of the forthcoming judgment or the desire to respect the intentions of the parties as they have been expressed in their choice-of-court agreement.

This does not mean that the connection between the substance of the dispute and the country of the forum should never play any role for the determination of jurisdiction, as the prospects of reaching a fair and just decision increase when due to that connection the evidence is easily available and the forum has good knowledge and understanding of the social and other background of the case, in particular if it finds that the dispute is to be decided by applying the familiar and well-known *lex fori*. It may even happen that the legislator chooses to regulate the issue of conflict of laws indirectly by jurisdictional rules or *vice versa*, in particular when pursuant to the private international law of the forum country a certain question is always governed by the *lex fori*[192] or — less frequently —

---

[191] This aspect of physical control is, naturally, considerably weaker when the dispute is not expected to result in a judgment that is amenable to enforcement in the physical sense, for example if the dispute concerns merely the determination or alteration of a legal status such as a marriage annulment, a declaration of death or an ascertainment of paternity.

[192] For example, adoption applications are in Sweden always decided by applying substantive Swedish law, see M. Bogdan, *Svensk internationell privat- och processrätt*,

when the jurisdiction regarding a certain question is restricted to those situations where that question is governed by the *lex fori* [193].

---

p. 231. Similarly, the intra-Nordic rules of private international law are largely based on the mandatory regulation of jurisdiction combined with the application of the *lex fori*.

[193] An example of the last-mentioned situation is the German rule according to which German authorities have jurisdiction to issue an inheritance certificate *(Erbschein)* only in those cases where the inheritance is governed by German substantive law, see E. Jayme, *Recueil des cours*, Vol. 251 (1995), p. 135. Similarly, Section 2, para. 1 (3), of the Swedish Act (1990:272) on International Questions concerning Property Relations between Spouses and Cohabitees provides for the jurisdiction of Swedish courts when the plaintiff has his habitual residence in Sweden *and* Swedish law is applicable pursuant to the Act's conflict rules.

CHAPTER V

DO ARBITRAL TRIBUNALS HAVE
A *LEX FORI*?

Treating the rules of private international law as parts of the legal system of the forum country presupposes, of course, that the forum country can be identified. This is usually not difficult in respect of courts belonging to the judiciary system of a particular country, but may give rise to serious doubts when the dispute is adjudicated by arbitrators[194].

Due to its practical advantages (informality, confidentiality, the possibility of choosing experts as arbitrators, world-wide recognition and enforcement, etc.), arbitration has become the preferred method of resolv-

---

[194] H. A. Grigera Naón, *Recueil des cours*, Vol. 289 (2001), pp. 373, footnote 448, suggests that "[i]t is not that international commercial arbitrators do not have a forum; in reality, the universe is their forum". In his view (*op. cit.*, p. 209), certain legal principles or norms enjoying wide international consensus should be considered to belong to "an incipient form of arbitral *lex fori* detached from any specific national legal system, and lead to dismissing the truism that international commercial Arbitral Tribunals lack a *lex fori* of their own". I. Fadlallah, *Recueil des cours*, Vol. 249 (1994), p. 383, admits that arbitrators do not have any *lex fori*, but suggests that the arbitrators are in need of a legal system of their own as a condition of their independence of State rules. He seems to be of the view that the *lex mercatoria* is a suitable replacement for the *lex fori* as far as international commercial arbitration is concerned. Cf. also Y. Loussouarn, *Recueil des cours*, Vol. 139 (1973), pp. 300-303; A. V. M. Struycken, *Recueil des cours*, Vol. 311 (2004), pp. 83-96; A. Bucher, *Recueil des cours*, Vol. 341 (2009), pp. 266-268.

ing international commercial disputes. Even though the decision of an arbitral tribunal is usually recognized and enforced by States, the tribunal itself is not an organ of any State but rather a private body, carrying out its work under a contract with the parties[195]. The tribunal is often composed of arbitrators coming from different countries with different systems of private international law and it may sit and work in yet another country, and these countries do not necessarily have any natural relation whatsoever to the parties and their dispute. For example, Sweden is frequently used as the place of arbitration for disputes between Russian and US companies. In contrast to the often very stringent jurisdictional rules binding on State courts, arbitration proceedings do not in principle require any natural connection with the country where they take place, mainly because arbitral proceedings are funded by the parties themselves and do not entail any financial or other burden for the taxpayers of that country. In fact, arbitration is usually a lucrative business for the arbitrators and arbitral institutions, as well as for the countries where the arbitral proceedings take place. This means that normally the question of jurisdiction of the arbitral tribunal does not arise in its usual private international law sense, albeit it may arise in other respects, for example regarding the extent of the material scope of the arbitration agreement.

Questions of applicable law do, on the other hand, often arise also in arbitration proceedings. Sometimes such questions concern the arbitration as such, for example when it has to be ascertained which legal system governs the validity and interpretation of the arbitration clause itself. Of even greater interest are the conflict-of-laws issues concerning the determination of

---

[195] See, for example, I. Fadlallah, *Recueil des cours*, Vol. 249 (1994), p. 382.

the law which is to govern the substance of the dispute. The arbitral tribunal is usually expected to resolve the dispute in accordance with rules of law and can decide the dispute *ex aequo et bono* or as *amiable compositeur* only if the parties have expressly authorized it to do so. It must be added that the State courts are normally not in a position to express an opinion about the arbitrators' decision regarding the law applicable to the substance of the dispute. In most, albeit not all, countries an arbitral award is final. It can be set aside by a court of law because of certain procedural defects, but not because of an erroneous decision of the arbitrators about the substance of the dispute, such as an erroneous decision on the legal system to be applied (unless the arbitrators have completely disregarded a choice-of-law clause in the contract, as such disregard can be considered to constitute a violation of the arbitrators' mandate [196]). Some national arbitration acts stipulate that in the absence of a choice of law by the parties the arbitral tribunal is entitled in essence to choose the applicable law using its own discretion [197],

---

[196] Choice-of-law clauses in arbitral agreements are sometimes indirect, for example they may refer to the rules of an arbitral institution which, in turn, contain a provision on applicable law. For example, Article 22 of the Arbitration Rules of the Arbitration Institute of the Stockholm Chamber of Commerce of 2007 provides that the Arbitral Tribunal shall decide the merits of the dispute on the basis of the law or rules of law agreed upon by the parties. In the absence of such agreement, it shall apply the law or rules of law "which it considers to be most appropriate". See also Article 33 (1) of the UNCITRAL Arbitration Rules of 1976, Article 28 of the UNCITRAL Model Law on International Arbitration from 1985 and Article 17 (1) of the Arbitration Rules of the International Chamber of Commerce of 1998.

[197] See, for example, Section 46 (3) of the UK Arbitration Act of 1996: "If or to the extent that there is no such choice or agreement, the tribunal shall apply the law

but such generally formulated provisions are seldom suitable for judicial review. This means that the State courts, including the highest judicial bodies, have very limited possibilities to correct the arbitrators in this respect and to guide them by setting precedents. As only a small fraction of all arbitral awards are published, nobody can claim profound knowledge of the general arbitral practice regarding the issue of applicable law.

This need not, of course, prevent legal writers from expressing their views as to what conflict rules the arbitrators should follow. Most of the proposals do not directly formulate the conflict rules as such, but prefer to recommend that the arbitrators follow certain methods to ascertain the conflict rules that should be used (one might say that most proposals suggest conflict rules for conflicts between various conflict rules). The most frequent and the most traditional of these suggestions is that in the absence of a choice-of-law clause, the arbitrators should abide by the private international law of the country where the arbitration proceedings take place, at least if the place of arbitration has been designated by the parties themselves. This solution, providing for a degree of foreseeability, is certainly more reasonable than the recommendation that each arbitrator follow the conflict rules of his own country, but there may be other suitable alternatives, such as the direct application of the substantive rules of the legal system having the closest connection with the legal relationship under scrutiny[198] or considered by the

---

determined by the conflict of laws rules it considers applicable." Article 1054 (2) of the Netherlands Code of Civil Procedure provides that if a choice of law has not taken place, "the arbitral tribunal decides according to the rules that it deems appropriate".

[198] See, for example, Article 187 (1) of the Swiss Act on Private International Law, which stipulates that the

arbitrators to be the most appropriate law (the so-called *voie directe*). This may be reasonable, in particular when the place (country) of arbitration has not been agreed on by the parties themselves.

It happens that the arbitrators succeed in avoiding the whole issue by pointing out that the substantive rules of all of the legal systems involved, or at least all of the conflict rules of these systems, lead to the same result[199].

To the extent the arbitrators decide to follow the private international law of the country where the proceedings take place, this includes not only the conflict rules in the narrow sense but even most of the general principles of private international law, such as the manner of classification or *renvoi*. As will be explained later, however, the arbitrators should not necessarily take into account the public policy *(ordre public)* reservation of the country of the proceedings[200].

---

arbitrators, in the absence of a choice of law by the parties, shall apply "les règles de droit avec lesquelles la cause présente les liens les plus étroits".

[199] H. A. Grigera Naón, *Recueil des cours*, Vol. 289 (2001), pp. 30-34, calls this "the false conflict technique".

[200] See Chapter X.7, *infra*.

CHAPTER VI

SHOULD CONFLICT RULES AND FOREIGN LAW BE APPLIED EX OFFICIO?

1. The Problem

A classical problem much debated among private international law specialists is whether courts should apply the forum country's conflict rules, and thus also the foreign law designated by those conflict rules, upon their own initiative (ex officio) or should disregard the conflict rules and apply the *lex fori* unless the application of foreign law is requested by at least one of the parties. In practice, this question can arise in various situations. One such situation occurs when the parties (or at least the party who would benefit from the application of foreign law) are simply unaware of the existence of the relevant conflict rule. It may also happen that the parties believe that the substantive rules of the applicable foreign law are in relevant respects the same as the corresponding rules in the *lex fori*. The private international law of many countries is relatively undeveloped, which means that reliance on its rules may often lead to unpredictable results, sometimes similar to opening Pandora's box. Finally, the parties may be of the opinion that the costs in terms of money and time of the application of foreign law would simply not be justified, for example in view of the limited value of the dispute.

This problem, which is, at least to some extent, of a procedural character, must not be confused with the question of whether the parties have the right to conclude, in advance, a binding agreement on the legal system that shall be applied to their potential future disputes. Such party autonomy is generally recognized in the area of contractual relations[201], but not only there[202]. The two issues are interrelated though, because judicial passivity meets fewer objections in those disputes where the parties have (or could have) designated the applicable law themselves (see *infra*).

The approach to the question of ex officio application of foreign law, which is seldom regulated by statutes and is frequently omitted in standard textbooks on private international law, differs from country to country and in many of them it is highly controversial and/or has undergone an interesting development in the recent decades. Opinons differ also with regard to the mandatory nature of the conflict rules in international conventions or EU law.

In theory, the discussion is on its face often about whether foreign law should be treated as law or as a mere fact, but such general and conceptualistic classification does not really solve the problem in all its complexity. It seems that those countries, where foreign law is ostensibly classified as a mere fact, regard it as a fact of a special type and in some respects treat it as if it were law, while in countries where foreign law is seen as law, it is seen as a law of a peculiar type and is in some respects treated as mere fact[203]. Besides, the

---

[201] See, for example, Article 3 of the EC Regulation No. 593/2008 of 17 June 2008 on the Law Applicable to Contractual Obligations (Rome I), OJ 2008 L 177; p. 6.

[202] See, for example, Article 14 of the EC Regulation No. 864/2007 of 11 July 2007 on the Law Applicable to Non-Contractual Obligations (Rome II), OJ 2007 L 199, p. 40.

[203] See, for example, U. P. Gruber and I. Bach, *Yearbook of Private International Law*, Vol. XI (2009), pp. 161-169; T. C. Hartley, 45 *International and Comparative Law Quarterly* 272-273 (1996); D. Girsberger *et al.*, *Zürcher Kommentar zum IPRG*, p. 228; R. Hausmann, *European Legal Forum*, 2008, pp. I-2-I-3; H. U. Jessurun

difference between treating foreign law as law and
treating it as fact[204] has several other aspects than the
issue of ex officio application, for example the questions whether it is the court or the parties that must
prove the contents of foreign law, whether an erroneous application of foreign law can be appealed to the
highest judicial instance, and whether a failure to prove
the contents of foreign law leads to the dismissal of the
case, application of the *lex fori* or has some other kind
of consequence.

From the viewpoint of comparative legal studies, it
is possible to divide the most common approaches to
foreign law roughly into three categories, namely passive, active and discretionary, depending on the role of
the judge. In the passive model the parties (or one of
them) must plead and establish the foreign law and the

d'Oliveira, *Revue hellénique de droit international*, 2008,
pp. 501-502; M. Jänterä-Jareborg, *Recueil des cours*,
Vol. 304 (2003), pp. 241 and 264-271.

[204] In practically all countries, situations can arise
where a foreign legal rule has to be treated as a fact, relevant pursuant to the legal system governing the disputed
issue. For example, the Swedish Supreme Administrative
Court examined in the case published in *Regeringsrättens
Årsbok*, 1985, 2:8, whether a rather exotic first name
could be registered for a Swedish child. The Court held
that the issue was governed by Swedish substantive law,
which requires that the name be suitable, but approved the
name anyway because the child had a close relationship
with a foreign country whose law accepted the name in
question. Foreign law was thus given effect within the
framework of the suitability test carried out pursuant to
Swedish law. Another example are the cases where the
violation of certain foreign legal provisions was held to
make a contract invalid because it amounted to a violation
of *bonos mores* pursuant to the *lex fori* or the legal system
governing the contract. See, for example, E. Jayme,
Recueil des cours, Vol. 251 (1995), pp. 87-88, about the
role of foreign law as *datum*.

judge will not raise these issues of his own motion. The opposite, active approach requires the judge to raise upon his own initiative the issue of application of foreign law and use all available resources, or at least exercise a reasonable effort, to ascertain the contents of the applicable foreign rule. In the intermediary, discretionary position, the judge has the right, but not the obligation, to raise and investigate foreign law issues[205].

This chapter focuses on the issue of ex officio application only, while the problems related to the establishment of the contents of foreign law will be dealt with in the next chapter.

The above-mentioned categorization of approaches into passive, active and discretionary is basically correct but somewhat oversimplified, as some legal systems fall within one group in some respects while belonging to another category in other respects, for example depending on the nature of the dispute. The grades of the judge's activism can, furthermore, be subdivided in a more detailed manner. Ex officio application of foreign law may, for example, mean very different things. In would certainly include the activist judge who is expected not only to give effect, upon his own initiative and regardless of the wishes of the parties, to the forum country's conflict rules and to the foreign law they designate, but also to conduct his own investigation looking for facts that may lead to the application of foreign law. A lesser grade of ex officio application can be exemplified by a judge who is obliged to apply foreign law of his own motion but is bound by the facts invoked by the parties and must not look for additional information himself that might lead

---

[205] See G. T. Yates, 18 *Virginia Journal of International Law* 728-729 (1977-1978); J. R. Brown, 9 *The Maritime Lawyer* 183-184 (1984).

to the application of foreign law. It is, in fact, possible
to speak about ex officio application also in those cases
where the judge, before he applies foreign law, is
obliged to bring, upon his own initiative, the conflicts-
of-law issue to the attention of the parties in order to
give them an opportunity to agree on the application of
the *lex fori* or to retract the pleading of the fact that
gives rise to that issue. This kind of ex officio application is very similar, and in practical effect probably
usually identical, to the seemingly opposite approach
where the court ostensibly will not apply foreign law
of its own motion but is, nevertheless, expected to
bring, upon its own initiative, the conflicts-of-law issue
to the attention of the parties in order to give each of
them the opportunity to request that foreign law be
applied. Finally, there is the passive model in its pure
form, where the court will totally ignore and keep
silent about the issue of applicable law and apply the
lex fori unless at least one of the parties discovers and
makes use of the possibility to plead foreign law.

2. The Approaches Used in Some Selected Jurisdictions

When reading the following summary presentations
of the approaches used in a selection of jurisdictions [206],
it should be kept in mind that the attitude towards foreign law depends to a large degree on and cannot be
seen as separate from the general principles of procedural law of the country concerned. The inquisitorial or
adversarial nature of the proceedings will obviously

---

[206] In view of the often diverging views even within
one and the same country and the limited access to sources
from some countries, the presentation is not guaranteed to
be correct in all details. Its main purpose is to illustrate the
various conceivable approaches to the problem.

have a deep impact on all aspects of the judicial handling of the disputes, including the treatment of foreign law. This is the reason why the Institut de droit international in its resolution recommending the ex officio application of conflict rules (and thereby also of the foreign law they designate) conditioned its recommendation to States by adding the words "to the extent that their general rules of procedure permit", even though the exact meaning of this reservation is not quite clear[207].

England is usually mentioned as a typical example of a country where foreign law is treated as a mere fact, which must be pleaded by the party interested in its application[208]. This is supposed to be due to certain accidental historical developments of the English common law courts system, but is certainly closely related

---

[207] See the resolution made by the Institut on 12 September 1989 (*Annuaire de l'Institut de droit international*, session de Saint-Jacques-de-Compostelle, Vol. 63 II, 1989, pp. 333-337):

> "Given the mandatory nature of choice of law rules, which select either foreign law or the law of the forum as applicable, it is recommended that, to the extent that their general rules of procedure permit, States require their competent authorities to raise *ex officio* the question of the application of the choice of law rule; and when that rule is applicable, apply *ex officio* the foreign law determined by it."

[208] See, for example, *Dicey and Morris on the Conflict of Laws*, p. 221; R. G. Fentiman, in *Comparative Law before the Courts*, p. 15; T. Hartley, 45 *International and Comparative Law Quarterly* 273 (1996); K. J. Hood, 2 *Journal of Private International Law* 182-183 (2006); C. M. V. Clarkson and J. Hill, *The Conflict of Laws*, pp. 13-15; Th. de Boer, *Recueil des cours*, Vol. 257 (1996), pp. 258-262; M. Jänterä-Jareborg, *Recueil des cours*, Vol. 304 (2003), pp. 276-277; K. Takahashi, [2002] *Singapore Journal of Legal Studies* 490.

to the English pragmatic and adversarial view of adjudication, which is seen more as a process of argument under the supervision of a passive judge than a process of discovery[209]. In fact, even English law (the *lex fori*), whether statutory or judge-made, must in principle be pleaded by the parties. There are some suggested exceptions though, in particular regarding disputes on personal status, where the result, such as a decree of nullity of a marriage, may affect the position of third parties[210]. As could be expected, the English approach is dominant in many common-law jurisdictions (for example in Australia[211], Canada[212] and India[213]) and even in some countries with a mixed common law-civil law legal heritage (for example in Israel[214]). It is unresolved whether the English approach is to be used also when the relevant conflict rule is based on an international treaty binding the United Kingdom or is contained in an EU Regulation[215].

In view of their English legal heritage, it might be expected that even American courts would follow the English model regarding the treatment of foreign law, but today the American approach is somewhat different. To begin with, since the amendment in 1966 of the Federal Rules of Civil Procedure, American federal

---

[209] See, for example, R. G. Fentiman, in *Comparative Law before the Courts*, p. 15; Th. de Boer, *Recueil des cours*, Vol. 257 (1996), p. 258.

[210] See T. C. Hartley, 45 *International and Comparative Law Quarterly* 286 (1996); R. Hausmann, *European Legal Forum*, 2008, p. I-6.

[211] See T. Einhorn, in *Essays Nygh*, p. 109.

[212] See, for example, J.-G. Castel, *Canadian Conflict of Laws*, 3rd ed., 1994, p. 147.

[213] See, for example, P. Diwan and P. Dewarn, *Private International Law : Indian and English*, 4th ed., 1998 p. 122.

[214] See T. Einhorn, in *Essays Nygh*, p. 109.

[215] See, for example, D. McClean, *Recueil des cours*, Vol. 282 (2000), pp. 225-227.

courts regard even foreign law as law. It has even been asserted that they are authorized to raise the conflict-of-law issue ex officio, even though without being obliged to do so[216]. In order to prevent unfair surprises, the amended federal rules require that the party intending to raise an issue concerning foreign law inform the court and the other party by "pleadings or other reasonable written notice"[217]. The requirement of "reasonable" notice has been interpreted to mean that even though the federal rules do not impose a definite cut-off date after which notice cannot be given, the issue of applicable foreign law should normally be raised already at the pre-trial stage, unless there are extenuating circumstances[218]. The failure to raise foreign law in a timely fashion may result in the application of the *lex fori*[219], and be equalled to a waiver of any objection based on the applicability of foreign law[220]. The notice must provide affirmative indication that the party believes that a specific foreign law ought to apply, so that a mere statement that there are serious doubts about the applicability of the *lex fori* is not sufficient[221]. As far as the state courts are concerned, it is possible to mention rule 4511 of the Civil Practice Law

---

[216] See G. T. Yates, 18 *Virginia Journal of International Law* 748 (1977-1978); M. Jänterä-Jareborg, *Recueil des cours*, Vol. 304 (2003), pp. 283-284.

[217] See Fed. R. Civ. P. 44.1; P. D. Trooboff, 29 *The National Law Journal* (2006).

[218] See *DP Aviation* v. *Smiths Industries*, 268 F. 3d 829 (9th Cir. 2001); P. D. Trooboff, 29 *The National Law Journal* (2006).

[219] See *DP Aviation* v. *Smiths Industries*, 268 F. 3d 829 (9th Cir. 2001); *Whirlpool* v. *Sevaux*, 96 F. 3rd 216 (7th Cir. 1996); P. D. Trooboff, *The National Law Journal* (2006).

[220] See *Whirlpool* v. *Sevaux*, 96 F. 3rd 216 (7th Cir. 1996).

[221] See *ibid*.

and Rules of New York, which allows courts to take, of their own motion, judicial notice of foreign law[222].

The German system seems to be the very opposite of the English approach. Foreign law is regarded as law and must be applied ex officio by German courts[223]. This seems to be rooted in the tradition, traceable to Savigny, that foreign law and the *lex fori* should be put on the same footing and treated equally, which means that foreign law cannot be "degraded" to a mere fact. There are, however, some German authors advocating a "fakultatives Kollisionsrecht"[224] and, in matters where the parties could have bound themselves by a choice-of-law clause, it may happen that if both parties plead only German law the court will, depending on the circumstances, interpret this as an implicit agreement on the application of German law[225]. In such cases, the court is considered obliged, pursuant to

---

[222] See 61 *The Record of the Association of the Bar of the City of New York*, No. 1, pp. 49-59 (2006); T. Einhorn, in *Essays Nygh*, p. 115.

[223] See, for example, G. Kegel and K. Schurig, *Internationales Privatrecht*, pp. 498 and 500-501; R. Hausmann, *European Legal Forum*, 2008, p. I-3.

[224] See, for example, A. Flessner, *Rabels Zeitschrift*, 1970, pp. 547-584; K. Zweigert, *Rabels Zeitschrift*, 1973, pp. 445-446 and 452. It should be noted that the proponents of this approach wish to abolish the *ex officio* application of foreign law even in those disputes where settlement is not permitted, see M. Jänterä-Jareborg, *Recueil des cours*, Vol. 304 (2003), pp. 248-251. A prominent partisan outside Germany of facultative choice of law is Th. de Boer, *Recueil des cours*, Vol. 257 (1996), pp. 223-421. See the critical comments by P. Lalive, *Recueil des cours*, Vol. 155 (1977), pp. 164-178.

[225] See, for example, the judgment of the German Federal Court on 18 January 1988, *Neue Juristische Wochenschrift*, 1988, p. 1592; T. C. Hartley, 45 *International and Comparative Law Quarterly* 276 (1996); R. Hausmann, *European Legal Forum* 2008, p. I-3.

Article 139 of the German Code of Civil Procedure, to draw the attention of the parties to the problem by asking them whether they really intend to make such a choice[226]. In disputes that can be resolved by settlement, the court is bound by the facts invoked by the parties, which can thus avoid foreign law simply by refraining from referring to circumstances that could lead to the application of foreign law[227]. It is important that German courts are required to designate the applicable legal system even when all potentially involved legal systems appear to lead to the same outcome, because an appeal to the Federal Court is traditionally permitted only regarding an incorrect application of German law (including, however, not only German substantive private law but also German private international law and German procedural law)[228].

The Japanese approach is in theory similar to the German one, which is not surprising in view of the close historical ties between German and Japanese legal systems. In practice, however, it happens that the theory is not followed and that the application of foreign law is avoided, for example by assuming that the applicable foreign law leads *in casu* to the same outcome as Japanese law[229]. The ex officio approach to foreign law appears to be an established principle also in China, at least in theory[230].

---

[226] See R. Hausmann, *European Legal Forum*, 2008, p. I-4.

[227] See *ibid.*, p. I-4.

[228] See, for example, the German Federal Court on 24 March 1987, *IPRax* 1988, p. 227, and on 29 June 1987, *IPRax*, 1988, p. 228; P. Gottwald, *IPRax*, 1988, pp. 210-212. About a possible change of German law on this point, see Chapter VII.2, *infra*.

[229] See K. Takahashi, [2002] *Singapore Journal of Legal Studies* 490-491.

[230] See Qingjiang Kong and Hu Minfei, 3 *Melbourne Journal of International Law* 425 (1996).

A similar attitude, i.e. ex officio application of foreign law, seems to prevail also in the Netherlands[231]. In disputes concerning rights and duties which the parties can freely dispose of, Dutch private international law normally permits the parties to agree during the proceedings on the application of the *lex fori*, even though it seems that the silence of the parties is not automatically interpreted as a tacit agreement of this kind. It appears that the Dutch courts are in such a case expected to raise, of their own motion, the question of the applicable law, thus bringing to the parties' attention the possibility of choosing Dutch law[232]. In the cases where the parties are not allowed to dispose freely of the dispute, such as most disputes concerning family-law status, Dutch courts must apply foreign law regardless of the wishes of the parties. Furthermore, the courts are in such cases not bound by the facts submitted to them, not even when they are undisputed by the parties[233].

In France, foreign law is deemed to be law, but law of a particular kind[234]. The prevailing French approach to the application of foreign law is derived from a number of judicial decisions. For many years the leading case was *Bisbal* v. *Bisbal*, decided by the French Supreme Court *(Cour de cassation)* on 12 May 1959[235].

---

[231] See, for example, P. M. M. Mostermans, *Netherlands International Law Review*, 2004, pp. 394-397.

[232] See, for example, P. M. M. Mostermans, *Netherlands International Law Review*, 2004, p. 405.

[233] See, for example, P. M. M. Mostermans, *Netherlands International Law Review*, 2004, pp. 407-408.

[234] See the case of *Coucke* v. *Hoste*, Cassation Court 13 January 1993, *Revue critique de droit international privé*, 1994, p. 78, with a note by Ancel.

[235] See Cassation Court 12 May 1959, *Revue critique de droit international privé*, 1960, p. 62, with a note by Batiffol; commented by Sialelli in *Journal du droit international (Clunet)* 1960, p. 810.

The case concerned a divorce between two spouses
who were citizens of Spain. Pursuant to the French
conflict rules at that time, French courts were supposed
to apply Spanish law which did not permit divorce, but
the lower court applied French law and dissolved the
marriage. One of the spouses lodged an appeal *(pour-
voi en cassation)*, but the Supreme Court rejected it on
the ground that French conflict rules, when prescribing
the application of foreign law, were not imperative
(d'ordre public) and that the trial court had not erred in
not applying them ex officio. On the other hand, less
than one year later, the same court held in the case of
Compagnie algérienne de crédit et de banque v. *Che-
mouny*[236] that it was permissible for the lower court to
investigate and apply foreign law upon its own initiative. It could thus be argued, on the basis of these two
judgments, that although French courts were not
required to apply foreign law ex officio, they were
allowed to do so. Subsequent developments led step by
step to a differentiated treatment of disputes depending
on whether the case concerned *droits disponibles*, i.e.
was of such nature that it could be resolved by a settlement (the parties were free to resolve it themselves
without the involvement of courts) or not. In 1984, the
Cassation Court approved in the case of *Société Thinet*
v. *Société Roque*[237] that the lower court had not applied
foreign law upon its own initiative, but the Cassation
Court founded its decision mainly on the fact that the
subject of the dispute was at the free disposal of the
parties, thus indicating that the decision may have been

---

[236] See Cassation Court 2 March 1960, *Revue critique
de droit international privé*, 1960, p. 97, with a note by
Batiffol.
[237] Cassation Court 24 January 1984, *Journal du droit
international (Clunet)*, 1984, p. 874, with a note by
Bischoff.

different if the dispute had concerned a matter where the judicial decision could not be replaced by a settlement. In two decisions made in October 1988[238], the Cassation Court made a rather far-reaching general statement that in view of Article 12, paragraph 1, of the New French Civil Procedure Code, obliging the courts to decide disputes in accordance with applicable legal rules[239], the courts had to give effect to the applicable foreign law ex officio, but soon thereafter, on 4 December 1990, in the case of *Coveco* v. *Versoul*[240] the same court took one step back and held that the courts are not under the duty to apply foreign law upon their own initiative when the parties have the free disposal of the subject of the dispute, unless the conflict rule originates in an international convention. This was confirmed on 26 May 1999 by the Cassation Court in the case of *Mutuelles du Mans* v. *Boedec*[241], even though the exception regarding international conventions (the same should apply to conflict rules in EC regulations) was restricted to those cases where the convention itself requires that its conflict rules be applied *ex officio* (most international conventions in

---

[238] See the paternity case of *Rebouh* v. *Bennour*, decided on 11 October 1988, and the money dispute in *Schule* v. *Philippe*, decided on 18 October 1988, both reported in *Journal du droit international (Clunet)*, 1989, p. 349, with a note by Alexandre; *Revue critique de droit international privé*, 1989, p. 368.

[239] "Le juge tranche le litige conformément aux règles de droit qui lui sont applicables." An English translation of Article 12 is provided by, for example, T. Einhorn, in *Essays Nygh*, p. 116.

[240] See *Journal du droit international (Clunet)*, 1991, p. 371, with a note by Bureau; *Revue critique de droit international privé*, 1991, p. 558, with a note by Niboyet-Hoegy.

[241] See *Revue critique de droit international privé* 1999, p. 707 with a note by Muir Watt.

the field of private international law, including the Hague Conventions, are silent on this point). In a case decided in June 2006, the Cassation Court seems to have reverted to its 1988 position, holding in a property dispute in the matter of *Wildenstein*[242] that the judges must apply, "au besoin d'office", the French conflict rule designating foreign law as applicable. The present French approach to the problem seems thus to be that the trial court must apply foreign law ex officio in disputes that are of such a nature that they cannot be resolved by a settlement (for instance, most status judgments of family-law nature)[243], but may perhaps have a discretion to do so or not to do so in the cases where the parties can freely dispose of their rights by settling the dispute. Nevertheless, the French case law is not sufficiently stable to permit a definite conclusion[244]. It should also be noted that Article 7 of the New Code of Civil Procedure proclaims, on the one hand, that the judge must not base his decision on facts

---

[242] Cassation Court 20 June 2006, *Journal du droit international (Clunet)*, 2007, p. 125, with a note by Gaudemet-Tallon. See, however, also Cassation Court 28 November 2006, *Revue critique de droit international privé*, 2007, p. 873, where the Court refused to annul the judgment of a lower court which had omitted to apply foreign law in a money dispute, as the party in question had not invoked that law in support of its claim.

[243] This was recently confirmed by the Cassation Court in its decision of 7 June 2006, *Revue critique de droit international privé*, 2007, p. 873.

[244] See, for example, B. Audit, *Droit international privé*, pp. 218-223; B. Fauvarque-Cosson, in *Comparative Law before the Courts*, pp. 4-6; Th. de Boer, *Recueil des cours*, Vol. 257 (1996), pp. 262-266; H. Gaudemet-Tallon, *Journal du droit international (Clunet)*, 2007, pp. 127-130; T. C. Hartley, 45 *International and Comparative Law Quarterly* 278-279 (1996); R. Hausmann, *European Legal Forum*, 2008, pp. I-4-I-5; M. Jänterä-Jareborg, *Recueil des cours*, Vol. 304 (2003), pp. 273-276.

that have not been introduced by the parties[245] and, on the other hand, that the introduced facts can be taken into consideration even if they have not been pleaded in support of the positions of the parties[246]; this means, *inter alia*, that the nationality and the addresses of the parties can always be taken into account as they are compulsory elements of the "dossier"[247]. A French court intending to apply foreign law ex officio is expected to notify the parties and give them the opportunity to argue the case on the basis of the applicable foreign law[248] or, if they so wish, to enter into a procedural agreement *(accord procédural)* in favour of the application of French law[249].

Such procedural agreements, in contrast to the usual choice-of-law clauses recognized by the private international law rules, cannot in a binding way be concluded in advance, but they seem possible in all disputes amenable to a settlement[250] and can today

---

[245] Article 7, para. 1, stipulates that "Le juge ne peut fonder sa décision sur des faits qui ne sont pas dans le débat."

[246] Article 7, para. 2, provides that "Parmi les éléments du débat, le juge peut prendre en considération même les faits que les parties n'auraient pas spécialement invoqués au soutien de leurs prétentions."

[247] See B. Audit, *Droit international privé*, pp. 223-224.

[248] See Article 16 of the New Code of Civil Procedure.

[249] See Article 12, para 3, of the New Code of Civil Procedure.

[250] See, for example, the decision of the French Cassation Court on 6 May 1997 in the case of *Hannover International* v. *Baranger*, *Revue critique de droit international privé*, 1997, p. 514, with a note by Fauvarque-Cosson, and *Journal du droit international (Clunet)*, 1997, p. 804, with a note by Bureau, as well as its decision on 1 July 1997 in the case of *Karl Ibold GmbH* v. *Société Lambert-Rivière*, *Revue critique de droit international privé*, 1998, p. 60, with a note by Mayer.

probably be concluded even tacitly, such as when despite having been made aware of the conflict issue both parties continue to argue on the basis of French substantive law[251]. When the legal systems involved had the same substantive contents[252], the Cassation Court has refused to reverse a judgment where the trial court had applied the wrong legal system[253] or where the lower court had refrained from choosing between potentially applicable legal systems[254].

As far as Switzerland is concerned, Article 16 (1) of the Federal Act on Private International Law of 1987

---

[251] See B. Audit, *Droit international privé*, pp. 224-225; B. Fauvarque-Cosson, in *Comparative Law before the Courts,* pp. 10-11; A. V. M. Struycken, *Recueil des cours,* Vol. 311 (2004), pp. 350-352. It seems that an *accord procédural* had originally to be concluded explicitly, see the case of *Roho* v. *Caron*, Cassation Court on 19 April 1988, *Revue critique de droit international privé*, 1989, p. 68, with a note by Batiffol. H. Gaudemet-Tallon, *Recueil des cours*, Vol. 312 (2005), pp. 295-296, is of the view that such procedural agreements should be respected also when they replace one foreign law with another foreign law or even when the French *lex fori* is to be replaced with foreign law, but she submits that the procedural agreement must be explicit and that the foreign law preferred by the parties must have a certain connection with the dispute.

[252] See B. Audit, *Droit international privé*, p. 226; B. Fauvarque-Cosson, in *Comparative Law before the Courts*, p. 8.

[253] Cassation Court on 11 July 1988, *Cassan* v. *Prince Vin Thuy*, concerning the action by Bao Dai, the former and last emperor of Vietnam, for annulment of a paternity acknowledgment, *Revue critique de droit international privé*, 1989, p. 81, with a note by Gautier.

[254] Cassation Court on 13 April 1999 in the case of *Compagnie royale belge* v. *Société Lilloise d'assurances*, *Revue critique de droit international privé*, 1999, p. 698, with a note by Ancel and Muir-Watt; *Journal du droit international (Clunet)*, 2000, p. 315, with a note by Fauvarque-Cosson.

deals on its face merely with the duty of the court to establish ex officio the content of the applicable foreign law (see *infra*), but that duty is considered also to imply the duty to apply foreign law of the court's own motion[255]. Nevertheless, the parties may agree on the application of Swiss law if the proceedings involve merely economic interests *("en matière partimoniale", "bei vermögensrechtlichen Ansprüchen")*, which is a category of disputes almost identical to disputes that can be resolved by a settlement[256]. If the court intends to apply foreign law which has not been pleaded by any of the parties, it must bring it to their attention and give them the opportunity to adapt their arguments accordingly (or, in cases involving merely economic interests, agree on the application of Swiss law)[257]. It seems that mere silence or passivity of the parties is not deemed to be equal to a tacit agreement on the application of Swiss law[258]. If the potentially relevant legal systems lead to the same outcome, the question of applicable law can be left unanswered by the court[259].

In spite of Article 12 (6) of the Spanish Civil Code of 1889 (as amended), which stipulates that Spanish courts must apply Spanish conflict rules ex officio[260],

---

[255] See, for example, B. Dutoit, *Droit international privé suisse*, p. 57; D. Girsberger *et al.*, *Zürcher Kommentar zum IPRG*, p. 220; T. C. Hartley, 45 *International and Comparative Law Quarterly* 277-278 (1996).

[256] See T. C. Hartley, 45 *International and Comparative Law Quarterly* 274 (1996).

[257] See B. Dutoit, *Droit international privé suisse*, pp. 58-59; D. Girsberger *et al.*, *Zürcher Kommentar zum IPRG*, p. 229.

[258] See D. Girsberger *et al.*, *Zürcher Kommentar zum IPRG*, pp. 220-221.

[259] See *ibid.*, p. 221.

[260] Article 12 (6): "Los Tribunales y autoridades aplicarán de oficio las normas de conflicto del derecho español."

the Spanish Supreme Court has traditionally treated foreign law as a fact. Foreign law could not be applied unless is had been invoked by the parties[261]. However, the new Spanish Civil Procedure Code *(Ley de Enjuiciamiento Civil)* of 2000 seems to have brought about a change in this respect. Even though the Code does not say so directly, it is interpreted to mean that as the application of foreign law in a specific case derives directly from the Spanish conflict rules, the pleading of foreign law by the parties is no longer a necessary pre-requisite of its application[262].

In Sweden, the view prevailing among legal writers[263] is that foreign law should be treated as law and not as a mere fact, but the treatment of the Swedish conflict rules and of the applicable foreign law depends to a large extent on whether the dispute is of a kind where the parties are free at any moment to reach a settlement or belongs to the category of disputes where a settlement cannot replace a judicial decision. In the cases belonging to the latter category, it seems clear that the court must follow the conflict rule on its own initiative and that it must even investigate on its own initiative the facts that may lead to the application of foreign law[264]. On the other hand, in those cases where the parties are the masters of the dispute, Swedish courts are explicitly forbidden to base

---

[261] See A.-L. Calvo Caravaca and J. Carrascosa González, *IPRax*, 2005, p. 170.

[262] See Article 281 (2) of the Code; A.-L. Calvo Caravaca and J. Carrascosa González, *IPRax*, 2005, p. 171; R. Hausmann, *European Legal Forum*, 2008, p. I-12.

[263] See, for example, M. Bogdan, *Svensk internationell privat- och processrätt*, pp. 42-46; M. Jänterä-Jareborg, *Recueil des cours*, Vol. 304 (2003), pp. 277-280.

[264] This does not happen very often though, as many important status issues, for example divorces and adoptions, are in Swedish private international law governed generally by the *lex fori*.

their decision on facts that have not been invoked by the parties[265]. This means that the Swedish judge must in such cases apply Swedish law even if he suspects, or even knows for a fact, that the circumstances *in casu* warrant the application of foreign law. Another question is, however, how the judge should act when the relevant circumstances have been invoked by a party, but without that party being aware of their consequences regarding the determination of the applicable law. It seems that the judge should in such a case ex officio inform the parties about the conflict rule in question and give them the opportunity to adapt their arguments to the applicable foreign legal system or to agree on the application of the *lex fori* (such agreement, reached at the time of the proceedings and similar to the French *accord procédural*, should be respected by the courts, provided the parties are masters of the dispute). Sometimes a tacit agreement on the application of the *lex fori* can even be presumed, for example when the parties, both having access to legal expertise, refer in their submissions exclusively to the *lex fori*[266].

The principle that foreign law should be applied upon the court's own initiative is confirmed or seems to be gaining ground in most of the relatively modern codifications of private international law[267].

---

[265] See Chapter 17, Section 3, of the Swedish Code of Judicial Procedure.

[266] See, for example, the Swedish Supreme Court, in *Nytt Juridiskt Arkiv*, 1977 p. 92.

[267] See Jänterä-Jareborg, *Recueil des cours*, Vol. 304 (2003), pp. 282 and 285, with references to Sections 1-3 of the Austrian Federal Act on Private International Law of 1978, Section 2 of the Turkish Act on Private International Law and International Civil Procedure of 1982, Article 2051 of the Peruvian Civil Code of 1984, Article 22 of the Paraguayan Civil Code of 1985, Article 60 of the Venezuelan codification of private international law of 1998, Article 1191 of the Russian Civil Code of 2002, etc.

After this summary and simplified survey of how the problem is dealt with in some selected jurisdictions, it is appropriate to ask which of the solutions is the most suitable one. As pointed out above, the solutions must be adapted to the rest of the legal system of the forum, in particular to the procedural principles prevailing there, but it is submitted that it is possible to make suggestions suitable for a more-or-less universal use. It is also submitted that even within the same country, different approaches can and should be used in different situations, the most fundamental difference in this respect being between those cases where the parties are the master of the dispute *(dominus litis)* entitled to resolve it by a settlement and those cases where a settlement cannot replace a judicial decision. The most typical example of the former category are pecuniary disputes, while family status matters are mostly of the latter type.

3. Suggestions for Disputes Where Settlement Is Not Permitted

There seems to be an almost general consensus that disputes which are not amenable to settlement, such as most status matters in family law, must be decided pursuant to the foreign law determined by the conflict rules of the forum and that this law must normally be applied upon the court's own initiative even if the parties, because of ignorance of private international law or other reasons, argue on the basis of the *lex fori* or even explicitly agree and request that the *lex fori* be applied. That is not all: the court should even be obliged to check and investigate the facts that may be relevant for the application of the conflict rules, for example it has to enquire about and take into account the foreign citizenship or habitual residence of the parties even if it has not been invoked by any of them.

The reason for this lies in the fact that it can be assumed that the dispute is not amenable to settlement because its resolution is deemed to be of direct interest not merely to the parties involved but also to third parties and perhaps also the society and State at large. To make the application of foreign law depend on the pleading of the parties would, in fact, make the outcome optional, which would be contrary to the nature of these disputes.

Assume, for example, that the forum has to decide on the formal validity of a marriage celebrated some years before in a foreign country by a local official fully authorized to do so by the applicable *lex loci celebrationis*. If both spouses after some years wish to avoid the trouble and expense of divorce proceedings and prefer to have the marriage declared null and void on the ground of the lack of authority on the part of the celebrating official, it seems inappropriate to let them achieve this by the simple expedient of not pleading foreign law.

4. Suggestions for Disputes Where Settlement is Allowed

Turning to those disputes which the parties are free to resolve by a settlement, for example most disputes about money, it must be noted that the society and the State are interested in such disputes too (otherwise there would be no point in using public resources in order to resolve them), but that their interest is merely secondary and can be summarized by saying that if the parties are content with the settlement or outcome then the public interest is in principle satisfied as well. This speaks in favour of leaving the matter of applicable law to the parties, provided that they, being the masters of the lawsuit, can agree on it at the time of the proceedings.

As the application of foreign law may cause delays and increase the costs of the procedure, which is particularly uncalled for when the pecuniary value of the matter in dispute is relatively small, the parties should have the right to agree, explicitly or implicitly, that the court should apply the *lex fori*, provided the agreement concerns a dispute that has already reached or is about to reach the courts *(accord procédural*[268]*)*.

As pointed out above, such procedural agreements must be distinguished from choice-of-law agreements concluded in advance[269]; while some agreements of the latter type are recognized and binding (for example choice-of-law clauses in commercial contracts having international character), the attitude may be less permissive with regard to, for example, a choice-of-law agreement between the mother and the father of a newly born child in respect of future maintenance payments.

The recognition of the freedom of the parties to agree, in a pending dispute amenable to a settlement, on the applicable law does not directly provide a solution for the situation where the parties seem not to have concluded any agreement on applicable law but they both argue on the basis of a legal system which the court does not consider applicable under the conflict rules of the forum country. A typical scenario is

---

[268] See, for example, B. Audit, *Droit international privé*, pp. 224-225 and 235; H. Gaudemet-Tallon, *Recueil des cours*, Vol. 312 (2005), pp. 293-297; A. V. M. Struycken, *Recueil des cours*, Vol. 311 (2004), pp. 350-352.

[269] See, for example, P. M. M. Mostermans, *Netherlands International Law Review* 2004, p. 396. An important difference between the two types of agreements about applicable law is that a procedural agreement should not bind the parties beyond the actual pending litigation, for example if the same issues arises in the future in a different context, see A. V. M. Struycken, *Recueil des cours*, Vol. 311 (2004), p. 351.

that both parties seem to assume that the *lex fori*
applies, although the private international law of the
forum designates another legal system. If both parties
are experienced businessmen with access to legal
experts, it might be possible to interpret their behaviour as proof of a tacit agreement on the application of
the *lex fori*[270], but this is hardly a good solution when
the court has reasons to believe that the parties simply
are not aware of the conflict rules and that their behaviour is a result of their ignorance rather than of a conscious choice[271].

It is submitted that in the last-mentioned situation
the courts should normally do exactly the same that
they would do if the parties to a purely domestic dispute (i.e. a dispute without any international implications) demonstrated a corresponding ignorance of the
substantive rules of private law. For example, it may
happen even in a purely domestic case that both the
buyer and the seller involved in a dispute about the
price of the goods sold rely in their pleadings on a
wrong section or article of the Sales Act or the Civil
Code. This mistake may be explicit or may be inferred
from the facts the parties refer to in support of their
respective positions. Can and should the court apply,
nevertheless, the correct relevant provision of law, or is
it bound by the parties' mistake?

The answer to this question varies substantially
from country to country, depending on several factors.
To a large extent, the attitude towards the application
of foreign law is a natural consequence of the general

---

[270] See, however, P. Lalive, *Recueil des cours*, Vol. 155
(1977), pp. 181-184.

[271] Of course, even in such cases one of the parties may
actually be aware of the private international law issue but
consciously refrains from mentioning it in its pleadings
because it prefers the application of the *lex fori*.

procedural or substantive legal principles of the country of the forum, such as on whether the civil procedure is mainly adversarial (for example in many common-law countries) or of mainly inquisitorial nature (for example in many countries on the European continent). It may be difficult or even inappropriate to suggest that foreign law be treated in a way that would deviate too much from the treatment of the *lex fori*, thus making foreign law a disturbing "irritant" within the legal procedure.

It seems that while even many civil-law countries have certain substantive rules that are not applied unless invoked by a party (for example the rules on time limitation for monetary debts), it is more common in these countries that rules of law are applied ex officio, including in those cases where settlement is permitted and where the court is bound by the facts pleaded by the parties. As far as Sweden is concerned, it has already been mentioned that Chapter 17, Section 3, of the Code of Judicial Procedure makes it clear that in the cases amenable to settlement the court is not allowed to base its decision on facts and circumstances that have not been invoked by a party in support of his claim or defence. However, it follows from the case law of the Swedish Supreme Court in purely domestic cases that once a party has invoked a certain fact, it is for the court to apply the appropriate Swedish legal provisions (the principle of *da mihi factum, dabo tibi jus*) and draw the appropriate legal conclusions, although the court is expected to bring the relevant provisions to the attention of the parties, so that they can start to plead using relevant arguments or perhaps even retract or amend some of the facts they have previously invoked in support of their arguments[272].

---

[272] See M. Bogdan, *Svensk internationell privat- och processrätt*, p. 48, with further references.

It is submitted that this is a reasonable approach, which is normally suitable even for the needs of private international law. If it is used in relation to the conflict rules, the result is twofold. On the one hand, the courts are not permitted, when determining the applicable law in disputes where settlement is allowed, to investigate and/or take into account facts and circumstances that have not been invoked by the parties. On the other hand, the private international law consequences of the facts invoked must in principle be drawn by the court itself, even though only after having informed the parties and given them the opportunity to reach a procedural agreement on the applicable law or amend (retract or add) the fact(s) that may be relevant for the court's choice of the legal system to be applied[273].

In order to illustrate this approach with the help of an example, one may imagine a Swedish family habitually residing in Sweden. In connection with the parents' divorce, a Swedish court applying Swedish law decides that the children should be entrusted into the sole custody of the mother while the father is obliged to pay a monthly sum for their maintenance. Due to a new marriage or a new employment, the mother, together with the children, move permanently from Sweden to a foreign country where the cost of life is substantially lower, whereupon the father brings an action in a Swedish court demanding that the amount of maintenance payments be reduced. A maintenance dispute is a dispute of a kind that can be resolved by a

---

[273] Such duty of the court to draw the attention of the parties to the law it intends to apply appears to exist in many countries, see M. Jänterä-Jareborg, *Recueil des cours*, Vol. 304 (2003), pp. 258-264; B. Audit, *Droit international privé*, p. 224; F. Vischer, *Recueil des cours*, Vol. 232 (1992), pp. 89-90.

settlement. The father bases his action on two facts, namely that the children now habitually reside in the foreign country in question and that the cost of living in that country is so much lower than in Sweden that a lower amount is sufficient to satisfy the children's needs. None of the parties demands that foreign law be applied or refers to the Swedish conflict rule pursuant to which maintenance is in principle governed by the law of the country where the child habitually resides. The new habitual residence of the children is invoked by the father in support of his demand, but merely in order to show that the needs of the children have changed (which is a circumstance relevant according to Swedish substantive law[274]); the father is perhaps not even aware of the Swedish conflict rule that says that Swedish law does not apply to his maintenance obligation any more because it has been replaced by the law of the foreign country where the children presently habitually reside. In this situation, it is submitted that the Swedish court must take account of the new residence of the children, because it was invoked by one of the parties (the father) in support of his request. It is, however, important that the court's decision on applicable law does not take the parties by surprise, as it might jeopardize their right to a fair hearing. The court should, in one way or another, inform the parties about the legal rules it intends to apply, as the parties must be given the opportunity to adjust their legal argumentation to the contents of the applicable law[275]. They

---

[274] See Chapter 7, Section 1, of the Swedish Children and Parents Code.

[275] According to Th. de Boer, *Recueil des cours*, Vol. 257 (1996), p. 324, and H. U. Jessurun d'Oliveira, *Revue hellénique de droit international*, 2008, p. 502, a failure of the court to give the parties a fair chance to adjust their pleadings in the light of the applicable law could amount to a violation of Article 6 ("Right to a Fair

should also be given a chance to agree on the application of Swedish law. If the new habitual residence of the children is relied on by the father only, he can achieve the same result by one-sidedly retracting his submission that the children are habitually resident in the foreign country. This can be described by saying that Swedish law shall be applied unless at least one of the parties, after having been informed about the conflict rule, prefers the application of foreign law, but the same method and the same result can, using other words, be described so that foreign law shall apply unless both parties, after having been informed about the conflict rule, prefer Swedish law.

What has just been said demonstrates that if the court is expected to inform the ignorant parties about the conflict rule and give them the opportunity to act on that information, then the difference between applying foreign law ex officio and applying it merely upon demand of a party is minimal and of a more theoretical than practical interest[276]. The crucial point is that the conflict rules, being parts of the legal system of the forum country, are to be treated in the same manner as other provisions of that legal system. They are as binding as substantive rules of private law and there are no reasons to assert that they should be treated differently, as some kind of second-rate rules, for example by being applied only upon the request of a party while the rules of domestic substantive law are applied upon the court's own initiative. It is a different matter that other factors, such as the difficulties in obtaining information about the content of the applicable foreign law,

Trial") of the European Convention for the Protection of Human Rights and Fundamental Freedoms of 1950.

[276] See, for example, B. Fauvarque-Cosson in *Comparative Law before the Courts*, pp. 10-11, comparing the English and the French system.

may in some cases force the court to refrain from its application[277].

5. Concluding Remarks

In the recommendations above, difference was made between two kinds of disputes, depending on whether they are of a type amenable to a settlement or not. To make such difference for the purpose of deciding on the application of foreign law may seem to constitute a vicious circle, because the question of whether a dispute can be resolved by the parties themselves is in principle to be answered by the applicable substantive law itself. Here it must again be recalled that private international law is a part of the legal system of the forum and that the recommended difference to be made in private international law between the two kinds of disputes reflects the differences in the degree of the forum country's interest in their resolution. Therefore, the line between the two kinds of disputes must *for the purposes of private international law* be drawn according to the *lex fori*. After the applicable law has been ascertained, it will, however, be its substantive rules that will decide whether the dispute can be settled or not.

In some countries, the court must state clearly and unequivocally which legal rules it applies in order to reach its decision, which means that it must determine the applicable legal system even when all conceivable alternative systems lead to exactly the same outcome. This seems to be a futile exercise and a waste of time and energy, in particular when the conflict rules are unclear and the determination of the applicable law requires a substantial effort[278]. It is submitted that

---

[277] See Chapter VII.3, *infra*.
[278] See, for example, G. Kegel and K. Schurig, *Internationales Privatrecht*, p. 497; G. Parra-Aranguren, *Recueil des cours*, Vol. 210 (1988), p. 27.

under such circumstances the court should be allowed to proceed to making its ruling on the merits while leaving the conflicts issue open, provided it clarifies that the outcome does not depend on which of the legal systems in question governs the matter in dispute[279]. This seems to be the approach chosen, for example, by the French Cassation Court[280]. In those countries where appeal to the highest court is not permitted regarding the allegedly erroneous application of foreign law[281], it may, however, be necessary to state clearly in the lower court's judgment whether the outcome is based on a foreign legal rule or on the *lex fori*[282]. Even in such countries it should be permitted for the lower courts to avoid the choice between a foreign rule and a rule of the *lex fori* by claiming that they are of identical contents; it is submitted that in this situation an appeal should be permissible, but merely to the extent the appellant asserts that the lower court's erroneous conclusion regarding the identical contents was caused by a misunderstanding of the contents of the *lex fori* (as opposed to a misunderstanding concerning the contents of the foreign rule).

---

[279] About this "non-election rule", see e.g. H. U. Jessurun d'Oliveira, *Revue hellénique de droit international*, 2008, pp. 499-520.

[280] See the decision of 13 April 1999 in the case of *Compagnie royale belge* v. *Société lilloise d'assurances*, *Revue critique de droit international privé*, 1999, p. 698, with a note by Ancel and Muir Watt; *Journal du droit international (Clunet)*, 2000, p. 315, with a note by Fauvarque-Cosson; B. Audit, *Droit international privé*, p. 226.

[281] See Chapter VII.2, *infra*.

[282] See P. Lalive, *Recueil des cours*, Vol. 155 (1977), p. 29.

CHAPTER VII

THE PRINCIPLE OF LOYAL APPLICATION
OF FOREIGN LAW

1. The Problem

It is an elementary principle that the provisions of
foreign law, which are to be applied due to the forum
country's conflict rules, must to the largest possible
extent be interpreted and applied loyally, i.e., as they
are interpreted and applied in their country of origin[283].
The use in this context of the term "loyally" must not
be misunderstood though. The court owes no loyalty in
the proper sense of that word to the foreign legislator,
but merely to the legislator of the forum country[284]. It
is the latter legislator who, by formulating and enacting
the conflict rule, has instructed the court to apply foreign law, and it must be assumed that this conflict rule
intends in principle to lead to the application of foreign
law as it really is. It would not make much sense to
prescribe the application of the law of a foreign country and then apply some imaginary rules not existing in
reality. The loyalty owed by the court to its own legislator leads thus indirectly also to an interpretation and
application of the foreign legal rules corresponding

---

[283] See, for example, M. Jänterä-Jareborg, *Recueil des
cours*, Vol. 304 (2003), pp. 307-308; G. van Hecke,
Recueil des cours, Vol. 126 (1969), pp. 514-518; G. Kegel
and K. Schurig, *Internationales Privatrecht*, pp. 504-505;
E. F. Scoles *et al.*, *Conflict of Laws*, p. 127.
[284] See M. Jänterä-Jareborg, *Recueil des cours*,
Vol. 304 (2003), p. 230; A. V. M. Struycken, *Recueil des
cours*, Vol. 311 (2004), pp. 59-60.

loyally to the interpretation prevailing in the foreign country itself. Such origin-conform interpretation may often necessitate that account be taken also of the political aims behind the foreign rule, even when those aims are not shared by the country of the forum.

It is, consequently, important and practically universally accepted that the court must use sources reflecting truthfully the state of the law in the foreign country. Whenever possible, the court should use the same primary and secondary sources of law that would be used by courts in the foreign country itself (statutory texts, precedents, preparatory legislative materials, customary law, legal literature etc.). This may, however, often be impossible, for example for linguistic reasons, in which case it is particularly crucial that the sources of information used (handbooks, digests, expert opinions, etc.) are reliable. The same methods of interpretation as those prevailing in the foreign country should be applied. It is, for example, a notorious fact that the courts in common-law countries traditionally tend to interpret statutory texts strictly according to the literal meaning of their wording, whereas continental judges prefer a more teleological interpretation[285]. A court applying foreign law should be cautiously conservative and it must resist the temptation to "improve" the foreign rules by interpreting them according to its own preferences. As it was put by one author, the court can be seen as a creative painter when applying the *lex fori*, but is not more than a mere photographer when it is applying foreign laws. Similarly, in order to avoid distorting the applicable foreign law, analogy and *e contrario* reasoning should be used only to the extent and in the manner they are used in the country of that law's origin.

---

[285] See, for example, M. Bogdan, *Comparative Law*, pp. 127-132.

Whether judicial precedents on the content of foreign law are binding depends in principle on the attitude towards precedents prevailing in the country of the applicable law rather than in the *lex fori*[286]. This theoretically undisputed principle is, however, not quite realistic. As the decisions of the French Cassation Court and the German Federal Court (the highest French and German judicial instances) do not constitute binding precedents, although they are published, carefully studied and normally followed, a Swedish court applying French or German law is in theory entitled to deviate from the French Cassation Court's or the German Federal Court's interpretation of a French or German rule if it finds that interpretation to be erroneous, but it is hardly probable that a Swedish court would consider itself to have a better understanding of French or German law than the highest judicial body of France or Germany. The interpretation prevailing in the decisions of the higher courts in the foreign country should thus normally be respected, regardless of whether they constitute binding precedents or not. For example, the Belgian Civil Code is historically the same Napoleonic Code that applies in France and the provisions of both codes are to a large extent identical even today, but a Swedish court applying one of such provisions as part of Belgian law must examine how it is understood and interpreted by Belgian courts and cannot rely on the interpretation prevailing in France, irrespective of the fact that neither Belgian nor French legal system recognizes the binding force of judicial precedents.

Similarly, should the question of compatibility of the applicable foreign rule with the Constitution of its

---

[286] See O. Kahn-Freund, *Recueil des cours*, Vol. 143 (1974), pp. 446-449; P. Lalive, *Recueil des cours*, Vol. 155 (1977), p. 233.

own country arise, a possible unconstitutionality of the foreign rule can be examined and given effect only if and to the extent it would be relevant in the eyes of the courts in the country of that rule's origin[287]. There are countries where many of the Constitution's provisions are political declarations that are mere decorations and are not intended to be applied by courts. Another problem is that the understanding of a foreign Constitution may be problematic unless there is an established case law in the foreign country declaring the rule in question to be constitutional or unconstitutional. The forum would be well advised to act with extreme moderation and care, as unconstitutionality issues are often highly political and difficult to understand and adjudicate for courts in countries other than that of the Constitution itself[288]. For example, Article 14 of Chapter 11 of the Swedish Constitution (the Instrument of Government) stipulates that if a court finds that a provision of law conflicts with the Constitution, that provision may not be applied; if the provision in question has been approved by the Parliament *(Riksdag)*, which is the case of practically all Swedish private-law legislation, it shall be refused application only if the incompatibility with the Constitution is manifest. Such delicate judicial review can hardly be properly carried out by a non-Swedish court.

An additional complication arises if the foreign

---

[287] A similar approach should be used when the foreign rule is accused of being contrary to the law of nations, in particular to an international convention binding on the country in question. See, for example, G. van Hecke, *Recueil des cours*, Vol. 126 (1969), pp. 517-518; G. Kegel and K. Schurig, *Internationales Privatrecht*, pp. 20-21.

[288] See, for example, G. Parra-Aranguren, *Recueil des cours*, Vol. 210 (1988), pp. 75-76; O. Kahn-Freund, *Recueil des cours*, Vol. 143 (1974), p. 451. Cf. E. Vitta, *Recueil des cours*, Vol. 162 (1979), pp. 79-80.

country in question has a special constitutional tribunal which is the only court authorized to examine the constitutionality of its laws; it does not seem quite appropriate for the forum to allow itself to interpret and give effect to the foreign constitution when a corresponding court in the foreign country would be merely allowed to refer the issue to that country's constitutional tribunal[289]. The forum as such cannot normally turn to the constitutional court of the foreign country whose law is applicable and ask for a judgment on that law's constitutionality. An existing final decision of a foreign constitutional tribunal on the constitutionality of a legal rule must be accepted as a part of the foreign legal system in question, regardless of whether the forum country normally recognizes foreign judgments or not.

Serious difficulties may arise in connection with the interpretation of foreign rules containing general qualitative value statements such as what is just, appropriate, fair, substantial, improper, manifestly inequitable or most compatible with the best interests of a child. The exact meaning of such general clauses is often unclear even in their country of origin and is, furthermore, subject to constant developments depending on the changes in the society there. It would, on the other hand, be wrong to interpret these clauses in accordance with the values prevailing in the country of the forum, as this may lead to disfigurement of the applicable foreign law[290]. If the foreign country is in cultural, religious, economical, political and other respects similar to the country of the forum, it may be reasonable to presume, in the absence of proof to the contrary, that

---

[289] See G. van Hecke, *Recueil des cours*, Vol. 126 (1969), p. 516; O. Kahn-Freund, *Recueil des cours*, Vol. 143 (1974), p. 449.
[290] See, for example, E. Jayme, *Recueil des cours*, Vol. 251 (1995), p. 244.

an interpretation pursuant to the values of the forum will correspond to the interpretation that the generally formulated clause would receive in the country of its origin. If there is reliable information about the interpretation prevailing in the country of origin, for example in a recent decision rendered by the highest court or unanimous legal writing there, it should not, however, be ignored.

As has been pointed out before[291], the applicable foreign legal rule is in some countries, for example in England, treated as mere fact, not as law[292]. An agreement between the parties regarding the contents of the applicable foreign law is in such countries normally binding on the court, at least in disputes that are amenable to settlement. In most countries, however, even foreign law is treated as law, which means, *inter alia*, that the parties cannot bind the court by agreeing on the contents of its mandatory rules (rules that are not mandatory can naturally be contracted out by the parties and replaced with whatever the parties agree on). Even in disputes that are amenable to settlement the outcome may sometimes depend on applicable foreign rules that are intended to be mandatory, for example rules on the protection of consumers or employees. The court may in such cases be bound by the *facts* that are not disputed by the parties, but it should not be bound by the agreement of the parties about the substantive contents of the foreign mandatory rules of consumer or labour law, regardless of whether that agreement was made during the proceedings or prior to them. This is consistent with the usual treatment in most countries of mandatory substantive rules of the

---

[291] See Chapter VI.6, *supra*.

[292] See, for example, C. M. V. Clarkson and J. Hill, *The Conflict of Laws*, pp. 13-15; *Dicey and Morris on the Conflict of Laws*, pp. 221-224.

lex fori and with the fact that the purpose of private international law is to subject the dispute to the most appropriate of the concerned legal systems and not to apply some kind of mutilated set of rules differing from the true content of the applicable foreign law.

The principle of loyal application of foreign law also requires that foreign law, applicable pursuant to the conflict rules of the forum, be applied as it is at the moment of its application[293]. This is true even if the conflict rule uses a connecting factor permanently fixed at some other point in time, for example if paternity is to be decided by the law of the country where the child became citizen or habitual resident at the moment of birth. Again, it must be remembered that the purpose of the conflict rule is to point out the most relevant and appropriate legal system and not to lead to the application of some outdated rules that do not constitute valid law anywhere any more. A conflict rule pointing to the law of the country where the child became a citizen at birth should thus normally be understood as having in mind the rules that are in force *today* in the country in question rather than the rules that applied there at the time when the child was born. The idea of "petrifying" the substantive rules of the applicable legal system should thus be rejected, but it is important to realize that the transitional provisions

---

[293] The situation is different when a foreign legal rule is applied not as as result of the forum's conflict rules but due to the freedom of contract provided by the applicable substantive law. For example, to the extent the rules of the applicable substantive law about contracts are not mandatory, the parties are free to agree that their mutual rights and obligations regarding the place and manner of performance will be governed by another legal system; it is then a matter of interpretation of their agreement to establish whether they had in mind the chosen law as it was at the time of contracting or as it is at the moment of adjudication.

regarding new legislation are also part of the valid law of today. This means that if the substantive rules on the determination of paternity in the applicable legal system have been amended, but the amendment is not intended to apply to children born before the entry into force of the new rules, then even the courts in other countries should respect that the older rules continue to constitute the valid law to be applied in relation to such children[294].

It must be admitted though that the main principle just described, according to which in the absence of transitional provisions stipulating otherwise foreign law is to be applied as it is at the time of its application, may sometimes lead to unsatisfactory results, as is demonstrated by the South African case of *Sperling* v. *Sperling* of 1975[295]. In this case, both spouses were domiciled in East Germany (German Democratic Republic) when they married there in 1954. They moved to South Africa in 1957. In 1965, the matrimonial property regime under East German family law was modified. The Appellate Division of the Supreme Court of South Africa had to apply East German law as the law of the first matrimonial domicile and, as the above-mentioned East German legislative amendment was intended to apply also to previously concluded marriages, this meant the application of the new East German rules. This solution does not seem to be reasonable, as the spouses broke off their contacts with the legal, social and political developments in East Germany many years before the legislative changes enacted in 1965. The unreasonable result must not,

[294] See, for example, B. Audit, *Droit international privé*, pp. 253-254; G. Parra-Aranguren, *Recueil des cours*, Vol. 210 (1988), p. 76.

[295] 1975 (3) SA 707; *Dicey and Morris on the Conflict of Laws*, p. 62.

however, be blamed on the principle that conflict rules refer to foreign law as it is today but rather on the unfortunate South African conflict rule, which used an immutable connecting factor (the first matrimonial domicile) even in situations where spouses many years ago had moved to and acquired domicile in a country with policies and views radically different from those prevailing in their country of origin.

A different, albeit related, problem arises in connection with the changes in the private international law of the forum country, if the new conflict rules do not contain clear transitional provisions. There are good reasons speaking in favour of the application of the new conflict rules even to older legal relationships, although exceptions may be in place with regard to the validity of legal acts performed in reliance of the older conflict rules. Furthermore, a kind of "retroactive" application is unavoidable when the new conflict rule is not statutory but judge-made, as such a rule can by definition only come into being by being applied in a particular case to a situation that has already arisen. Judge-made conflict rules are thus in principle created retrospectively, while statutory conflict rules are usually — albeit not always — prospective and future-oriented[296].

In theory, the ambition of the forum should be to maintain the same quality standards in its work irrespective of whether it is applying the *lex fori* or foreign law, but it must be admitted that this ideal is often difficult to uphold. The risk of mistakes and misunderstandings is obviously much higher when the court applies foreign law. The procurement of correct, up-to-date and complete information about the contents of foreign law can be difficult and sometimes even

---

[296] See *Dicey and Morris on the Conflict of Laws*, p. 55.

impossible. Better than pretending that this problem does not exist is to admit frankly that the standards of knowledge of law may be somewhat lower when foreign law applies. Exceedingly high requirements in this respect might at a superficial glance seem to be an expression of respect for foreign law, but they can in practice lead (and are in some cases perhaps even intended to lead) to the opposite result, where foreign law is refused application and is replaced by the *lex fori*, ostensibly because the content of the foreign law has not been "sufficiently" established[297]. The fact that many countries exclude the possibility of appealing to the highest court when the issue concerns an erroneous application of foreign law[298] is, by itself, an indication that the ambitions regarding the quality of application of foreign law are somewhat lower than those regarding the application of the *lex fori*.

In spite of what has just been said about the need not to under-estimate the difficulties involved in the work with foreign rules, such difficulties should not be overestimated either. In my experience, both judges and practising lawyers are often afraid of foreign law and suspect that it will be totally different from their own law, incomprehensible and devoid of all logic and common sense. In reality, there are often surprisingly significant similarities between the existing legal systems as far as the substantive contents of the legal rules are concerned, in particular within private law. Professor Max Rheinstein, who made a research on this similarities some 40 years ago, came to the conclusion that approximately 80 per cent of private-law cases would reach the same result regardless of

---

[297] Cf. M. Jänterä-Jareborg, *Recueil des cours*, Vol. 304 (2003), p. 308.
[298] See, for example, K. J. Hood, 2 *Journal of Private International Law* 189-192 (2006).

whether they arose and were decided in the United States, Canada, France, Argentina or Japan[299]. Due to the ongoing general globalization process that number might be even higher today. This similarity is confirmed by everyday experience. Even people who have not studied law at all travel abroad and dare to engage there in legal transactions such as purchasing goods, renting cars or hotel rooms, travelling by public transportation, etc. They assume instinctively that such contracts, although relatively complicated, are made and function in roughly the same way as equivalent contracts in their own country. While the applicable foreign rules have to be studied with utmost care, there are thus normally no reasons to be afraid of their contents.

2. Procurement of Information about the Content of Foreign Law

A crucial issue is how the forum can obtain correct and complete information about the content of the applicable foreign legal system, and in particular who is responsible for procuring that information.

In almost all Continental legal systems, the judge (the court) is in principle supposed to possess the necessary knowledge of the legal rules of the *lex fori* (the principle of *jura novit curia*). This does not, of course, mean that the judge is expected to know the whole legal system by heart, but rather that it is one of his tasks to procure, in each individual case, the necessary information by studying both primary and secondary

---

[299] See M. Rheinstein, in Rotondi (ed.), *Inchieste di diritto comparato 2. Buts et méthodes du droit comparé*, Padua-New York 1973, p. 553. About the so-called *preaesumptio similitudinis* see for example, M. Bogdan, *Comparative Law*, pp. 97-98.

sources, such as statutes, precedents, legal literature, etc. In most Continental countries, the judge cannot normally demand that the parties provide him with information about his own legal system[300], although the parties have usually the right to argue in favour of their interpretation of the law and support it by submitting legal opinions written by experts or other types of evidence. All this is in principle true about the application of the *lex fori*, but may be difficult to uphold in situations where the court has to apply foreign law.

In theory, there are two alternative possibilities: either the court investigates the contents of the foreign rules by itself or the investigation and presentation of foreign law is carried out by the parties[301]. In practice, the matter is much more complicated, as the two alternatives are not mutually exclusive and are seldom used in their pure form. Different countries implement various combinations of the two methods, and the approaches may vary even within the same country, depending on the nature of the dispute or the discretion of the court. It is not uncommon that the two approaches are combined and used simultaneously even within the same proceedings. When the proof

---

[300] See, for example, Chapter 35, Section 2, of the Swedish Code of Judicial Procedure.

[301] The question about whether it is the court or the parties who has to prove the contents of the applicable foreign law must be distinguished from the previously discussed question of whether the court can and should apply foreign law ex officio or merely upon request by at least one of the parties. For example, Th. de Boer, *Recueil des cours*, Vol. 257 (1996), pp. 416-417, argues that foreign law should be applied only if the parties raise the choice-of-law issue, but if the issue is raised the judge should in his view bear the full responsibility for applying the foreign law "as best it can" (even though he welcomes information about the content of the foreign law offered voluntarily by the parties).

regarding the content of foreign law is submitted by the parties or one of them, the kinds of evidence admitted may, but do not necessarily have to, depend on the general rules of evidence of the country of the forum.

To start with England, it should be recalled that in principle foreign law is by English private international law seen as mere fact, which means that it must normally be proved by the parties[302]. The burden of proof is usually placed on the party relying on the foreign law and alleging that it differs from English law[303]. An exception can be made when the content of the foreign legal system is a "notorious fact"[304] or when the content of the foreign rule relied on by one of the parties is admitted expressly or tacitly by the other party[305]. The normal method of proof of foreign law in English courts is the testimony of expert witnesses (usually foreign legal practitioners or academics[306]), who can be

---

[302] There seem to be a few examples of judgments where an English court discussed and applied foreign law although the report of the case does not mention any evidence about its content having been given, see for instance *Re Cohn*, [1945] Ch. 5.

[303] See *Dicey and Morris on the Conflict of Laws*, p. 232.

[304] See *Saxby* v. *Fulton*, [1909] KB 208, on p. 211, where Bray J. said the following:

"I was asked to assume, in the absence of evidence, that the law in Monte Carlo is the same as in England as regards gaming, but I decline to make this assumption; it is notorious that at Monte Carlo roulette is not an unlawful game."

See also *Dicey and Morris on the Conflict of Laws*, p. 222.

[305] *Ibid.*, p. 223.

[306] See Section 4 (1) of the Civil Evidence Act 1972:

"It is hereby declared that in civil proceedings a person who is suitably qualified to do so on account of his knowledge or experience is competent to give expert evidence as to the law of any country or territory out-

subjected to cross-examination. A mere citing or submission by the parties of foreign statutes or judicial
decisions is normally not sufficient, since an English
court is not expected to be able to evaluate and interpret them without the guidance and assistance by an
expert (who may, however, rely on such material in
order to support his evidence)[307]. Due to the strict
English rules on evidence, the judge is normally not
entitled to conduct his own research to ascertain the
content of applicable foreign law and he is not even
allowed to make use of his or her own knowledge of
foreign law[308].

This means that if the experts of both parties are in
agreement, the court is normally not allowed to deviate
from their view, unless it is obviously false or absurd[309].
It is only when the experts disagree that the court may
— and must — form its own opinion on the basis of
the evidence (case law, statutory law, etc.) presented in
connection with the witness testimony[310].

Nevertheless, foreign law is in some respects treated
as if it were law. Thus, it follows from Section 4 (2) of
the Civil Evidence Act of 1972 that where a question

---

side the United Kingdom or of any part of the United
Kingdom other than England and Wales, irrespective of
whether he has acted or is entitled to act as a legal prac-
titioner there."

[307] See *Dicey and Morris on the Conflict of Laws*,
p. 225.
[308] See *Dicey and Morris on the Conflict of Laws*,
p. 227; T. C. Hartley, 45 *International and Comparative
Law Quarterly* 283-284 (1996). For an outsider, it is easy
to agree with K. Takahashi, [2002] *Singapore Journal of
Legal Studies* 492, who describes the English evidence
rules as "saddled with dogmatism".
[309] See *Dicey and Morris on the Conflict of Laws*,
p. 227.
[310] See *Dicey and Morris on the Conflict of Laws*,
pp. 228-229.

as to foreign law has been decided by one of the higher English courts, that decision will, if reported or recorded in citable form, constitute admissible evidence in future cases for the purpose of proving the foreign law in question; it will also be presumed to be correct unless the contrary is proved[311]. This differs sharply from the judicial treatment of other facts. To give evidentiary value, even though in the form of a mere presumption of correctness, to previous findings about foreign law is surprising, especially as the previous finding may have been based on mere admission by the parties rather than on any real evidence[312]. Another difference in England between the treatment of foreign law and the treatment of other facts is that while English appellate courts normally respect the findings of fact made by the trial courts, this does not seem to apply to findings about the content of foreign law[313]. Furthermore, in those rare civil cases where an English court conducts a jury trial, questions of foreign law are nowadays (since 1920) decided by the judge and not by the jury[314].

---

[311] See T. C. Hartley, 45 *International and Comparative Law Quarterly* 283 (1996); R. Hausmann, *European Legal Forum*, 2008, p. I-13; K. J. Hood, 2 *Journal of Private International Law* 184 (2006); M. Jänterä-Jareborg, *Recueil des cours*, Vol. 304 (2003), pp. 293-296.

[312] See T. C. Hartley, 45 *International and Comparative Law Quarterly* 283 (1996).

[313] See, for example, *Attorney General of New Zealand v. Ortiz*, [1984] AC 1 (House of Lords); T. C. Hartley, 45 *International and Comparative Law Quarterly* 284-285 (1996); R. Hausmann, *European Legal Forum* 2008, p. I-3.

[314] See Section 69 (5) of the Supreme Court Act of 1981:

"When for the purpose of disposing of any action or other matter which is being tried in the High Court by a judge with a jury it is necessary to ascertain the law of any country which is applicable to the facts of the

As a vestige of their English roots, American courts also used to treat foreign law as mere fact and refused to apply it unless its provisions were properly pleaded and proved by the parties in accordance with the technical rules of evidence; independent research by the judge was prohibited and he was not allowed to rely on his personal knowledge of foreign law[315]. All this was radically changed for the federal courts with the adoption, in 1966, of Rule 44.1 of the Federal Rules of Civil Procedure, which allowed federal judges to determine the content of foreign law as a question of law[316]. The current wording of the relevant part of the rule deserves to be quoted:

> "In determining foreign law, the court may consider any relevant material or source, including testimony, whether or not submitted by a party or admissible under the Federal Rules of Evidence. The court's determination must be treated as a ruling on a question of law."

This means, *inter alia*, that federal judges ascertaining the content of foreign law are free — albeit not obliged — to undertake, of their own motion, any research they find appropriate. They can admit any evi-

---

case, any question as to the effect of the evidence given with respect to that law shall, instead of being submitted to the jury, be decided by the judge alone."

See also the corresponding provision in Section 68 of the County Courts Act of 1984; T. C. Hartley, 45 *International and Comparative Law Quarterly* 284 (1996).

[315] See J. R. Brown, 9 *The Maritime Lawyer* 180-181 (1984).

[316] See, for example, J. R. Brown, 9 *The Maritime Lawyer* 188-195 (1984); T. Einhorn, in *Essays Nygh*, pp. 115-116; M. Jänterä-Jareborg, *Recueil des cours*, Vol. 304 (2003), pp. 302-303; the Committee on International Commercial Disputes, in 61 *The Record of the Association of the Bar of the City of New York*, Vol. 1, pp. 49-59.

dence they find relevant (a frequently used proof is an affidavit submitted by an expert) and are bound neither by the strict and formal Federal Rules of Evidence nor by the evidence presented by the parties. The findings of trial courts on foreign law are subject to full review by appellate courts.

The traditional French approach to the problem used to be to put the burden of proving foreign law on the party whose claim was governed by it, irrespective of which party relied on it (the so-called Lautour-Thinet rule, named after the cases where it was formulated [317]). The Lautour-Thinet rule meant, for example, that a plaintiff suing under a contract governed by foreign law had to prove the content of that law. This was the case even if he preferred French law and it was the defendant who relied on foreign law [318]. Today, French courts use different approaches depending on whether the dispute is of a kind where settlement is permitted or not [319]. In the leading case of *Société Amerford* v. *Compagnie Air France*, decided in 1993 [320], the Cassation Court held that, in the cases amenable to a settle-

---

[317] See *Lautour* v. *Guiraut*, Cassation Court on 25 May 1948, *Revue critique de droit international privé*, 1949, p. 89, with a note by Batiffol; *Société Thinet* v. *Société Roque*, Cassation Court on 24 January 1984, *Journal du droit international (Clunet)* 1984, p. 874, with a note by Bischoff.

[318] See T. C. Hartley, 45 *International and Comparative Law Quarterly* 280 (1996); R. Hausmann, *European Legal Forum* 2008, p. I-10.

[319] See B. Fauvarque-Cosson, in *Comparative Law before the Courts*, pp. 6-7; T. C. Hartley, 45 *International and Comparative Law Quarterly* 280-282 (1996); M. Jänterä-Jareborg, *Recueil des cours*, Vol. 304 (2003), pp. 291-293.

[320] Cassation Court on 16 November 1993, *Revue critique de droit international privé*, 1994, p. 332, with a note by Lagarde; *Journal du droit international (Clunet)*, 1994, p. 98, with a note by Donnier.

ment, it is for the party relying on foreign law to show that pursuant to that law the outcome would differ from that under French law; otherwise, French law will apply. On the other hand, in the cases where the parties are not permitted to resolve their dispute by a settlement, the ascertainment of the content of foreign law is a task of the court itself, even though the parties are free to argue and submit evidence as well. Some recent decisions of the Cassation Court indicate that French courts are obliged to investigate the content of the applicable foreign law even in disputes that are amenable to settlement[321]. There are no restrictions regarding the methods of proof[322], but the usual way of proving foreign law is to present expert opinions (so-called *certificats de coutume*) written by foreign legal experts. With regard to appeals, foreign law is treated as a fact, which means that an erroneous interpretation of foreign law cannot normally be subject of appeal to the Cassation Court[323].

It follows from Article 281 (2) of the Spanish Code of Civil Procedure that in contrast to Spanish substan-

---

[321] See, for example, two decisions of the Cassation Court rendered on 28 June 2005 *(Aubin* v. *Bonal* and *Société Itraco* v. *Fenwick Shipping Services)*, *Revue critique de droit international privé*, 2005, p. 645, with a note by Ancel and Muir Watt, where the Court said that

"il incombe au juge français qui reconnaît applicable un droit étranger d'en rechercher, soit d'office, soit à la demande d'une partie qui l'invoque, la teneur, avec le concours des parties et personnellement s'il y a lieu, et de donner à la question litigieuse une solution conforme au droit positif étranger".

[322] See R. Hausmann, *European Legal Forum*, 2008, p. I-11.

[323] See, for example, the decision of the Cassation Court on 26 May 1999 in the case of *Société Moureau* v. *Société Lanvin*, *Revue critique de droit international privé*, 1999, p. 713, with a note by Muir Watt.

tive law the content of the applicable foreign law must be proved[324]. As a general rule, it is for the parties to prove foreign law, but as foreign law is seen as law rather than as a mere fact, it must be proved even if the parties agree upon its content. The burden of proof seems to be on the party relying on foreign law. In the cases involving a particularly strong interest on the part of the legislator (such as the cases where the parties are not allowed to resolve the dispute by a settlement), the court must step in and investigate the content of foreign law ex officio if satisfactory evidence is not provided by the parties. Any relevant evidence can be used and the judge is permitted to use his private knowledge as well.

Article 14 (1) of the Italian Private International Law Act of 1995 provides that the judge has to as-certain the applicable foreign law upon his own initiative[325].

From the previously described German view, according to which foreign law is law rather than a mere fact, it is considered to follow that it is for the German courts to ascertain the content of applicable foreign law. The judges are thus allowed to use their own knowledge of foreign law[326], even though in contrast to situations where German law is applicable the

---

[324] See A.-L. Calvo Caravaca and J. Carrascosa González, *IPRax*, 2005, pp. 171-173; R. Hausmann, *European Legal Forum*, 2008, p. I-12.

[325] R. Hausmann, *European Legal Forum*, 2008, p. I-11.

[326] See Section 293 of the German Code of Civil Procedure:

"The law which is in force in another state, customary law and by-laws require proof only to such extent as they are unknown to the Court. In the establishment of these legal norms, the Court is not limited to the evidence brought forward by the parties; it is empowered to make use of other sources of knowledge and to order whatever is necessary for the purpose of such utilization."

courts are permitted to ask the parties for assistance in this respect[327]. The court cannot shift the burden of proving foreign law to the parties, but if a party fails to provide the requested support, for example refuses to present legal texts that are easily accessible to it, then the court may draw conclusions from such behaviour[328]. If both parties agree on the content of the applicable law, the court may refrain from further investigation, but it is not bound to do so and it will not accept an agreement that is based on a manifestly erroneous understanding of the foreign rules[329]. There are no formal restrictions regarding the means of evidence that can be used, but the preferred proof of foreign law is most frequently an expert opinion *(Gutachten)* from a university or a research institution such as the Max-Planck-Institut für ausländisches und internationales Privatrecht in Hamburg or even an individual expert. German courts can also use two unofficial but valuable and continuously updated loose-leaf systems containing German translations of most foreign rules on marriage, parental issues and successions[330]. As an appeal on a point of law to the highest German court (the Federal Court) could until recently only be made on a point of German federal law or other German law of supra-regional importance[331], appeals

---

[327] See, for example, T. C. Hartley, 45 *International and Comparative Law Quarterly* 275-276 (1996); R. Hausmann, *European Legal Forum*, 2008, pp. I-2 and I-7-I-9; M. Jänterä-Jareborg, *Recueil des cours*, Vol. 304 (2003), pp. 289-291.

[328] See R. Hausmann, *European Legal Forum*, 2008, p. I-9.

[329] See *ibid.*, pp. I-3, I-7 and I-9.

[330] See Bermann/Ferid/Henrich, *Internationales Ehe- und Kindschaftsrecht*, and Ferid/Firsching/Dörner/Hausmann, *Internationales Erbrecht*.

[331] See Section 545 (1) of the German Code of Civil Procedure, as it was until 1 September 2009.

concerning misunderstanding of the content of foreign law could not go beyond the intermediate appellate courts (as opposed to incorrect use of, for example, German conflict rules). As of 1 September 2009, the wording of Section 545 (1) of the German Code of Civil Procedure was amended, so that every violation of law can be the subject of an appeal to the Federal Court. Even though this amendment was carried out for other reasons and without a real discussion about its relevance for foreign law, the reform is understood by some German authors to mean that such appeals are now indeed allowed even on aspects of foreign law [332].

Section 4 (1) of the Austrian Act on Private International Law of 1978 stipulates that the content of the applicable foreign law must be ascertained ex officio [333]. There are no restrictions regarding admissible evidence. Section 4 (1) states that the co-operation of the parties, information from the Federal Ministry of Justice and expert opinions can "also" be used. A similar approach is used in other Central European countries. For example, Section 53 of the Czechoslovak Act No. 97 of 1963 concerning Private International Law and the Rules of Procedure Relating Thereto, which appears to continue to apply in the Czech Republic and in Slovakia, stipulates that the judicial organ "shall take all necessary measures to ascertain the provisions of a foreign law"; if such provisions are not known to such an organ, it may request the information for this purpose from the Ministry of Justice.

Just like in Germany, the principle of *jura novit curia* is also supposed in Japan to apply even in relation to foreign law, meaning that the Japanese courts are expected to extend their best efforts, within the

---

[332] See Eichel, *IPRax*, 2009, pp. 389-393.
[333] See M. Jänterä-Jareborg, *Recueil des cours*, Vol. 304 (2003), pp. 303-304.

framework of available time and resources, to investigate ex officio the content of foreign law[334]. The courts may, however, request the parties to provide assistance. Any relevant and reliable evidence can be used, and is evaluated on a case-by-case basis.

The situation in China seems to be similar to that in Japan, at least in theory[335]. The rules of the applicable foreign law should thus be identified ex officio by the court, but in practice Chinese courts appear to rely on the parties to do so.

Dutch courts are also expected to determine the content of the applicable foreign law ex officio[336]. The courts may order a party to co-operate in ascertaining the foreign law, but they are not bound by the information obtained from the parties. On the other hand, errors in the application of foreign law are not subject to review by the Dutch Supreme Court.

Article 16 of the Swiss Federal Act on Private International Law stipulates that the contents of the foreign law must be established by the court of its own motion, even though the court may request the co-operation of the parties and, in matters involving merely an economic interest *(en matière patrimoniale, bei vermögensrechtlichen Ansprüchen)*, it may also order the parties to assist the court on this point[337]. Such request or order is always at the discretion of the court and does not discharge the court of its duty of applying foreign law correctly, but it can make its burden of investiga-

---

[334] See K. Takahashi, [2002] *Singapore Journal of Legal Studies* 491 and 492-493.

[335] See Qingjiang Kong and Hu Minfei, 3 *Melbourne Journal of International Law* 425 (2002).

[336] See P. M. M. Mostermans, *Netherlands International Law Review*, 2004, pp. 405-407.

[337] See B. Dutoit, *Droit international privé suisse*, pp. 57-62; D. Girsberger *et al.*, *Zürcher Kommentar zum IPRG*, pp. 222-228.

tion easier to bear. The main difference between a request and an order seems to be that the ordered party may be subjected to pecuniary sanctions if it refuses to co-operate. The efforts required of the court and of the parties must be reasonable and proportional in view of the circumstances in the individual case. When the court has carried out its own investigation of the content of foreign law, it must give the parties the opportunity to comment on its result and the same applies when the court wishes to rely on the information provided by only one of the parties. There are in principle no restrictions as to the admissible evidence and the judge is permitted to use any personal knowledge of foreign law he may possess. It is not unusual that the evidence consists of an expert opinion submitted by the Institut suisse de droit comparé in Lausanne.

The procedural law of the Nordic countries is based on the principle that the court knows the law and that no proof thereof is, consequently, required[338]. Although even foreign law is deemed to be law, it is treated in a different manner. Chapter 17, Section 3, of the Finnish Code of Judicial Procedure, Article 191 of the Norwegian Code of Civil Procedure and Chapter 35, Section 2, of the Swedish Code of Judicial Procedure stipulate that the court, if it does not know the content of the applicable foreign law, may request a party to prove it. The court may carry out its own investigations too. Any relevant and reliable evidence is admissible.

In Russia, the main principle is that it is the task of the court to ascertain the content of the applicable foreign law, but in business disputes the burden of proving foreign law may be vested by the court in the parties[339].

---

[338] See, for example, M. Jänterä-Jareborg, *Recueil des cours*, Vol. 304 (2003), pp. 296-298.

[339] See Article 1191 (2) of the Russian Civil Code; M. Jänterä-Jareborg, *Recueil des cours*, Vol. 304 (2003), p. 305.

In my opinion, the court should be both permitted and expected to exercise reasonable efforts to procure information about foreign law and to use the knowledge of foreign law it happens to possess, regardless of whether the dispute is of a type where settlement is permitted or where the parties cannot dispose of the disputed matter by settling it. Further, in both types of disputes the parties should be provided with the opportunity to comment on the court's understanding of the applicable foreign law and disprove it. It is, however, true that frequently it may be more practical and appropriate to demand that the parties or one of them assist the court by presenting evidence about the contents of the foreign law to be applied. Such request should not be mandatory for the court but merely permissible and it should not be made unless the court finds it necessary and appropriate. This should be possible in all kinds of disputes, but is probably of particular importance in commercial disputes where the human and financial resources of the parties are often far superior to those of the court itself. In any case, each party should be given the opportunity to disprove the information submitted by the opposing party.

If and to the extent the court wishes to request the assistance of the parties, the question arises as to which of the parties should be asked to procure the information about the contents of the applicable foreign law and what sanction the court can use in order to compel this party to obey that request. It is submitted that the request should normally be addressed to both parties, but the relevant differences between them should be taken into account when evaluating the information provided by them and when deciding about the consequences of a failure by a party to provide reasonable amount of co-operation in the ascertainment of the content of the applicable law (see *infra*). It might frequently be reasonable to put most of the burden of proof on the party relying on the foreign law and alleging that the application of the foreign law leads to a result different from the *lex fori*, but it may sometimes be more practical to demand more co-operation of the party residing habitually in the foreign country in question or having otherwise an easier access to information about the contents of the applicable law. The court should not be formally bound by the information about foreign law furnished by a party, not even when that information is not disputed by the other party.

3. What Should Be Done When the Content of Foreign Law Remains Unknown?

The obligation, whether of the court or of the parties, to procure information about the content of the applicable foreign law can hardly amount to more than the duty to do one's best and spend reasonable resources in terms of time and money. These days, in view of the wealth of information available on the Internet, the well-functioning communications by electronic mail or fax and the improved linguistic skills of judges and legal practitioners, one might be tempted to believe that procuring the necessary information has become relatively easy even in those cases where it is not possible to use any of the established international systems created for the purpose, such as the Council of Europe Convention on Information of Foreign Law (London 1968)[340] or the European Judicial Network on Civil and Commercial Matters[341].

---

[340] See, for example, M. Jänterä-Jareborg, *Recueil des cours*, Vol. 304 (2003), pp. 314-318.
[341] See the Network's homepage <http://ec.europa.eu/civiljustice>, and M. Jänterä-Jareborg, *Recueil des cours*, Vol. 304 (2003), pp. 318-321. See also the new European e-Justice Portal, <e-justice.europa.eu>.

It may, nevertheless, happen that in spite of all reasonable efforts the content of the applicable foreign
law remains unknown or unclear. For example, the
applicable legal system may belong to a distant, closed
and obscure country, or the situation in the foreign
country may be so chaotic due to a civil war between
two competing regimes operating two different legal
systems that it is simply not possible to determine what
is the valid law there. One conceivable solution in such
situations might be to dismiss the case or at least to
stay the proceedings and postpone the judgment until
the contents of the applicable legal system can be
established. However, this method could often lead to
unacceptable delays, in particular in family-law matters, and might in fact result in a denial of justice. It
would, for example, hardly be acceptable to leave a
child to live without maintenance or with unclear
paternity merely because the contents of the applicable
law could not be shown with sufficient clarity due to a
chaotic situation in the foreign country in question[342].

The most obvious method of dealing with a situation where the content of the applicable foreign law
remains unknown seems to be to apply the *lex fori*,
which in the private international law context is in
several respects often considered to serve as a general
residuary (substitute, auxiliary) law[343]. It must, again,
be recalled that foreign law is in principle applied in
the interest of the forum country and that foreign legislators have normally no right to demand that their laws
be applied. They cannot, consequently, object to their
rules being substituted by the *lex fori*, in particular

---

[342] See P. Lalive, *Recueil des cours*, Vol. 155 (1977),
p. 243.
[343] See, for example, Th. de Boer, *Recueil des cours*,
Vol. 257 (1996), pp. 313-315; P. Lalive, *Recueil des cours*,
Vol. 155 (1977), pp. 243-244 and 246.

when the reason of the substitution is the obscurity of their law.

The application of the *lex fori* seems in most countries to be the generally preferred method of dealing with the problem[344]. In some older French decisions, the plaintiff's failure to show the content of the applicable foreign law resulted in a rejection of his claim, but today (since the *Amerford* decision in 1993, see *supra*), such failure would merely result in the application of the *lex fori* (French law) as a substitute, at least when the dispute is of a kind where settlement is permitted[345]. A similar approach is used in many other countries too, usually based on case law[346], but sometimes it is even prescribed by a statute. For example, Article 16 (2) of the Swiss Act on Private International law stipulates that Swiss law applies if the contents of the foreign law cannot be established[347]. Sometimes this solution is disguised as a presumption that the for-

---

[344] See M. Jänterä-Jareborg, *Recueil des cours*, Vol. 304 (2003), pp. 328-331.

[345] See T. C. Hartley, 45 *International and Comparative Law Quarterly* 280-281 (1996); R. Hausmann, *European Legal Forum*, 2008, p. I-10; M. Jänterä-Jareborg, *Recueil des cours*, Vol. 304 (2003), pp. 292 and 326.

[346] In addition to France, this is the case in, for example, England, see K. J. Hood, 2 *Journal of Private International Law* 185-189, in Spain, see A.-L. Calvo Caravaca and J. Carrascosa González, *IPRax*, 2005, p. 174, and in China, see Qingjiang Kong and Hu Minfei, 3 *Melbourne Journal of International Law* 426 (2002).

[347] "Le droit suisse s'applique si le contenu du droit étranger ne peut pas être établi." See B. Dutoit, *Droit international privé suisse*, p. 62; D. Girsberger *et al.*, *Zürcher Kommentar zum IPRG*, pp. 228 and 237-238. See also Section 4 (2) of the Austrian Act on Private International Law of 1978; Article 14 (2) of the Italian Private International Law Act of 1995; Article 2809 of the Civil Code of Québec; Chapter 17, Section 3, of the Finnish Code of Judicial Procedure, etc.

eign law is identical with the *lex fori*[348], but mostly the method needs no such defending and is rather seen as the most natural and expedient manner of dealing with the problem.

In spite of its practical advantages, the application of the *lex fori* has also some serious drawbacks, such as the risk of applying substantive rules that are clearly unsuitable for the case under scrutiny. The substance of the dispute may be totally unrelated to the country of the forum and the application of the *lex fori* can be manifestly incompatible with the expectations of the parties, for example if Swedish family law were to be applied merely because the family law of a distant Moslem country could not be ascertained. Besides, the content of the applicable foreign legal system remains very often unknown regarding a rather narrow specific point only. The application of the *lex fori* to that specific point, while the applicable foreign law continues to govern all the other issues, can create problems of mutual inconsistency, and this may occasionally require that in order to preserve the coherence of the solution, the *lex fori* be applied also to some neighbouring issues[349].

A possible alternative solution, which seems to be suitable in some special cases only, is the application of a surrogate rule taken from another (third) legal system which is so closely related to the applicable law that it can be assumed to be identical or at least very similar ("neighbour law", *"droit voisin"*)[350]. For example, English law could be used as a substitute for the

---

[348] See, for example, T. Einhorn, in *Essays Nygh*, p. 109.

[349] Cf. D. Girsberger *et al.*, *Zürcher Kommentar zum IPRG*, p. 237.

[350] See, for example, P. Lalive, *Recueil des cours*, Vol. 155 (1977), pp. 244-245; K. Siehr, *Yearbook of Private International Law*, Vol. VII (2005), p. 47.

applicable rule of New Zealand or French law as a substitute for the law of Luxembourg[351]. This method is, however, legitimate only when there are reasons to assume that there really exists a similarity in the particular field of law, so that, for example, the use of French or English law as a secondary source of information about the law of their former colonies may be an acceptable solution in the field of commercial law but hardly in the fields of family law or land law, which are usually based on traditional local customary rules rather than on the law inherited from the former colonial power. The probability of similarity is presumably higher when the question to be answered pertains to the more general aspects of the legal system, such as the method of interpretation of the sources of law, than when it concerns some detail of positive private law, such as the calculation of damages or the validity of dismissal of an employee[352]. It must be seriously doubted whether it was reasonable of the District Court of Tokyo to presume, in its decision of 19 March 1976, that the content of North Korean law regarding postmortal acknowledgment of a child corresponded to Czechoslovak, Polish and Soviet laws, on the ground that they all belonged to the socialist legal family[353].

---

[351] Cf. E. Jayme, *Recueil des cours*, Vol. 251 (1995), pp. 125-126, who submits, for example, that Islamic law is an appropriate substitute for Tunisian law and praises a German judgment from 1936 where Danish and Norwegian law were considered to be suitable substitutes for the law of Iceland.

[352] See, for example, B. Audit, *Droit international privé*, pp. 233-234; Th. de Boer, *Recueil des cours*, Vol. 257 (1996), pp. 310-312; T. Einhorn, in *Essays Nygh*, pp. 117-118; M. Jänterä-Jareborg, *Recueil des cours*, Vol. 304 (2003), pp. 331-333; G. Kegel and K. Schurig, *Internationales Privatrecht*, pp. 512-513.

[353] Information about this Japanese decision is taken from a presentation by Professor Yuko Nishitani, prepared

There are other possible alternative solutions as well, for example the application of another legal system (the next best choice) having close relationship to the dispute, for example the *lex domicilii* instead of the *lex patriae* of unknown contents[354], or the application of some uniform principles or rules elaborated by a widely respected international body such as UNIDROIT[355].

A reasonable compromise, when the contents of the applicable foreign law cannot be established, seems to be the application of *lex fori* unless the circumstances in the individual case warrant the application a third legal system or a refusal to adjudicate. This flexible compromise solution would make it possible to take into account the nature of the dispute, the position of the parties and which of the parties should bear the risk that the content of the applicable law remains unknown. Often — albeit not necessarily always — this risk should be borne by the party relying on the foreign law in question (it is therefore natural that this party will frequently be asked to procure information about the content of that law, see *supra*). Applying the *lex fori* as a sanction against a non-cooperative party relying on foreign law is, however, not appropriate in those disputes that cannot be resolved by a settlement (for example divorces or adoptions, if and to the extent they are governed by foreign law), where the determination of the applicable law should not depend on the procedural behaviour of the parties or, even worse, of merely one of them.

---

for an expert meeting at the Hague Conference on Private International Law in February 2007.

[354] See, for example, Th. de Boer, *Recueil des cours*, Vol. 257 (1996), pp. 352-353.

[355] See A. V. M. Struycken, *Recueil des cours*, Vol. 311 (2004), pp. 233-235.

The problem discussed in the previous paragraphs must be distinguished from those cases where reliable information about the applicable foreign law is available but the problem under scrutiny has simply not yet found a solution there, i.e., the applicable law contains an unregulated gap *(lacuna)*. Such gap should in principle be filled in the same manner as it would be filled by the courts in the country of the legal system concerned[356], for example by looking for an answer among the general principles of that system or in an analogous application of the existing rules thereof. It is also possible to seek answer in another, closely related legal system, in particular when it is known that it exercises considerable influence in the country in question (for example, the courts in many small common-law jurisdictions are known to fill the gaps by seeking guidance in English law). Looking for answers in universal natural law or "general principles of law recognized by civilized nations" (such as the principle *pacta sunt servanda*[357]) is generally not a good solution, as it usually amounts merely to a covert application of the *lex fori*[358].

It must also be realized that the lack of statutory or judge-made rules on a particular issue does not necessarily amount to a real gap. If the applicable foreign legal system has no rules about, for example, the determination of paternity regarding children born out of

---

[356] See, for example, B. Dutoit, *Droit international privé suisse*, p. 61; D. Girsberger *et al.*, *Zürcher Kommentar zum IPRG*, p. 237; G. Kegel and K. Schurig, *Internationales Privatrecht*, pp. 506-507; P. Lalive, *Recueil des cours*, Vol. 155 (1977), p. 242.

[357] See, for example, G. Kegel and K. Schurig, *Internationales Privatrecht*, p. 513.

[358] Cf., for example, the notorious award in the case of *Petroleum Development Ltd.* v. *Sheikh of Abu Dhabi*, 18 *International Law Reports* 144 (1951).

wedlock, this may be a reflection of the fact that judicial determination of paternity is consciously and intentionally not allowed (such attitude is not unusual in, for example, Islamic countries). It is hardly possible to argue in such a case that the matter is "left unregulated" or that there is a "gap".

CHAPTER VIII

CLASSIFICATION

1. The Problem

Just like any other legal rules, even the terms used in conflict rules are subject to interpretation, which is not always unproblematic. The conflict rules of private international law of the forum country categorize and divide among themselves the branches and subbranches of substantive law or, more correctly expressed, the substantive legal problems and issues [359]

---

[359] Cf., however, G. Kegel and K. Schurig, *Internationales Privatrecht*, pp. 312-313, and C. M. V. Clarkson and J. Hill, *The Conflict of Laws*, pp. 10 and 457-458, who seem to be of the view that classification involves the categorization of legal rules *(Rechtsnormen)* and/or factual situations *(Sachverhälte or Lebensverhältnisse)*. B. Audit, *Droit international privé*, pp. 82 and 171, speaks about classifying *le type de situation juridique*, which appears to be a combination composed of both facts and their legal consequences *(les faits contemplés par la règle . . . et les conséquences qu'elle en tire)*. A. Philip, *Recueil des cours*, Vol. 160 (1978), p. 39, writes about the characterization of facts ("the facts are characterized as being of the nature indicated in the scope of application-element of the choice of law rule"). I am inclined to agree with E. Jayme, *Recueil des cours*, Vol. 251 (1995), p. 107, according to whom the classification pertains rather to the legal issue itself: "c'est plutôt la question juridique même qui doit être classée", and A. E. von Overbeck, *Recueil des cours*, Vol. 176 (1982), p. 91: "il s'agit de déterminer la nature juridique de la question qui se pose". On the other hand, W. Wengler, *Recueil des cours*, Vol. 104 (1961), pp. 349-350, appears to attribute decisive importance to the wording of the conflict rule involved, i.e. whether it says that a certain type of claims is governed by a certain law or that

that may arise in connection with private-law disputes. For example, the right to inheritance may be governed by the law of the country of the last habitual residence of the deceased, non-contractual damages may be governed by the law of the country where the direct damage occurred, procedural issues are to be decided by the *lex fori*, etc. This gives rise to the notorious problem of classification (also called characterization or qualification), related to the obvious need to classify the issue to be decided as belonging to the subject-matter scope of application of a particular conflict rule of the forum. For example, it has to be decided whether the issue at hand concerns, in the terminology of the conflict rules, the right to inheritance, non-contractual liability, procedure, or falls within the subject-matter scope of application of one of the other conflict rules.

In the huge majority of cases, classification is relatively simple and straightforward. If the court has to decide which surviving relatives are entitled to the estate of a deceased person, it is usually not difficult to ascertain that this is a matter of inheritance law (in some instances a matter of matrimonial property regime) and not a matter of, say, contract, non-contractual liability or procedure. However, the classification is not always that easy, in particular when the question to be resolved is closely related to more than one

---

a certain type of rules govern a certain claim. These rather superficial and formalistic differences between various authors are, however, of little significance for the substance of the classification problem, as the classification of legal issues and the classification of facts, legal rules or their consequences are merely different sides of the same coin. If, for example, a particular legal issue is classified as procedural, then the situation giving rise to that issue, the legal rules governing that issue and the consequences of those rules must logically be classified as procedural too (and vice versa). Cf. *Dicey and Morris on the Conflict of Laws*, pp. 34-35.

branch of law and these are subject to different conflict rules. As long as the scopes of the various branches of the law are defined merely for pedagogical or other similar purposes they are not legal concepts defined by the law, but in private international law the same scopes take on a legal meaning. As private international law consists of "rules about applicable rules", the terms used to define their respective scopes of application ("procedural matters", "matters relating to the right of inheritance", "matters relating to non-contractual obligations", etc.) are legal terms, usually "borrowed" from the substantive *lex fori*[360]. These terms may have different meaning in different countries and their exact meaning may be unclear even in the *lex fori*. There are many questions that are difficult to classify because they are on the borderline between two or even more conflict rules.

Assume, for example, that a Dutch tourist has been assaulted and physically injured in China by a Brazilian tourist. The victim sues the assailant in a Brazilian court (the *forum domicilii* of the defendant), claiming compensation for pain and suffering. While the case is pending, the victim dies. Assume that pursuant to both Chinese and Brazilian law the victim's estate or his heirs can take over his claim, while we also assume that according to Dutch law such claims for non-economic damage, in contrast to other claims, disappear if the victim dies prior to the judgment. Whether the Brazilian court will allow the heirs to take over the claim will thus depend on whether it will apply Chinese, Brazilian or Dutch law. This will, in turn, depend on how the court will classify the issue. Is it an issue of procedure, governed by the Brazilian *lex fori*? The right of the heirs or of the estate to continue the

---

[360] See M. F. Yasseen, *Recueil des cours*, Vol. 116 (1965), p. 440.

proceedings has, no doubt, a procedural aspect. Or is it rather an issue of substantive inheritance law, to be decided by Dutch law as the personal law of the deceased? This may seem to be a plausible alternative, as the problem is about the right of the heirs to inherit an asset (a claim). Or is it more natural to see the issue as a matter of non-contractual liability, governed by the Chinese *lex loci damni*? After all, it can be argued that the whole problem is caused by the tort-related features of compensation for non-economic damage rather than by procedural considerations or considerations of inheritance law.

The answer to these questions is far from self-evident, unless the legal concepts used to define the scope of application of the forum country's various written or unwritten conflict rules have a clearly defined meaning, which is unusual in the private international law of most countries. As far as the Member States of the European Union (except Denmark) are concerned, the notorious classification problem arising in the example above has, however, been solved by Article 15 *(e)* of the EC Regulation Rome II[361], stipulating that the question whether a right to claim damages may be transferred by inheritance shall be governed by the law applicable to the non-contractual obligation in question (and thus not by the law governing the inheritance). In many non-European countries the question remains open though.

There are authors denying the very raison d'être of classification, even calling it a conceptualist "self-inflicted embarrassment"[362], but the objective existence

---

[361] Regulation No. 864/2007 of 11 July 2007 on the Law Applicable to Non-Contractual Obligations (Rome II), OJ 2007 L 199, p. 40.

[362] See, for example, F. K. Juenger, *Recueil des cours*, Vol. 193 (1985), pp. 191-194.

of classification problems cannot be denied as long as private international law of the forum country consists of various binding conflict rules — irrespective of whether statutory or judge-made — for various categories of legal issues. Naturally, if and to the extent this system of conflict rules is replaced with one single conflict rule, covering all kinds of legal issues, the problem of classification will disappear[363]. It is also true that sometimes the classification problem arises but is not mentioned and even less discussed by the parties and the courts, who seem not to have noticed the possibility of a characterization different from that which appeared closest at hand at a superficial glance[364].

---

[363] Such a rule is theoretically conceivable, for example a single conflict rule stipulating that any legal problem of any kind whatsoever shall be governed by the legal system with which it is most closely connected or which leads to the most reasonable substantive result.

[364] For example, in the Swedish Supreme Court decision in *Nytt Juridiskt Arkiv* 1969, p. 163, the law of the country where the tort occurred imposed certain restrictions on compensation claims between spouses (the so-called spousal immunity). These restrictions were applied due to the Swedish conflict rule designating the *lex loci delicti* as the law applicable to torts. Nobody seems to have noticed the possibility that special liability restrictions between spouses could be classified as belonging to the field of family law, governed by the law applicable to matrimonial relations of personal nature. Cf. the American case of *Haumschild* v. *Continental Casualty Co.*, 95 NW 2d 814 (Wisconsin 1959), where such liability was held to be a matter of family law rather than tort law. As far as EU Member States are concerned, this classification problem has probably — but not certainly — been solved by Article 15 *(b)* of the Rome II Regulation No. 864/2007 of 11 July 2007 on the Law Applicable to Non-Contractual Obligations, OJ 2007 L 199, p. 40, stipulating that the grounds for exemption from liability are governed by the law applicable to the non-contractual obligation in question (thus not by the law governing the effects of marriage).

It would be a mistake to believe that all classification issues could easily be resolved if the forum country decided to clarify by legislation the exact meaning of the concepts and terms appearing in the forum country's conflict rules[365]. To begin with, it is probably impossible to predict and regulate all classification problems that conceivably may arise. Furthermore, even when it is known how a particu-lar issue is classified in the *lex fori*, for example even if it is generally accepted that the problem in the example above is in the forum country's private law treated as belonging to the field of tort law, the classification in private international law is complicated by the fact that it could be — and in fact it has been — argued that the court should not always automatically follow the classification in accordance with the legal concepts and terms of the *lex fori* but should rather take into account the classification prevailing in the country whose law is to be applied (the so-called classification pursuant to the *lex causae*)[366] or carry out the classification on the basis of

---

[365] Such statutory classification can sometimes be found in international istruments, for example in Article 5 of the Hague Convention of 5 October 1961 on the Conflicts of Laws relating to the Form of Testamentary Dispositions:

"For the purposes of the present Convention, any provison of law which limits the permitted forms of testamentary dispositions by reference to the age, nationality or other personal conditions of the testator, shall be deemed to pertain to matters of form."

A provision of substantive national law stipulating that a will made by a minor requires the presence of a public notary while not imposing such a requirement on wills made by adults is thus classified as pertaining to form, even though its purpose might make it more natural to see it as pertaining to matters of legal capacity of the testator.

[366] D. F. Cavers, *Recueil des cours*, Vol. 131 (1970), p. 135, appears to consider — incorrectly — such classification to be a mere variant of *renvoi* (cf. Chapter IX, *infra*).

comparative studies, i.e. by giving terms in conflict rules an autonomous and universal meaning without being bound by the terminology and established classification in the *lex fori*, the *lex causae* or any other particular legal system.

2. *Classification Based on a Comparative Approach*

The last-mentioned classification method, which is usually traced back to the famous German legal scientist Ernst Rabel[367], is undoubtedly attractive and corresponds in some respects to the needs of our globalized world. It is particularly valuable with regard to the interpretation of conflict rules that stem from an international convention or some other type of international legislative co-operation, as such uniform conflict rules would lose much of their uniformity if they were given varying scopes depending on the different interpreta-

---

[367] See his statement in *Zeitschrift für ausländisches und internationales Privatrecht*, 1931, p. 283: "Für das System des internationalen Privatrechts ergibt sich die Notwendigkeit, eigene Begriffe zu bilden." See also G. Barile, *Recueil des cours,* Vol. 116 (1965), p. 345, who writes that

"le sens des expressions employées par les règles de rattachement afin de déterminer leur objet ne doit pas être déduit d'une façon immédiate et automatique du droit matériel interne, mais, autant que possible, des caractères universels des différents instituts juridiques, de sorte que les expressions en question assumant par là même un sens indéterminé et générique, d'un côté tendent à correspondre à celles qu'adoptent les règles de rattachement d'ordres juridiques étrangers, et de l'autre, puissent être référées à des rapports et à des instituts, même partiellement différents, prévus par les droits matériels . . ."

See also P. G. Vallindas, *Recueil des cours*, Vol. 101 (1960), p. 358, who spoke in this context about the "autonomy" of conflict rules.

tions by courts in different countries. However, some
kind of uniform classification could be used even in
respect of purely national conflict rules. This can be
illustrated by a decision of the Swedish Supreme Court
of 6 December 1990[368], where it had to be decided
whether an insurer's right of recourse against the tortfeasor was to be classified as a contractual matter
falling within the scope of application of the law governing the insurance contract (*in casu* German law) or
as a matter of tort, governed by the *lex loci delicti* (*in
casu* Swedish law). After having pointed out that the
solution for this classification issue could be found neither in Swedish legislation nor in the previous Swedish
case law, the Supreme Court decided to subject the
recourse to the law governing the insurance contract.
Among the arguments supporting this classification,
the Supreme Court mentioned that it would be in
accordance with the judicial practice "in many countries" and also conform to the conflict rule on subroga-
tion of contractual claims in Article 13 of the 1980 EC
Convention on the Law Applicable to Contractual
Obligations (the so-called Rome Convention, to which
Sweden was not a party in 1990)[369].

However, the Court did not give an account of the
"many countries" it had looked at, and it is doubtful

---

[368] See *Nytt Juridiskt Arkiv*, 1990, p. 734.

[369] This classification problem has subsequently been
solved, as far as EU Member States (except Denmark) are
concerned, by Article 19 of the Rome II Regulation
No. 864/2007 of 11 July 2007 on the Law Applicable to
Non-Contractual Obligations, OJ 2007 L 199, p. 40, which
provides that where a person (the creditor) has a non-contractual claim upon another person (the debtor), and a third
person (e.g. an insurer) has a duty to satisfy the creditor,
the law governing the third person's duty (e.g. an insurance contract) shall determine whether the third person is
subrogated to the creditor's rights and can exercise them
against he debtor.

whether a proper large-scale comparative investigation can be carried out every time there is a classification issue facing the court[370]. It can also be argued that a compulsory comparative characterization method would build a watertight wall between the concepts in the substantive and conflict rules, which would be undesirable in view of the close connection between the two and the common legislative aims they normally pursue in the country of the forum[371].

3. *Classification Pursuant to the* Lex Causae

Classification pursuant to the *lex causae* has also had its champions, arguing that

> "French law classifies French legal rules, Italian law Italian rules, and an English court examining the applicability of French rules will have to take the French classification into consideration"[372].

In practice this would mean, for example, that an issue should be classified as pertaining to a contract if in the country whose law governs the contract it is deemed to be contractual; it should, instead, be treated as pertaining to a tort if that is the view in the country whose law is applicable to torts. The idea behind this approach seems to be that the manner of classifying is part of how a legal system looks at a certain issue, i.e. part of the "spirit" of that legal system, and disregarding that spirit would amount to an erroneous application thereof.

---

[370] See M. F. Yasseen, *Recueil des cours*, Vol. 116 (1965), pp. 448-450.

[371] Cf. B. Audit, *Droit international privé*, pp. 174-175.

[372] See M. Wolff, *Private International Law*, pp. 154-155 (it should be noted that he spoke about the classification of "rules" rather than legal issues). Cf. G. Kegel and K. Schurig, *Internationales Privatrecht*, pp. 341-342.

In the 1990 Swedish case above, this approach
would require that the question of whether the insurer's
right of recourse is governed by the German law governing the insurance contract be answered by German
law, while the question whether the insurer's right of
recourse is governed by the Swedish *lex loci delicti* be
answered by Swedish law. This could obviously lead to
problems of inconsistency, some of them logically
impossible to solve[373], for instance if German law classifies the insurer's right of recourse to be a matter of
tort, while Swedish law considers it to be a contractual
matter. A consistent classification pursuant to the *lex
cause* would under such circumstances mean that the
issue would fall between two chairs into some kind of
a legal vacuum (in German called *Normenmangel*), as
it would be considered to be beyond the scopes of
application of both the conflict rule on contracts and
the conflict rule for torts. In the opposite case, where
German law classifies the issue as contractual while
Swedish law sees it as belonging to the field of tort
law, a consistent classification pursuant to the *lex
causae* would lead to the simultaneous application of
both German and Swedish rules to the same issues (in
German *Normenhäufung*), which might turn out to be
impossible due to the mutual incompatibility of
German and Swedish substantive law. It is, therefore,
hardly surprising that this method of classification has
not won many adherents among judges and legal
writers; it may be noted that the Swedish Supreme
Court in the above-mentioned 1990 case decided to
classify the issue as contractual without giving any
particular weight to whether this view was shared by

---

[373] See, for example, B. Audit, *Droit international
privé*, pp. 90-91 and 173; G. A. L. Droz, *Recueil des
cours*, Vol. 229 (1991), p. 334; G. Kegel and K. Schurig,
Internationales Privatrecht, p. 342.

German law which was the law governing the insurance contract concerned.

Nevertheless, there are examples of cases where the *lex causae* approach was used by the courts, such as the English decision *In re Cohn* of 1945[374]. The case concerned the succession to the estate of a woman who was considered to have been domiciled in Germany at the time when she was killed, together with her daughter, in London by a German bomb. Due to her German domicile, the succession was governed by German law, according to which she and her daughter were presumed to have died simultaneously, while English substantive law presumed that the daughter, being younger, had survived her mother long enough to inherit under the mother's will. The court faced the question whether this issue was a procedural matter of evidence (in which case the English *lex fori* would have applied) or a substantive matter of succession (in which case it would have been governed by German law). The court first took a look at the English legal system and came to the conclusion that the English presumption had to be characterized as a rule of substantive law and, therefore, was not to be applied. The court then turned to German law and found, based on the location of the German presumption in the German Civil Code, that the presumption was part of the German substantive law on succession. Therefore, the court concluded that the German presumption was applicable. It remains an open question what the court would have done if the two legal systems had characterized their presumptions in different ways, for example if the presumption under scrutiny had been

---

[374] [1945] Ch. 5. See also C. M. V. Clarkson and J. Hill, *The Conflict of Laws*, p. 461; *Dicey and Morris on the Conflict of Laws*, pp. 37-39; O. Kahn-Freund, *Recueil des cours*, Vol. 143 (1974), pp. 369-371.

classified in English law as procedural while in German law as substantive (in which case both English and German presumption would have claimed application), or if it in German law had been characterized as procedural while in English law as substantive (in which case none of them would have applied).

Such potentially absurd consequences of classification in accordance with the *lex causae* can be illustrated by the notorious decision made in 1882 by the German *Reichsgericht*[375], dealing with the time limitation period for a monetary claim governed by foreign law. Despite the fact that that period has lapsed pursuant to both the German *lex fori* and the foreign *lex causae*, the claim was held to be enforceable, as the foreign time limitation rule was characterized as procedural and thus inapplicable while the corresponding German rule was characterized as substantive and thus inapplicable to a claim governed by foreign law!

Another English case frequently discussed in connection with the problem of characterization is *Re Maldonado* of 1954[376]. A person domiciled in Spain but owning movable property in England died without leaving any relatives or a will. Pursuant to English private international law, the succession to movables was governed by the law of the last domicile of the deceased, i.e. by Spanish law, which stipulated that the property would be inherited by the Spanish State as sole and universal heir. On the other hand, if the property were seen as *bona vacantia* (property without an

---

[375] *Entscheidungen des Reichsgerichts in Zivilsachen*, Vol. VII, p. 21. See also *Dicey and Morris on the Conflict of Laws*, pp. 38-39; T. C. Hartley, *Recueil des cours*, Vol. 319 (2006), pp. 190-191; O. Kahn-Freund, *Recueil des cours*, Vol. 143 (1974), pp. 372-373.

[376] *State of Spain* v. *Treasury Solicitor*, [1954] P. 223 (CA); *Dicey and Morris on the Conflict of Laws*, pp. 39-40.

owner), its fate would be governed by English law as the *lex rei sitae*, pursuant to which it would be vested in the British crown. The Court of Appeal held that the property only became *bona vacantia* if the deceased died leaving no successors according to Spanish law or if the Spanish State sought to assert a right not as successor but by a *jus regale* which the English courts would not recognize as having extraterritorial validity. The Court examined the relevant Spanish rule and came to the conclusion that it was applicable because it treated the Spanish State as the true final heir *(ultimus heres)* rather than the holder of a prerogative right under public law to confiscate ownerless assets. The Spanish State had thus become entitled to the property on the death of the deceased and the English rule on *bona vacantia* did not apply because the property was never ownerless. If the Spanish legislator had attempted to reach the same result using a different, public-law terminology, the outcome would have been the opposite and the property would have gone to the British Crown. As put in the Dicey and Morris handbook [377], it is questionable whether it is desirable that the outcome in this case, regarding the right to property in England, should depend on a foreign verbal formulation with no real content. In Sweden, for example, this particular problem happens to be regulated by a special statutory provision. Even though rights to inheritance are in Sweden in principle governed by the law of the country of which the deceased was a citizen at the time of his death, if a foreigner dies intestate and leaves no relatives entitled to inherit under the applicable foreign law, the assets situated in Sweden are not handed over to the foreign State or other public institution entitled to the property pursuant to the foreign law in question but are vested in the Swedish General

---

[377] See *Dicey and Morris on the Conflict of Laws*, p. 40.

Inheritance Fund to be used for certain humanitarian purposes[378]. This can be considered to be an expression of characterization pursuant to the *lex fori*: these kinds of claims by foreign States or other public entities are in accordance with Swedish view in principle to be treated as belonging to the field of public law even when the foreign legal system applicable to succession characterizes them as inheritance governed by private law.

The purpose of the conflict rule may sometimes require that it be interpreted in some respects in accordance with foreign law. For example, one of the reasons why there are often special conflict rules subjecting matters concerning real (immovable) property to the law of the country where that property is situated, is that most countries insist on the application of their own substantive law to real property within their borders and would probably refuse to recognize foreign judgments based on another law. In order to fulfil their purpose in this respect, the conflict rules on real property should therefore normally be interpreted to have in mind property which is immovable pursuant to the law of the country where it is situated rather than pursuant to the *lex fori*[379].

---

[378] See Chapter 1, Section 11, of the Swedish Act (1937:81) on Some International Relationships concerning Estates of Deceased Persons.

[379] See the English case of *In re Hoyles. Row* v. *Jagg*, [1911] 1 Ch. 179; E. Bartin, *Recueil des cours*, Vol. 31 (1930), pp. 597-599; C. M. V. Clarkson and J. Hill, *The Conflict of Laws*, p. 465; D. J. L. Davies, *Recueil des cours*, Vol. 62 (1937), p. 499; O. Kahn-Freund, *Recueil des cours*, Vol. 143 (1974), p. 381; A. E. von Overbeck, *Recueil des cours*, Vol. 176 (1982), pp. 101-102; J. M. Trias de Bes, *Recueil des cours*, Vol. 62 (1937), p. 51. Cf., however, also B. Audit, *Droit international privé*, p. 176; G. A. L. Droz, *Recueil des cours*, Vol. 229 (1991), pp. 334-337.

4. *Classification Pursuant to the* Lex Fori

In practice, most scholars and the courts of most countries prefer to classify legal problems in accordance with the *lex fori*, even though some of them do so with various reservations and exceptions[380]. Some authors discard classification pursuant to the *lex fori* but present a theory of their own which at a closer look turns out to be a mere variety of the *lex fori* approach[381]. Indeed, at least in relations between legal systems belonging to the same legal culture, in nine cases out of ten the classification according to the *lex*

---

[380] See, for example, R. Ago, *Recueil des cours*, Vol. 58 (1936), pp. 313-330; B. Audit, *Droit international privé*, pp. 173-174; E. Bartin, *Recueil des cours*, Vol. 31 (1930), p. 589; H. Batiffol, *Recueil des cours*, Vol. 97 (1959), pp. 451-456; D. F. Cavers, *Recueil des cours*, Vol. 131 (1970), p. 136; C. M. V. Clarkson and J. Hill, *The Conflict of Laws*, pp. 10 and 458-460; D. J. L. Davies, *Recueil des cours*, Vol. 62 (1937), pp. 501-502; *Dicey and Morris on the Conflict of Laws*, pp. 35-36; G. A. L. Droz, *Recueil des cours*, Vol. 229 (1991), pp. 323-342; H. Gaudemet-Tallon, *Recueil des cours*, Vol. 312 (2005), pp. 187-188; O. Kahn-Freund, *Recueil des cours*, Vol. 143 (1974), pp. 369-382; G. Kegel and K. Schurig, *Internationales Privatrecht*, pp. 337 and 339; H. Lewald, *Recueil des cours*, Vol. 69 (1939), pp. 79-84; J. Maury, *Recueil des cours*, Vol. 57 (1936), pp. 484-496; *Restatement of the Law Second. Conflict of Laws 2d*, Vol. 1, §7, pp. 17-18; E. Vitta, *Recueil des cours*, Vol. 162 (1979), pp. 61-63; M. F. Yasseen, *Recueil des cours*, Vol. 116 (1965), pp. 438-446.

[381] See, for example, K. Lipstein, *Recueil des cours*, Vol. 135 (1972), p. 200, who discards the approach based on the *lex fori* and suggests that the forum must analyse the nature of the claim or defence expressed according to some system of laws in the light of its function within that legal system, but thereafter should relate the claim or defence so analysed to that among its own (the forum's) rules of private international law which "upon a broad interpretation" are capable of covering the claim in question.

fori does not create any hesitation or doubt. Classification pursuant to the *lex fori* might even seem to be the obvious and natural solution, because classification is basically a matter of interpretation of the conflict rules of the country of the forum[382]. These conflict rules have been formulated by the legislator (irrespective of whether by the Parliament or by some precedent-making judges) of the forum country and it is, therefore, quite natural that they should be interpreted in accordance with the intentions of that legislator, who may even explicitly instruct the courts on how certain issues should be classified[383]. It can be argued that if the forum country renounces on the application of its own law in favour of a foreign law, then the limits and contents of this renunciation should be set by the *lex fori*. The freedom of the courts to interpret the scope of application of a conflict rule is in principle limited by the clear wording of that rule and by its obvious purpose, as well as by the other principles of interpretation generally accepted in the country of the forum[384].

This reasoning, seemingly leading to the conclusion that classification should always be done in accordance with *lex fori*, may appear uncontroversial, but it does not really answer the fundamental question. It can namely be argued that the legislator of the forum country does not always intend that the terms defining the subject-matter scope of the conflict rules be understood

---

[382] See, for example, A. Philip, *Recueil des cours*, Vol. 160 (1978), p. 39.

[383] See, for example, the above-mentioned Article 15 *(e)* of the EC Regulation Rome II, stipulating that the question whether a right to claim damages may be transferred by inheritance shall be governed by the law applicable to the non-contractual obligation in question (and thus not by the law governing the inheritance).

[384] See A. Philip, *Recueil des cours*, Vol. 160 (1978), pp. 20-21.

as having exactly the same meaning as they have in the domestic substantive *lex fori*[385]. "Habit and the poverty of language"[386] may lead the legislatures and courts to express conflict rules in the terms they are accustomed to, i.e. terms in the conflict rules are borrowed from the forum country's own substantive law, but their interpretation should take into account the international context and the fact that the conflict rules have a specific purpose which differs from the function of the substantive provisions.

To begin with, the forum must take into consideration that some of the conflict rules are based on international instruments and should be interpreted in accordance therewith. This follows from the general principles of public international law on the interpretation and implementation by States of their treaty obligations[387] and is only exceptionally spelled out in the treaty itself, one such exception being Article 16 of the Hague Convention of 22 December 1986 on the Law Applicable to Contracts for the International Sale of Goods, which provides that "[i]n the interpretation of the Convention, regard is to be had to its international character and to the need to promote uniformity in its application".

---

[385] See, for example, *Dicey and Morris on the Conflict of Laws*, p. 36; G. Kegel and K. Schurig, *Internationales Privtrecht*, p. 334; G. S. Maridakis, *Recueil des cours*, Vol. 105 (1962), p. 398; A. Philip, *Recueil des cours*, Vol. 160 (1978), pp. 39-40; E. Vitta, *Recueil des cours*, Vol. 162 (1979), pp. 62-63; M. F. Yasseen, *Recueil des cours*, Vol. 116 (1965), pp. 443-444.

[386] See E. E. Cheatham, *Recueil des cours*, Vol. 99 (1960), p. 323.

[387] See, in particular, Article 31 of the 1969 Vienna Convention on the Law of Treaties, providing that a treaty shall be interpreted in good faith in accordance with the ordinary meaning to be given to the terms of the treaty in the context and the the light of its object and purpose.

The conflict rules in the instruments of EU law (such as the Rome I and Rome II Regulations) will, furthermore, be authoritatively interpreted by the Court of Justice of the European Union, whose interpretation will have to be respected by the national courts of the Member States. There are no reasons to believe that the ECJ will not follow the same interpretation method it has developed in respect of most provisions of the 1968 Brussels Convention on Jurisdiction and the Enforcement of Judgments in Civil and Commercial Matters. Pursuant to this method, in the interpretation of that Convention's concepts [388],

> "reference must not be made to the law of one of the states concerned but, first, to the objectives and scheme of the Convention and, secondly, to the general principles which stem from the corpus of the national legal systems".

But even those terms and concepts that are used in the conflict rules of purely national origin may often have to be interpreted more extensively than according to their usual meaning in the *lex fori*. A very illustrative example of a classification pursuant to the *lex fori* but differing radically from the concepts in the forum country's domestic law is the English Foreign Limitation Periods Act of 1984 [389]. As the expiry of the time limitation does not extinguish the claim but only makes it unenforceable in courts, the time limitation used to be classified in England traditionally as a matter of procedure rather than of substantive law. This meant that English courts always applied English rules on time limitation and refused to apply foreign limitation

---

[388] *LTU Luftransportunternehmen GmbH* v. *Eurocontrol* (case 29/76, decided on 14 October 1976).

[389] See C. M. V. Clarkson and J. Hill, *The Conflict of Laws*, pp. 467-468.

rules. However, the 1984 Act provides that where any matter is governed by the law of a foreign country, then that country's limitation rules shall apply. It must be stressed that this does not amount to any classification pursuant to the *lex causae*, as the foreign time-limitation rules are applied irrespective of whether time limitation is in the law of their own country classified as a substantive or procedural matter. The traditional common-law characterization of statutes of limitation as being procedural continues to prevail in the United States; it is true that the Uniform Conflict of Laws Limitations Act introduces a substantive characterization for the purposes of private international law, but it has been adopted by very few States only[390].

In the ideal world, the sum of all conflict rules of the forum would cover all private-law issues that may conceivably arise and divide all such issues into clearly delineated categories ("boxes") that would not overlap each other[391]. We do not, alas, live in such a fictitious ideal world. Difficult classification problems may arise in particular when characterization pursuant to the *lex fori* has to be carried out regarding foreign legal phenomena that are unknown in the *lex fori*[392]. Thus, a Swedish appellate court has treated the Islamic *mahr* (a kind of bride-price, promised to the bride in the mar-

---

[390] See E. F. Scoles *et al.*, *Conflict of Laws*, pp. 129-131.

[391] Cf. M. Dogauchi, *Recueil des cours*, Vol. 315 (2005), pp. 38 and 108.

[392] See, for example, B. Audit, *Droit international privé*, pp. 169-170; C. M. V. Clarkson and J. Hill, *The Conflict of Laws*, pp. 459-460; G. A. L. Droz, *Recueil des cours*, Vol. 229 (1991), pp. 331-332; E. Jayme, *Recueil des cours*, Vol. 251 (1995), pp. 114-115; G. Kegel and K. Schurig, *Internationales Privatrecht*, p. 338; A. E. von Overbeck, *Recueil des cours*, Vol. 176 (1982), pp. 94-95; M. F. Yasseen, *Recueil des cours*, Vol. 116 (1965), p. 447.

riage contract by the bridegroom) as falling within the field of application of the Swedish conflict rule on maintenance, thus extending the concept of maintenance in this conflict rule far beyond the concept of maintenance in Swedish domestic family law[393]. Another Swedish appellate court preferred, however, to treat *mahr* as falling within the field of application of the Swedish conflict rule on matrimonial property relations, thus giving the concept of matrimonial property relations in that conflict rule a meaning much wider than it has in domestic Swedish law[394]. It might also be conceivable to classify *mahr* as a mere contract or — if the wife claims her *mahr* after her husband's death — as a phenomenon governed by the law applicable to succession.

5. Concluding Remarks

It follows from the aforesaid that it is impossible to apply one single approach mechanically to the classification problem, which has to be dealt with flexibly. In the words of Audit[395], "la meilleure attitude à l'égard du conflit de qualifications est de ne pas se prononcer par une disposition générale sur la question". Trevor Hartley has suggested that the optimal approach is to give up theorizing, and to decide each case as it comes along in the way that produces the best results, i.e. to choose the characterization that best gives effect to the policies and purposes of the law[396]. A similar view has

---

[393] See *Rättsfall från hovrätterna*, 1993:116. A similar classification of *mahr* has been made by the German Federal Court on 28 January 1987, see *IPRax*, 1988, p. 109, and E. Jayme, *Recueil des cours*, Vol. 251 (1995), pp. 114-115.

[394] See *Rättsfall från hovrätterna*, 2005:66.

[395] See B. Audit, *Droit international privé*, p. 178.

[396] See T. C. Hartley, *Recueil des cours*, Vol. 319 (2006), p. 191.

been expressed by A. A. Ehrenzweig, according to whom characterization is merely one element in the process of interpreting forum law and policy "which may or may not take into account foreign characterization"[397]. This is undoubtedly a sensible advice on a general level, but it provides very little guidance in actual cases. It is, in any case, the nature of the disputed issue as perceived by the forum rather than the formulations used by the foreign law or by the parties that must decide how the issue is to be characterized[398].

The optimal principle can perhaps be formulated so that the terms and concepts in the conflict rules of the forum can normally be presumed to mean the same as in the substantive *lex fori*, but this presumption may and should be disregarded if it appears from the origin or purpose of the conflict rule that its interpretation should follow foreign law or deviate from the *lex fori* in some other manner. The *lex fori* is thus a mere starting point *(point de départ, Ausgangsbasis)* for a closer examination[399]. The classification according to the *lex*

---

[397] See A. A. Ehrenzweig, *Recueil des cours*, Vol. 124 (1968), p. 235.

[398] See the English case of *Macmillan Inc.* v. *Bishopgate Investment Trust (No. 3)*, [1996] 1 WLR 387 (CA), on p. 407 (Auld L.J.):

"Subject to what I shall say in a moment, characterisation or classification is governed by the lex fori. But characterisation or classification of what? It follows from what I have said that the proper approach is to look beyond the formulation of the claim and to identify according to the lex fori the true issue or issues thrown up by the claim and defence."

See also G. Sperduti, *Recueil des cours*, Vol. 122 (1967), p. 283, who stresses that it is not the terminology used by the foreign law but the substance of its dispositions that is decisive.

[399] See, for example, G. Kegel and K. Schurig, *Internationales Privatrecht*, p. 339.

fori should not be mechanical but, in the words of Otto Kahn-Freund, "enlightened"[400]. In practice, this means usually an extension of the scope of the conflict rules for the purpose of accommodating even those foreign legal phenomena that do not fit into the concepts of the forum country's municipal law[401]. Such extensive characterizations of phenomena unknown in the *lex fori* are both acceptable and necessary, provided they are based on the examination of and comparisons between the roles (functions) and the legal contents of both the foreign legal phenomenon and the potentially relevant conflict rule(s) of the forum[402]. In this way, comparative law can be of use even when the classification is carried out pursuant to the *lex fori*. It is submitted that whenever possible the scope of the conflict rules should be defined in a manner sufficiently wide to accommodate corresponding or closely related foreign legal phenomena, rather than couched in narrow technical legal terms taken from the substantive *lex fori*. "Responsibility for the person and upbringing of minors" seems thus normally preferable to technical terms such as "custody", even though, as shown above, a similar result can be achieved by interpreting "custody" in a conflict rule as having a wider meaning than it has in the substantive private law of the country of the forum[403].

Admittedly, all this gives the court a great deal of

---

[400] See O. Kahn-Freund, *Recueil des cours*, Vol. 143 (1974), pp. 373-377.

[401] See, for example, J. Maury, *Recueil des cours*, Vol. 57 (1936), pp. 496-504.

[402] See, for example, Chapter XIII, *infra*, and E. Jayme, *Recueil des cours*, Vol. 251 (1995), p. 107; F. Schwind, *Recueil des cours*, Vol. 187 (1984), pp. 64-66.

[403] See, for example, G. S. Maridakis, *Recueil des cours*, Vol. 105 (1962), pp. 400-401; A. E. von Overbeck, *Recueil des cours*, Vol. 176 (1982), p. 119.

discretion and it cannot be ruled out that the court will use it to achieve the result it wishes to achieve, whether it is a "just" substantive outcome of the dispute or simply the application of the *lex fori*[404]. For example, the court may characterize a certain issue to be of procedural nature in order to escape the need to apply foreign law, not necessarily because it dislikes its effects in the individual case (characterization can in fact occasionally be used as a substitute for *ordre public*) but possibly rather because it wants to avoid the practical difficulties involved in application of foreign law in general.

It would be an illusion to believe that a strict characterization pursuant to the *lex fori* would be a simple task. In most legal systems, probably including the *lex fori*, the borderlines between various areas of law are not quite clear. For example, as mentioned above, in some countries claims for compensation regarding non-economical damage resulting from a tort, such as pain and suffering, cannot be inherited, while in other countries there are no such restrictions. When the forum has to decide whether such restrictions imposed on the right to inherit certain tort claims are an issue of tort law or inheritance law, it will probably find no statutory definitions in the *lex fori* of the scopes of these two branches of private law[405]. The fact that a certain problem is dealt with in the forum country's Inheritance Act and not in its Torts Act (or in the chapter of the civil code dealing with inheritance and not in the chapter dealing with torts) is hardly conclusive evi-

---

[404] See, for example, B. Audit, *Droit international privé*, p. 171.
[405] Cf., however, Article 15 *(e)* of the EC Regulation No. 864/2007 of 11 July 2007 on the Law Applicable to Non-Contractual Obligations (Rome II), OJ 2007 L 199, p. 40.

dence of how that problem should be classified for the purposes of private international law, even though it undeniably constitutes some indication thereof[406]. The fact that a certain problem is discussed in the standard textbooks on inheritance law rather than in the textbooks on torts is even less conclusive, as it may depend on purely pedagogical considerations and/or purely pragmatic arrangements between the authors. The legal categories used in the *lex fori* have often no objectively fixed meaning carved in stone, but depend to a large extent on the purpose they are used for. Even if an attempt were made in the forum country to divide the legal system into categories defined by statutes (statutory characterization), it would be unlikely to deal with phenomena unknown in the *lex fori*; even if the "correct" characterization of the above-mentioned restriction concerning inheritance of tort claims might be well-established in the legal system to which that restriction belongs, it is not probable that it is established (by statute or otherwise) in countries where such (or similar) restrictions are unknown[407].

Perhaps the most important characterization issue in many legal systems involves the drawing of the line between procedural questions, which are pursuant to the *forum regit processum* principle practically always governed by the *lex fori*, and substantive issues, which, depending on the forum's conflict rules and the cir-

---

[406] See, for example, B. Audit, *Droit international privé*, p. 167; *Dicey and Morris on the Conflict of Laws*, p. 36; G. Kegel and K. Schurig, *Internationales Privatrecht*, p. 344.

[407] Cf., however, Article 15 *(e)* of the EC Regulation No. 864/2007 of 11 July 2007 on the Law Applicable to Non-Contractual Obligations (Rome II), OJ 2007 L 199, p. 40, which applies in all EC Member States (except Denmark), regardless of whether their domestic law limits inheritance rights regarding certain tort claims or not.

cumstances *in casu*, may potentially be governed by foreign law. In some countries, most notably in England and other countries with a common-law legal system, the concept of procedure is given a very wide meaning, maybe to some extent unconsciously or even consciously due to the temptation to avoid the application of foreign law [408]. The procedural or substantive nature of a legal issue is, of course, nothing that can be observed and measured with scientific accuracy, but lies to a significant degree rather in the eyes of the beholder. It is submitted that the main criterion for the dichotomy between procedural and substantive law should be related to the reason why procedural and substantive issues are not treated in the same way in private international law (this means logically also that this division does not have to be the same when procedural and substantive law have to be separated for other purposes, for example in order to achieve a pedagogically optimal structure of the curriculum of a law school) [409]. For the purposes of private international law, the procedural "label" should be put on those — and only on those — matters that affect less the substantive outcome of the dispute than the smooth functioning of judicial proceedings (they relate more *ad litis ordinationem* than *ad litis decisionem*); another characteristic feature of many procedural matters is that it would be highly inconvenient and impractical to let them be governed by foreign law. These two features are interconnected: as the procedure is in theory

---

[408] See *Dicey and Morris on the Conflict of Laws*, p. 157.

[409] See *Dicey and Morris on the Conflict of Laws*, pp. 164-165, who point out that to characterize a provision of law as procedural for the purposes of private international law merely because it had previously been characterized as procedural for some purposes of domestic law is to lose sight of the purpose of the characterization.

normally not expected to affect the substantive outcome, the benefit of learning and implementing foreign
procedural rules would simply be outweighed by the
huge increase in costs in terms of both money and time
that would arise for the courts, the attorneys and the
parties. Due to the rather technical character of many
procedural rules (presentation of evidence, the prescribed time and form for written submissions, etc.)
there would also be a substantial risk that the parties
and/or the court would commit procedural mistakes
with far-reaching adverse consequences. Keeping all
this in mind, one must disagree with the traditional
English view that, for example, the nature of the available remedies (monetary damages, specific performance, etc.) and the quantification of damages (such as a
ceiling imposed on the amount of damages) are matters
of procedure to be determined by the *lex fori*[410]. A step
in the right direction was taken in England in 1984,
when a special statute (the above-mentioned Foreign
Limitation Periods Act) introduced the general principle that the English time limitation rules, albeit traditionally characterized as procedural, are not applied
unless the claim is governed by English law as the *lex
causae* and that foreign time limitation rules are
applied when the claim is governed by foreign law[411].

It must be stressed that after the process of characterization has been carried out and it has been established that the issue under scrutiny is to be classified as
belonging to the field of, say, tort law, then the substantive rules of the legal system governing the tort
pursuant to the conflict rule of the forum should apply
regardless of whether they are, in that legal system,

---

[410] See, for example, *Dicey and Morris on the Conflict
of Laws*, pp. 159 and 170-172.
[411] See *Dicey and Morris on the Conflict of Laws*,
pp. 172-176.

considered to belong to tort law, inheritance law or some other field of law. Some scholars discuss the question of whether the conflict rules of the forum refer to a particular foreign rule or a particular foreign legal system (rule selection versus system selection)[412]. This seems to me to be a strange question, as every rule must be understood against the background of the whole legal system to which it belongs and everything in the applicable legal system affecting the issue under scrutiny is part of the "rule" in a wide sense of the word. The legal question to be answered by the applicable foreign legal system should thus be governed by that system *in toto*, regardless of the classification prevailing in its own country[413]. It is submitted that this approach is preferable to the concept of "secondary classification" or *"qualification de second degré"*[414], according to which the court should merely apply those rules of the applicable foreign legal system that are in that system itself classified in the same way as in the *lex fori*. The proponents of such secondary classifications seem to suggest, for example, that the court, after having classified the issue pursuant to the *lex fori* as being one of tort law, should have a look at the applicable *lex loci delicti* and apply only those of its substantive rules that are in the *lex loci delicti* considered to belong to tort law. In my opinion, if the court has decided that the issue under scrutiny is, for example, an issue of tort law, then all those substantive rules that belong to the *lex loci delicti* and deal with that issue

---

[412] See, for example, A. A. Ehrenzweig, *Recueil des cours*, Vol. 124 (1968), pp. 260-261.

[413] See, for example, J. Maury, *Recueil des cours*, Vol. 57 (1936), pp. 504-512; P. G. Vallindas, *Recueil des cours*, Vol. 101 (1960), p. 375; M. F. Yasseen, *Recueil des cours*, Vol. 116 (1965), pp. 435-437.

[414] Cf., for example, F. Schwind, *Recueil des cours*, Vol. 187 (1984), p. 66.

must obviously be considered to be rules on torts, at least in the eyes of the forum[415].

Interpretation problems concerning conflict rules are not limited to those parts of the conflict rules which determine the subject-matter scope of their application. The connecting factor used in a conflict rule may be an undisputable pure fact, for instance the place where a tangible asset (an immovable or a chattel) is situated or where an act was performed, but is very frequently rather a legal concept (for instance the domicile of a person or the place where an intangible asset is deemed to be situated). The legal concepts used as connecting factors can give rise to doubts and may be understood differently in different countries, for example with regard to whether domicile or habitual residence pre-supposes sojourn for a certain minimum period of time, or whether for the purposes of a conflict rule referring to the *lex rei sitae* a monetary claim is to be treated as situated in the country of the debtor or that of the creditor. Although it is, in these cases, hardly correct to speak of classification or characterization, there seems to be little doubt that the connecting factors too should normally be understood and interpreted in accordance with the *lex fori*[416]. It is, furthermore, up

---

[415] Cf. Article 13 of the Swiss Act of 18 December 1987 on Private International Law: "La désignation d'un droit étranger par la présente loi comprend toutes les dispositions qui d'après ce droit sont applicables à la cause."

[416] See, for example, the English case *In re Annesley. Davidson* v. *Annesley*, [1926] Ch. 629, where due to the English concept of domicile a person was considered to be domiciled in France, irrespective of the fact that she never obtained a formal French domicile according to French law. See also R. Ago, *Recueil des cours*, Vol. 58 (1936), pp. 354-361; C. M. V. Clarkson and J. Hill, *The Conflict of Laws*, pp. 12 and 465-466; O. Kahn-Freund, *Recueil des cours*, Vol. 143 (1974), pp. 388-389; H. Lewald, *Recueil des cours*, Vol. 69 (1939), pp. 85-94; K. Lipstein, *Recueil*

to the *lex fori* to decide whether a particular connecting factor, for example domicile, has the same meaning in all conflict rules or is understood in various ways depending on the purpose of the particular conflict rule under scrutiny[417]. It deserves to be repeated that the whole problem concerns the interpretation of conflict-of-law rules of the forum country and that those connecting factors used in these rules that have been "borrowed" from the terms and concepts in the substantive law of the forum are presumably — albeit not necessarily — intended to retain the meaning they had there. The same applies when the conflict rule uses a very "soft" general connecting factor, such as the "closest connection"[418] or the "most significant relationship" dominating the American Second Restatement of the Conflict of Laws[419]. What is close or significant should in these cases depend on the *lex fori*. There are, how-

---

des cours, Vol. 135 (1972), p. 197; J. Maury, *Recueil des cours*, Vol. 57 (1936), pp. 512-518. Cf., however, also G. Barile, *Recueil des cours*, Vol. 116 (1965), pp. 354-357; E. F. Scoles *et al.*, *Conflict of Laws*, pp. 126-127.

[417] See, for example, O. Kahn-Freund, *Recueil des cours*, Vol. 143 (1974), pp. 404-406.

[418] See, for example, Article 15 (1) of the Swiss Act of 18 December 1987 on Private International Law:

"Le droit désigné par la présente loi n'est exceptionnellement pas applicable si, au regard de l'ensemble des circonstances, il est manifeste que la cause n'a qu'un lien très lâche avec ce droit et qu'elle se trouve dans une relation beaucoup plus étroite avec un autre droit."

[419] See, for example, *Restatement of the Law Second. Conflict of Laws 2d*, Vol. 1, § 145 (1), p. 414:

"The rights and liabilities of the parties with respect to an issue in tort are determined by the local law of the state which, with respect to that issue, has the most significant relationship to the occurrence and the parties under the principles stated in § 6."

ever, exceptions, where it is appropriate to give the
connecting factors a meaning independent of the *lex
fori*. An obvious example are the connecting factors
imposed by an international instrument, where the need
of uniform interpretation deserves special regard.
Further, the nationality (citizenship), frequently used in
many countries as a connecting factor for the purpose
of designating the applicable law in matters of family
and inheritance, cannot be construed in accordance
with the citizenship legislation of the forum, as that
legislation cannot determine whether a person is a
citizen of a certain foreign country or not. References
in conflict rules to the law of the country of which the
person involved is a citizen must, therefore, be understood to have in mind citizenship pursuant to the
nationality laws of the country in question rather than
pursuant to the *lex fori*[420].

---

[420] See, for example, O. Kahn-Freund, *Recueil des
cours*, Vol. 143 (1974), pp. 389-391; K. Lipstein, *Recueil
des cours*, Vol. 135 (1972), p. 197; P. Lagarde, *Recueil des
cours*, Vol. 196 (1986), pp. 66-68. In this respect, nationality differs normally from the concept of domicile or habitual residence which, if used in the conflict rules of the
forum country, is normally to be interpreted pursuant to
the *lex fori*, see for example, P. Lagarde, *Recueil des
cours*, Vol. 196 (1986), pp. 69-70. A Swedish court may
thus consider an illegal immigrant, living since many years
in California, to have his habitual residence for the purposes of private international law in California, even if due
to the absence of a residence permit he is not recognized
as habitual resident by Californian law (cf., for example,
the above-mentioned English case of *In re Annesley.
Davidson* v. *Annesley*, [1926] Ch. 629, where due to the
English concept of domicile a person was considered to be
domiciled in France, irrespective of the fact that she never
obtained a formal French domicile according to French
law). Some exceptions can be found in international
instruments, such as in the last paragraph of Article 1 of
the Hague Convention of 5 October 1961 on the Conflicts

Questions concerning the interpretation of conflict rules, whether regarding their subject-matter scope or the connecting factors they use, must be distinguished from the interpretation of the applicable substantive foreign law once it has been identified[421]. The applicable foreign law must to the largest possible extent be interpreted loyally in accordance with how it is interpreted in its own country of origin[422]. To the extent the forum country accepts *renvoi*[423], the foreign conflict rules, too, should be interpreted in accordance with the meaning they are given in their own country[424].

Turning to the procedural parts of private interna-

---

of Laws relating to the Form of Testamentary Dispositions, which provides that the determination of whether or not the testator had his domicile in a particular place will be governed by the law of that place. Cf. also Niboyet, *Traité de droit international privé français*, Vol. I, pp. 561-562:

> "Il appartient à chaque Etat de décider, à l'exclusion de tout autre, quels sont les individus domiciliés chez lui, de même qu'il dénombre seul ses nationaux . . . Inversement, il ne lui appartient plus de décider si un individu est domicilié en pays étranger, pas plus qu'il ne peut affirmer, par le jeu de ses propres lois, qu'un individu doive posséder telle nationalité étrangère; tout ce que la loi française peut faire c'est de disposer que l'on est domicilié en France, ou au contraire que l'on n'y est pas domicilié."

This approach is normally not suitable for conflict rules, but may be legitimate when domicile or habitual residence is to be established for jurisdictional purposes, where foreign concepts have sometimes to be taken into account in order to avoid negative jurisdictional conflicts (see *infra*).

[421] See, for example, B. Audit, *Droit international privé*, p. 176; E. F. Scoles *et al.*, *Conflict of Laws*, p. 127.

[422] See Chapter VII, *supra*.

[423] See Chapter IX, *infra*, and G. Kegel and K. Schurig, *Internationales Privatrecht*, p. 409.

[424] See, for example, K. Lipstein, *Recueil des cours*, Vol. 135 (1972), pp. 197-198.

tional law, it is submitted that the forum country's
jurisdictional rules and rules on recognition and
enforcement of foreign judgments are normally to be
interpreted pursuant to the *lex fori*, unless they origi-
nate from an international convention or some other
form of international legislative co-operation. It cannot
be excluded, however, that even terms and concepts in
purely national provisions may sometimes be intended
to have a meaning that differs from their contents in
the domestic procedural law of the forum country. For
example, Chapter 10, Section 1, paragraph 5, of the
Swedish Code of Judicial Procedure stipulates that a
person with no known habitual residence in or outside
Sweden may be sued at the place in Sweden where he
is sojourning (the so-called vagabond forum or *forum
deprehensionis*). The purpose of this jurisdictional rule
is to avoid a negative conflict of competences, where a
person with no habitual residence could not be sued
anywhere. In order to serve its purpose, the concept of
habitual residence in this provision must sometimes be
understood as meaning something different from the
concept of habitual residence in domestic Swedish procedural law[425] and it may even have to be interpreted
in accordance with foreign law, so that a person can be
deemed to have no known habitual residence at all
even though according to the usual Swedish under-

---

[425] It may, in fact, have to be interpreted differently
from the concept of habitual residence in the rest of
Swedish private international law as well. It should be
noted that some international instruments stipulate that the
domicile of a person for the purposes of jurisdiction or
recognition/enforcement of judgments is to be established
pursuant to the law of the country where that person is
(allegedly) domiciled, see for example Article 59 of the
EC Regulation No. 44/2001 of 22 December 2000 on
Jurisdiction and the Recognition and Enforcement of
Judgments in Civil and Commercial Matters (the Brussels
I Regulation), OJ 2001 L 12, p. 1.

standing of habitual residence he has such residence in a particular foreign country. This is of practical importance in particular when the person in question cannot be sued in the foreign country concerned because the courts there use a more restrictive concept of habitual residence and do not, therefore, consider him to be a local habitual resident. Because of similar reasons, the classification of property as moveable or immoveable for the purpose of the forum's jurisdictional rules might reasonably be done in accordance with the law of the country where the property is situated rather than strictly according to the corresponding concepts in the *lex fori*.

CHAPTER IX

RENVOI

1. The Problem

A typical conflict rule normally designates the legal system which, in the eyes of the legislator of the forum country, is particularly suited to deal with the issue at hand. If this reference is to a foreign law, it can be understood in two ways, namely either as referring merely to rules of substantive law (in German called *Sachnormverweisung*) or as even (or rather[426]) referring to the conflict rules of the foreign legal system in question (in German *Gesamtverweisung*). For example, a conflict rule of the forum country stipulating that inheritance should be distributed pursuant to the law of the country of which the deceased was a citizen can be understood to refer exclusively to the rules of substantive succession law of the country of citizenship, but it is also possible to argue that the reference has rather in mind that country's private international law. If the conflict rules of the country of citizenship differ from those of the country of the forum (for instance by subjecting the distribution of inheritance to the law of the country where the deceased habitually resided), the question arises whether the forum should take into account the foreign conflict rule and apply the legal system it points to. As most international legal relationships involve two countries only, the question arises typically in situations where the foreign conflict rule

---

[426] See, for example, G. Sperduti, *Recueil des cours*, Vol. 122 (1967), p. 228.

points back to the law of the forum. Such "remission", in German called *Rückverweisung*, is generally known under its French name of *renvoi*, perhaps because it was a French case, *Forgo* v. *Administration des domaines*, decided by the Cassation Court in 1878, that made many lawyers aware of the problem and its practical importance[427]. The *Forgo* case concerned the estate of a deceased Bavarian national living in France, whose only survivors were certain relatives of his natural mother. These relatives were entitled to inheritance pursuant to Bavarian, but not French, law. According to French conflict rules, Bavarian law applied, but Bavarian conflict rules designated French law as applicable.

The French Cassation Court decided to accept this remission, applied French law and the assets became vested in the French public treasury.

Of course, it may happen that the conflict rule of the legal system applicable pursuant to the private international law of the forum does not point back to the law of the forum but designates the law of a third country. Such special type of *renvoi*, called "transmission"[428], *Weiterverweisung*[429] or *renvoi au second degré*[430], could occur in the fictitious example above if the deceased resided habitually in a country other than the country of his citizenship and none of these two countries was the country of the forum.

It should be noted that the problem of *renvoi*, as described above, cannot arise if and to the extent the

---

[427] See, for example, J. Dolinger, *Recueil des cours*, Vol. 283 (2000), pp. 242; R. De Nova, *Recueil des cours*, Vol. 118 (1966), pp. 486-487.

[428] See C. M. V. Clarkson and J. Hill, *The Conflict of Laws*, p. 13; E. F. Scoles *et al.*, *Conflict of Laws*, p. 138.

[429] See G. Kegel and K. Schurig, *Internationales Privatrecht*, p. 390.

[430] See B. Audit, *Droit international privé*, p. 180.

private international law of the forum country adheres
strictly to the unilateralist approach and does not refer
to foreign law but merely defines the scope of application of the *lex fori*[431]. Whereas the doctrine of *renvoi*
deals with the effect to be given to the conflict rules of
the particular foreign legal system designated by the
conflict rules of the forum, the pure unilateralist
approach would rather consider the conflict rules of all
foreign legal systems having some connection with the
case and ask whether any of them aspire(s) to be
applied[432].

The attitude towards *renvoi* varies considerably
from country to country. It is, for example, to some
extent accepted by German private international law.
Article 4 (I) of the Introductory Act to the German
Civil Code provides that the conflict rules of the country designated by a German conflict rule are to be followed whenever they point back to German law; if
they point to a third legal system they are to be followed as well, unless it would be contrary to the purpose and meaning of the German conflict rule in question[433]. An even more flexible approach can be found
in Section 35 of the Czech Act No. 97/1963 concerning
Private International Law and the Rules of Procedure
Relating Thereto, which provides that references in
foreign law back to Czech law or to the law of a third
State "may be accepted if it is in keeping with a reasonable and just settlement of the relations involved".

---

[431] See P. Lalive, *Recueil des cours*, Vol. 155 (1977),
p. 279.

[432] See Chapter IV.1, *supra*.

[433] "Art. 4. (I) If referral is made to the law of another
country, the private international law of that country
shall also be applied, insofar as this is not incompatible with the meaning of the referral. If the law of
another country refers back to German law, the
German substantive provisions shall apply."

Subject to certain exceptions, *renvoi* appears to be accepted in the case law of the French Cassation Court[434]. It seems to be seldom used by English courts, even though there are decisions where it was applied[435]. It seems to be losing ground in England and, as one English author put it, the doctrine of *renvoi* is fast approaching its sell-by date[436]. In the United States, the Second Restatement favours in its §8 *renvoi* in two situations only, namely if the purpose of the particular conflict rule is that the forum reach the same result as would the courts of another State[437] or if the forum State has no substantial relationship to the issue or the parties and all other interested countries would apply the same law. As far as the Nordic countries are concerned, the attitude towards *renvoi* is generally negative in Sweden and Denmark, while the situation seems

---

[434] See, for example, B. Audit, *Droit international privé*, p. 185-187.

[435] See, for example, C. M. V. Clarkson and J. Hill, *Conflict of Laws*, pp. 473-474. The operation of *renvoi* can be illustrated using the case *In re Annesley. Davidson* v. *Annesley*, [1926] Ch. 692, where an English court had to decide who was entitled to the movable property left in England by deceased person domiciled in France. Under the relevant English conflict rule this had to be decided by French law and the court took this to mean that its decision had to be the same as a French court would decide. By French conflict rules, the succession was governed by English law, but as a French court also was assumed to accept *renvoi*, the court ultimately applied French law. This case is thus an example of a "total *renvoi*" (see *infra*).

[436] See C. M. V. Clarkson and J. Hill, *The Conflict of Laws*, p. 479.

[437] See *Restatement of the Law Second. Conflict of Laws 2d*, Vol. 1, §8, pp. 21-31. See also §260, stipulating that the devolution of interests in movables upon intestacy is determined by "the law that would be applied by the courts of the state where the decedent was domiciled at the time of his death".

to be less clear in Norway[438]. *Renvoi* has been rejected several times by the Swedish Supreme Court, the leading decision dating from 1969[439]. The case concerned a married couple, both citizens and habitual residents of Sweden. During a car trip in Europe, the husband caused a traffic accident in the Netherlands and his wife was injured. At that time, Swedish conflict rules regarding non-contractual liability designated the law of the place of the harmful act, i.e. Dutch law, which restricted tort liability between spouses. The wife argued that Swedish law should be applied, and pointed out that pursuant to Dutch private international law, the common personal law of the parties (i.e., Swedish law) was applicable. The Supreme Court applied Dutch substantive law and declared explicitly that for the purposes of Swedish private international law it was irrelevant that Dutch courts would apply Swedish law. The *renvoi* in favour of Swedish law was thus rejected.

2. *Advantages and Disadvantages of* Renvoi

Renvoi seems to have a certain attraction from the point of view of some courts and judges, because it often offers them increased possibilities to avoid foreign law and apply the *lex fori*[440]. Nevertheless, some

---

[438] See, for example, in Sweden, M. Bogdan, *Svensk internationell privat- och processrätt*, pp. 59-63; in Norway, Thue, *Internasjonal privatrett*, pp. 117-146; in Denmark, Nielsen, *International privat- og procesret*, pp. 60-61.

[439] *Nytt Juridiskt Arkiv*, 1969, p. 163.

[440] See, for example, B. Audit, *Droit international privé*, p. 182; C. M. V. Clarkson and J. Hill, *The Conflict of Laws*, p. 477; G. Kegel and K. Schurig, *Internationales Privatrecht*, p. 395; M. F. Yasseen, *Recueil des cours*, Vol. 116 (1965), pp. 430-432.

see in it an instrument of universalism, as it involves taking into account the conflict rules of other countries[441]. The partisans of *renvoi* also argue sometimes that it contributes to an increased uniformity of decisions in different countries[442], as it means that the forum shall apply the same law that would be applied by the courts in the country whose legal system is designated as applicable by the conflict rule of the forum. This reasoning is, however, far from flawless. It is true, of course, that if each court follows its own conflict rules only, then courts in different countries will often apply different legal systems, leading to different outcomes. The uniformity argument disregards, however, the possibility that the courts in the country whose law is applicable pursuant to the conflict rule of the forum may also accept *renvoi*, as can be illustrated by the following example.

Imagine that the dispute concerns the distribution of an estate after a deceased foreign national habitually residing in the forum country. Assume further that according to the conflict rule of the forum, the distribution is governed by the law of the country of the deceased person's citizenship, while the private international law of the country of citizenship points to the law of the country of the deceased person's habitual residence. If both countries accept *renvoi*, each court will ultimately apply its own substantive law. In fact, if *renvoi* is used consistently and without limitation, the reference back to the *lex fori* will not provide the final

---

[441] See, for example, J.-M. Jacquet, *Recueil des cours*, Vol. 292 (2001), pp. 188-189. Valladão, *Recueil des cours*, Vol. 133 (1971), pp. 474-475, sees in *renvoi* an expression of solidarity and respect for the foreign legal systems and equals the refusal of *renvoi* to an amputation of the applicable law.

[442] See, for example, J. M. Trias de Bes, *Recueil des cours*, Vol. 62 (1937), p. 62.

answer, because the conflict rule of *lex fori* refers, again, to the same foreign law which refers back to the *lex fori*, and so on. In order to prevent a situation where such "total *renvoi*" would create a vicious circle (some authors speak of a *circulus inextricabilis*, *chassé-croisé*, a stalemate, *cercle vicieux*, a cabinet of mirrors, or an endless game of ping pong or tennis)[443], the private international law of some countries, for example England, accepts *renvoi* only if it is not accepted by the foreign country in question, so that the game stops after the first round, but this ingenious solution (the co-called "foreign court theory")[444] is of no avail if it is used by the foreign country as well. There is obviously a risk of reasoning in an endless circle where the conflict rule of each country prescribes the application of the law that would be applied by the courts of the other country. Paradoxically, this means

---

[443] See, for example, R. Ago, *Recueil des cours*, Vol. 58 (1936), pp. 402-405; B. Audit, *Droit international privé*, pp. 182 and 184; A. Bucher, *Recueil des cours*, Vol. 341 (2009), pp. 235-236; C. M. V. Clarkson and J. Hill, *The Conflict of Laws*, pp. 475-476 and 479; G. A. L. Droz, *Recueil des cours*, Vol. 229 (1991), pp. 307-308; J.-M. Jacquet, *Recueil des cours*, Vol. 292 (2001), p. 183; E. Jayme, *Recueil des cours*, Vol. 251 (1995), p. 96; F. K. Juenger, *Recueil des cours*, Vol. 193 (1985), p. 198; G. Kegel and K. Schurig, *Internationales Privatrecht*, pp. 393-394; E. F. Scoles *et al.*, *Conflict of Laws*, p. 139. F. Rigaux, *Recueil des cours*, Vol. 213 (1989), p. 147, uses the metaphor of two polite gentlemen who do not manage to get through a door because each of them obstinately refuses to go first.

[444] The essence of this solution is that if the foreign law refers back to English law (the *lex fori*) and rejects the doctrine of *renvoi*, the substantive rules of the English *lex fori* will be applied, whereas if the foreign law refers back to English law and adopts *renvoi*, the substantive rules of the foreign legal system will be used. See *Dicey and Morris on the Conflict of Laws*, p. 72.

that uniformity of decisions will be achieved only if the attitudes of the two countries towards *renvoi* differ[445]. The "foreign court theory" and other similar approaches cannot thus be proposed for general use, as they would not work if accepted internationally[446]. As it was put by some authors, it is difficult to justify a doctrine whose existence is premised on the assumption that no other country in the world adopts it[447]: "si la méthode est bonne, tous les pays devraient l'adopter"[448]. The German legislator has solved the problem by stipulating that when accepting *renvoi*, the foreign conflict rule is treated as referring to German substantive law only, i.e. the foreign country's attitude to *renvoi* is disregarded[449].

---

[445] See, for example, B. Audit, *Droit international privé*, p. 184; G. Kegel and K. Schurig, *Internationales Privatrecht*, p. 398; F. Rigaux, *Recueil des cours*, Vol. 213 (1989), p. 146. B. Audit discusses the possibility of achieving uniformity of decisions with the help of the theory of *"double renvoi"*, where the court examines the approach to *renvoi* in the foreign country in question and then proceeds to do the opposite: "il fait alors lui-même le contraire afin d'aboutir à une véritable harmonie de solutions". Cf. also P. Lagarde, *Recueil des cours*, Vol. 196 (1986), pp. 159-163.

[446] See, for example, B. Audit, *Droit international privé*, p. 185.

[447] See C. M. V. Clarkson and J. Hill, *The Conflict of Laws*, p. 479; *Dicey and Morris on the Conflict of Laws*, p. 78; G. A. L. Droz, *Recueil des cours*, Vol. 229 (1991), pp. 308-309; O. Kahn-Freund, *Recueil des cours*, Vol. 143 (1974), p. 433.

[448] See P. Mayer, *Recueil des cours*, Vol. 327 (2007), p. 270.

[449] See Article 4 (I) of the Introductory Act to the German Civil Code; G. Kegel and K. Schurig, *Internationales Privatrecht*, pp. 399-400. See also E. Jayme, *Recueil des cours*, Vol. 251 (1995), pp. 98-99, about Article 13 of the Italian Act on Private International Law from 1995.

It is worth noting that modern international codifications of private international law do not favour *renvoi*. For example, Article 20 of the EC Regulation No. 593/2008 of 17 June 2008 on the Law Applicable to Contractual Obligations of 1980 (the Rome I Regulation)[450], which is applied regardless of whether the law specified by the Regulation's conflict rules is or is not the law of a Member State, stipulates that the application of the law of any country specified by the Regulation means the application of the rules of law in force in that country "other than its rules of private international law". The same formulation is found in Article 34 of the EC Regulation Rome II[451]. In other words, only the substantive rules of the legal system designated by the conflict rules of these instruments are to be applied and it is irrelevant which legal system would be applicable pursuant to the designated foreign system's own conflict rules.

It is submitted that in principle this is a sound approach. The conflict rules of the forum country have probably been enacted in order to provide for the application of the legal system which, according to the opinion of the legislator of the forum country, has the closest and most relevant relationship to the disputed issue. If, for example, the legislator of the forum country is of the view that it is most reasonable and appropriate to hold a wrongdoer liable to pay compensation in accordance with the law of the country where he committed the wrongful act, why should the court subordinate this conflict rule and the policy considerations behind it to a different view, embraced by the legislator of the country of the wrongful act, according to which

---

[450] OJ 2008 L 177, p. 6.

[451] Regulation No. 864/2007 of 11 July 2007 on the Law Applicable to Non-Contractual Obligations, OJ 2007 L 199, p. 40.

it is more reasonable and appropriate to apply the law of the country of the resulting damage or of the victim's domicile? It is submitted that the policy considerations underlying the conflict rule of the forum country should normally be allowed to prevail[452]. The fact that the refusal of *renvoi* can lead to a situation where foreign law is applied in spite of not being considered applicable by the foreign legislator himself[453] is not as absurd as it might seem[454], provided it is recalled that foreign law is not applied as a service rendered to foreign countries because their law "wishes to be applied" ("se veut applicable"), but rather in the interest of the country of the forum and pursuant to the commands of the forum country's own legislator. The country of the designated foreign law can and will hardly complain that its law is used against its will.

In any case, the possible advantages of *renvoi* seem normally to weigh much less than the theoretical complications and practical difficulties it gives rise to. It is, for example, sufficiently difficult to obtain reliable information about the content of foreign substantive

---

[452] See, for example, R. Ago, *Recueil des cours*, Vol. 58 (1936), p. 398; B. Audit, *Droit international privé*, p. 179; C. M. V. Clarkson and J. Hill, *The Conflict of Laws*, pp. 13 and 478; G. S. Maridakis, *Recueil des cours*, Vol. 105 (1962), pp. 425-426; P. Mayer, *Recueil des cours*, Vol. 327 (2007), pp. 329-333; A. Philip, *Recueil des cours*, Vol. 160 (1978), p. 48; G. Sperduti, *Recueil des cours*, Vol. 122 (1967), p. 222; M. F. Yasseen, *Recueil des cours*, Vol. 116 (1965), p. 427.

[453] To some extent, the doctrine of *renvoi* might seem to be related to unilateralist approaches, as its main idea, namely that the law of a State should not be applied against that State's will, makes the application of foreign law depend on the wish of the foreign legislator to have his law applied, see F. Vischer, *Recueil des cours*, Vol. 232 (1992), pp. 38-39.

[454] See, for example, B. Audit, *Droit international privé*, p. 89.

rules; the need to find such information about foreign conflict rules makes the task even more difficult, especially when the "foreign court theory" and other similar theories necessitate that the forum seek information about complicated and controversial issues, such as whether the foreign country in question also accepts the doctrine of *renvoi*. As it was put by an English author[455], a court should not undertake the onerous task of trying to ascertain how a foreign private international law would decide the question, unless the situation is an exceptional one and the advantages of doing so clearly outweigh the disadvantages. In most situations, the balance of convenience lies clearly in interpreting the reference to foreign law to mean its substantive rules only.

There seems, however, to be practical reasons to accept *renvoi* in certain special situations, where a refusal to do so would lead to unnecessary multiplication of limping legal relationships. If, for example, a family status such as a marriage exists in the eyes of the foreign country whose law, pursuant to the forum's conflict rules, is applicable to its existence, it seems reasonable to recognize it in the forum country as well, regardless of whether its validity in the foreign country in question depends on that country's substantive law or on some other law designated by that country's conflict rules[456]. For instance, it is an almost universally accepted principle that a marriage is valid with regard to form (including the authority of the celebrating official) if it has been entered into in accordance with the

---

[455] See *Dicey and Morris on the Conflict of Laws*, pp. 78-79.

[456] See, for example, *Dicey and Morris on the Conflict of Laws*, pp. 74-75; H. Lewald, *Recueil des cours*, Vol. 69 (1939), pp. 58-59; P. Mayer, *Recueil des cours*, Vol. 327 (2007), pp. 269-271.

formal requirements of the country where the marriage ceremony took place. The main objective of this rule (the rule of *locus regit actum*) is to avoid a situation where married couples would be compelled to go through a new marriage ceremony in each country where they wished to be considered married. This purpose is best served if a marriage ceremony is universally recognized not only if it was performed according to the law of the country where it took place (the *lex loci celebrationis*) but also if it was performed pursuant to some other legal system (e.g., the law of the country of which both contracting parties were citizens), provided that it is recognized as valid in the country of celebration due to that country's conflict rules. This means, in fact, that the forum should in such cases take into account the private international law of the country of celebration, which amounts to a certain hidden acceptance of *renvoi*. Such acceptance, which seems to be advocated by the American Restatement (Second) of the Conflict of Laws[457], may nevertheless sometimes become complicated due to the risk of getting entangled in the above-mentioned endless "game of tennis", for example where the private international law of the country of celebration recognizes the marriage as valid if it is valid in the country of citizenship, while the private international law of the country of citizenship recognizes the validity of the marriage if it is valid in the country of celebration.

---

[457] See *supra*. See also Chapter 1, Section 7, of the Swedish Act (1904:26) on Certain International Marriage and Guardianship Relationships.

CHAPTER X

PUBLIC POLICY
AND OVERRIDING MANDATORY RULES

1. The Problem

The instruction, contained in the forum country's conflict rules, to apply foreign law is occasionally described using the metaphor of a leap into an unknown dark space, *saut dans l'inconnu* (Batiffol), *Sprung ins Dunkle* (Raape). Traditional bilateral conflict rules refer to foreign legal systems without knowing their contents. The legislator formulating a conflict rule which is intended to apply in relation to hundreds of foreign legal systems cannot reasonably be expected to be aware of the content of their substantive provisions, and even if such knowledge were available at the time of the enactment of the conflict rule, there is no way of predicting how foreign laws will be changed in the future. A rigid application of the conflicts rules might thus sometimes lead to results that are unacceptable from the point of view of the forum country, for example if it results in the application of rules discriminating against persons of a certain race or gender or violating human rights in some other respect. The risk that this will happen is relatively small in connection with regional conflict rules which can lead to the application of certain closely related legal systems only, such as some conflict rules in Denmark, Finland, Iceland, Norway and Sweden which concern merely intra-Nordic family and succession cases. Most conflict rules apply, however, in relation to all legal systems without any geographical limitation, creating a non-negligible potential risk of unacceptable results. Similar risks arise also in connection with the forum country's rules on recognition and enforcement of foreign judgments, even as between closely co-operating countries such as the Member States of the European Union[458].

It deserves to be repeated that foreign law is in principle applied in the interest of the forum country and that the application of foreign law does not mean that the forum country is indifferent to the outcome of the dispute. If the forum country were indifferent, it would probably refrain from adjudicating at all, i.e. its courts would have no jurisdiction. There is thus practically always some connection between the dispute and the forum country, even though not necessarily a very close one, and this makes the forum country interested in resolving the dispute in a manner that will not be perceived as manifestly unjust or otherwise shocking from the forum country's point of view.

In order to avoid the risk of unacceptable results arising out of the application of foreign law or the recognition and enforcement of foreign judgments, the private international law of practically all countries contains an explicit or implicit reservation, according to which foreign law both can and must be refused application, and foreign decisions both can and must be refused recognition and enforcement, whenever the application, recognition or enforcement would be manifestly incompatible with the fundamental principles (public policy, *ordre public*) of the forum country. This public policy reservation is intended to protect the fundamental values of the forum country, such as its concepts of morality, decency, human liberty or justice[459], against being harmed by foreign laws and decisions.

---

[458] See, for example, the ECJ judgment *Krombach* v. *Bamberski* (case C-7/98, decided on 28 March 2000); R. M. Moura Ramos, *Yearbook of Private International Law*, Vol. II (2000), pp. 25-39.

[459] See C. M. V. Clarkson and J. Hill, *The Conflict of Laws*, pp. 487-488.

The purpose of the *ordre public* reservation goes beyond the protection of the interests of the parties in the actual dispute. It protects also — and perhaps even in the first place — the dignity of the court and of the forum country itself. The reservation should, therefore, be considered ex officio, i.e., even if none of the parties relies on it[460]. It can be mentioned, for example, that Article V of the 1958 New York Convention on the Recognition and Enforcement of Foreign Arbitral Awards, listing the legitimate grounds for refusing recognition and enforcement of foreign arbitral decisions, in respects of most such grounds requires that they be relied on and proved by the party against whom the foreign award is invoked, whereas incompatibility with the public policy of the forum may lead to a refusal regardless of the attitude of the party in question.

In many countries, express public policy reservations can be found in statutes dealing with private international law[461], but it seems that this reservation is

---

[460] See, for example, A. V. M. Struycken, *Recueil des cours*, Vol. 311 (2004), pp. 398.

[461] See, for example, Article 17 of the Swiss Act on Private International Law of 1987, which provides that the application of provisions of a foreign law is excluded if the outcome *(résultat)* would be incompatible with Swiss public policy *(ordre public suisse)*; Section 36 of the Czech Act No. 97 of 1963 concerning Private International Law and the Rules of Procedure Relating Thereto, stipulating that foreign rules must not be applied if the effects of such application would be contrary to those principles of the Czech social and governmental system whose observance must be required without exception; Article 6 of the Introductory Act to the German Civil Code, providing that a provision of the law of another country shall not be applied where its application would lead to a result which is manifestly incompatible with the fundamental principles of German law, in particular with civil rights. Public policy reservations are found also in the EC regulations in the

to such an extent considered to be a fundamental principle that it can usually be used even without direct statutory support.

In most cases, the *ordre public* reservation is discussed with regard to the negative effects of the application of foreign substantive private law. However, in countries accepting the doctrine of *renvoi*, public policy may intervene also against the application of a foreign conflict rule, for example if that rule is discriminatory or otherwise unacceptable. Foreign procedural law may be reprobated as well, in particular in connection with the recognition and enforcement of a foreign decision rendered in violation of precedural guarantees considered essential in the country of the forum.

2. Public Policy Reservation and International Treaties

It appears that some courts and judges feel that even in the absence of a treaty obligation to apply foreign law or to recognize/enforce a foreign decision, a refusal of application or recognition/enforcement on grounds of public policy could somehow violate the legitimate rights of the foreign country concerned. Such fears are normally groundless though. Apart from international conventions and the like, foreign States have no right to demand that their laws be applied or their judgments be recognized/enforced at all, as such application or recognition/enforcement results from the forum country's conflict and recognition/enforcement

---

field of private international law. For example, Article 21 of the EC Regulation No. 593/2008 of 17 June 2008 on the Law Applicable to Contractual Obligations (Rome I), OJ 2008 L 177, p. 6, stipulates that the application of foreign law designated by the Regulation's conflict rules may be refused "if such application is manifestly incompatible with the public policy *(ordre public)* of the forum".

rules, which have normally been enacted due to unilateral considerations made by the legislator of the that
country in accordance with its own values and interests. As foreign States normally have no right to have
their laws applied and their judgments recognized or
enforced, a refusal to do so in exceptional cases on the
grounds of public policy can hardly, *per se*, constitute
a violation of any such right. There are thus no legal
reasons why the courts should not openly rely on the
public policy reservation when they find that there are
good reasons to do so. A totally different matter is that
many judges fear that a judicial statement, to the effect
that the application of a foreign rule or the recognition
or enforcement of a foreign decision would *in casu* be
manifestly incompatible with the public policy of the
forum, might be perceived as discourteous to that foreign country ("like throwing stones at your neighbour's
house"[462]) or at least lead to unnecessary publicity and
become an embarrassment for the Government of the
country of the forum.

Most private international law treaties contain an
express public policy reservation, usually in the form
of a special public policy clause[463]. This clause differs

---

[462] See, for example, C. V. M. Clarkson and J. Hill, *The
Conflict of Laws*, pp. 487, with further references.

[463] See, for example, Article 21 of the Hague Convention of 2000 on the International Protection of Adults,
which provides that the application of the law designated
by the Convention's conflict rules "can be refused only if
this application would be manifestly contrary to public
policy". Article 22, point 2 *(c)*, of the same Convention
stipulates that the recognition of measures taken by the
authorities of a contracting State may be refused "if such
recognition is manifestly contrary to public policy of the
requested State, or conflicts with a provision of the law of
that State which is mandatory whatever law would otherwise be applicable". See further J. Dolinger, *Recueil des
cours*, Vol. 283 (2000), pp. 298-303.

from the other treaty provisions, which are supposed to be interpreted as uniformly as possible, because the public policy clause is intended to refer to the fundamental values and principles in the contracting State of the forum, which may legitimately differ from the fundamental values and principles in other contracting countries.

There are, nevertheless, limits to the forum's freedom of action, as the clause must not be used arbitrarily and must be restricted to exceptional cases. It would certainly be contrary to the international obligations assumed under a treaty if a contracting State abused the public policy clause in order to systematically and routinely deprive the treaty's conflict rules of their intended effect.

A different question is whether it is possible for the forum country to abstain, for example by means of an international treaty, from the right to rely on its public policy.

The *ordre public* reservation appears to exist in all national systems of private international law and it may perhaps be regarded as one of the "general principles of law recognized by civilized nations" in the sense of Article 38 of the Statute of the International Court of Justice [464], but it is hardly a part of *jus cogens*

---

[464] See, for example, Judge Sir Hersch Lauterpacht's votum in the notorious case of *The Netherlands* v. *Sweden* (the *Boll* case), decided by the International Court of Justice in 1958, *ICJ Reports* 1958, p. 55. In Lauterpacht's view,

"the exception of *ordre public* is a reason for the exclusion of foreign law . . . generally — or rather universally — recognized . . . so much so that the recognition of the part of *ordre public* must be regarded as a general principle of law . . .".

Cf. also O. Kahn-Freund, *Recueil des cours*, Vol. 143 (1974), pp. 173-174.

and it can, therefore, be excluded[465] or restricted[466] by a treaty. The public policy reservation is, however, so deeply and universally rooted that such a waiver would probably have to be explicit. A mere silence, i.e. the lack of an express public policy clause, does not necessarily amount to a waiver. Public policy can thus normally be invoked even without explicit support in the treaty's text, even though there may be exceptions where the *travaux préparatoires* of the treaty or other circumstances indicate that a waiver was indeed intended[467].

In some cases a waiver, whether explicit or silent, should be interpreted to have in mind merely the application of foreign substantive rules existing at the time

---

[465] See, for example, A. Philip, *Recueil des cours*, Vol. 160 (1978), p. 62, and cf. the Swedish judgment in the case *Nytt Juridiskt Arkiv*, 1978, C 480, where the Swedish Supreme Court has held that public policy cannot bar the recognition in Sweden of an Icelandic adoption, because Article 22 of the intra-Nordic Convention containing Rules of Private International Law on Marriage, Adoption and Guardianship of 1931 stipulated that such a decision had to be recognized "without examination of whether it is correct".

[466] Thus, modern private international law conventions permit the use of the public policy reservation only if the effects of the application of foreign law would be "manifestly" incompatible with the *ordre public* of the forum, see for example Articles 21 and 22, point 2 *(c)*, of the 2000 Hague Convention on the International Protection of Adults. Cf. also Article 35, point 3, of the EC Regulation No. 44/2001 of 22 December 2000 on Jurisdiction and the Recognition and Enforcement of Judgments in Civil and Commercial Matters (the Brussels I Regulation), OJ 2001 L 12, p. 1, forbidding the use of the public policy test in relation to the jurisdiction of the court in another Member State that has rendered the judgment whose recognition is under scrutiny.

[467] See, for example, A. Bucher, *Recueil des cours*, Vol. 239 (1993), p. 76.

of the making of the treaty, but not subsequently introduced rules that could not be anticipated at that time. A rather sad chapter in the history of Swedish private international law concerns the application by Swedish authorities of the racist marriage impediments imposed by German law during the Nazi period. Pursuant to the opinion prevailing at that time, these impediments could not be avoided on the basis of Swedish public policy because both Germany and Sweden were parties to the Hague Marriage Convention of 1902 that required Sweden to apply German law to German nationals and contained no public policy reservation[468]. The absence of a general public policy clause in the 1902 Hague Convention was not an oversight but rather the result of a conscious intention of the contracting States to avoid the legal insecurity created by such clauses. The contracting States decided to replace the general public policy clause with more specific reservations. For example, the Convention stipulated that the contracting States were under no obligation to give effect to foreign marriage impediments based on different religions of the couple[469]. Racist impediments of the Nazi type were not mentioned, probably because nobody anticipated them at that time. It is, therefore, submitted that Sweden could, in spite of being bound in relation to Germany by the 1902 Hague Convention,

---

[468] See A. Jarlert, *Judisk "ras" som äktenskapshinder i Sverige. Effekten av Nürnberglagarna i Svenska kyrkans statliga funktion som lysningsförrättare 1935-1945*, Malmö, 2006. About the absence of public policy reservations in the early Hague conventions see, for example, G. Parra-Aranguren, *Recueil des cours*, Vol. 210 (1988), pp. 94-95. It seems that the Netherlands, which was also one of the parties to the 1902 Hague Convention, encountered the same difficulties, see A. V. M. Struycken, *Recueil des cours*, Vol. 311 (2004), pp. 401-402.

[469] See Article 3 of the Convention.

refuse to apply the racist German rules on the basis of the principle of *rebus sic stantibus*, but the whole issue was and still is rather controversial and the discussion is more of political than legal nature.

3. The Content of the Public Policy Reservation

The public policy reservation is usually conceived as the "last line of defence" or *ultimum remedium* for the preservation of the basic values and fundamental principles of the *lex fori*. It is to be relied on in exceptional situations only. If it is used routinely against everything that differs from the *lex fori*, then the forum will, in fact, apply the *lex fori* and nothing else, which would go against the spirit and the whole idea of private international law. While the reservation is in some countries perhaps used too often, the judges in some other countries, for example Sweden, are very cautious in this respect. There are numerous Swedish decisions declaring that the application of the foreign law or the recognition/enforcement of the foreign decision *in casu* is not manifestly incompatible with the Swedish public policy, but there are almost no published decisions where a foreign law has been openly refused application or a foreign decision has been openly refused recognition/enforcement because of such incompatibility. This does not mean that Swedish courts are extremely tolerant towards foreign laws and foreign decisions, but reflects rather the tendency among Swedish judges to do their utmost to avoid repugnant foreign rules and decisions by other means without resorting explicitly to public policy, for instance by re-characterizing the issue or altering the previous judge-made conflict rule in order to be able to claim that the repugnant foreign rule is not applicable at all[470]. It is

---

[470] See, for example, the Swedish Supreme Court in *Nytt Juridiskt Arkiv*, 1964, p. 1.

also obvious that the space for the application of public policy decreases to the extent that the most "sensitive" areas of law are subjected to the *lex fori*.

For example, as questions such as the capacity to marry, divorce and adoption are pursuant to Swedish private international law governed in principle by Swedish substantive law with very limited space and effects being given to foreign law, there are very limited opportunities to invoke Swedish public policy on these points.

The ascertainment of those fundamental principles of the forum country that are protected by the public policy reservation is usually left to the courts. Such principles vary, of course, from country to country and have a tendency to vary in time as well. Much depends on the standards and opinions of the individual judge or other official having to apply foreign law or recognize/enforce foreign judgments. The public policy clauses are usually couched in general terms which can mean different things at different points of time, but it is the public policy at the time of the adjudication that is decisive[471]. Public policy is the policy of the day, and any attempt to exhaustively enumerate its content once and for all would be doomed to fail[472]. Something that was acceptable at the time of the enactment of a conflict rule need not be acceptable at the time of its implementation, and vice versa. The equality of the sexes is today an almost sacred principle in practically all Western countries, but one does not have to go back many decades to see that this is is a relatively recent

---

[471] See, for example, B. Audit, *Droit international privé*, p. 264; A. Bucher, *Recueil des cours*, Vol. 239 (1993), pp. 45-46; H. Gaudemet-Tallon, *Recueil des cours*, Vol. 312 (2005), p. 273; A. Philip, *Recueil des cours*, Vol. 160 (1978), p. 58.

[472] See G. Parra-Aranguren, *Recueil des cours*, Vol. 210 (1988), p. 95.

approach[473]. Such developments can take place quite
quickly. For example, in Sweden children born out of
wedlock did not obtain the right to inherit their father
and other paternal relatives until 1970, but almost
immediately thereafter it was suggested by some that
the application of a foreign inheritance rule discriminating against such children would be contrary to
Swedish *ordre public*. Most of the fundamental values
and principles of law protected by the public policy
reservation are, however, relatively stable and unlikely
to change dramatically within a short period of time.

Only the really fundamental principles of the *lex
fori* (some speak in this context of the "core" of the *lex
fori*[474]) deserve the protection afforded by the public
policy reservation, and in most countries the reservation is to be used only if the violation of the forum's
public policy is manifest, i.e. obvious. The last-mentioned requirement means that the public policy reservation should not be used in those cases where one
doubts the incompatibility itself (this question must, in
turn, be distinguished from the question of whether the
incompatibility is serious or grave). As pointed out
above, the whole existence of private international law
would be meaningless if the mere fact that the foreign
substantive rule deviates from the *lex fori* were sufficient for a refusal of its application[475], as such attitude
would lead to the general and exclusive application of
the *lex fori*. The negative effects of the use of the public policy exception, such as increased unpredictability
and lack of uniformity, demand that it should be relied

---

[473] See A. V. M. Struycken, *Recueil des cours*, Vol. 311
(2004), p. 46.

[474] See, for example, A. Bucher, *Recueil des cours*,
Vol. 239 (1993), p. 25.

[475] See, for example, G. Kegel and K. Schurig,
Internationales Privatrecht, p. 529; E. F. Scoles *et al.*,
Conflict of Laws, p. 143.

on only if the consequences of the application of a foreign rule would be unacceptable and pass the threshold of the intolerable[476].

The incompatibility of a foreign legal rule with the mandatory rules (i.e., rules that cannot be derogated from by the parties) of the *lex fori* does not, by itself, amount to incompatibility with the public policy of the forum country. This means that even the mandatory provisions of the *lex fori* should normally be set aside when foreign law applies, unless they are of the overriding type (see *infra*). Many rules of family law, such as those regarding the capacity to marry or the determination of paternity, are often of mandatory character, but this does not mean that such matters must always be governed by the *lex fori*. The borderline between the tolerable and the intolerable may lie elsewhere. It is possible, for example, that the mandatory age limit stipulated in the *lex fori* for marrying is eighteen years while the minimum age which the public policy of the forum can tolerate is fifteen. Swedish private international law contained until 2004 an explicit provision to that effect and it could be argued that this provision[477], being *lex specialis*, precluded the use of the general public policy clause with regard to the age requirement imposed in respect of the capacity to marry[478].

Even though it is in principle a matter for the *lex fori* to decide which of its principles are so fundamen-

---

[476] See A. Bucher, *Recueil des cours*, Vol. 239 (1993), p. 27.

[477] See the pre-2004 wording of Chapter 1, Section 3, of the Swedish Act (1904:26) on Some International Marriage and Guardianship Relationships.

[478] Cf., however, E. Jayme, *Recueil des cours*, Vol. 251 (1995), p. 231, who seems to be of the view that specialized public policy rules *(les règles spéciales de l'ordre public)* do not preclude or restrict the application of the general *ordre public* reservation.

tal that they deserve the protection of the public policy reservation, it must not be forgotten that some parts of those fundamental principles may have their roots in international instruments, such as the human rights conventions ratified by the forum country[479]. If the application of a foreign rule or the recognition or enforcement of a foreign judgment would lead to a result violating an internationally protected human right, then the forum country cannot escape its responsibility for this violation by putting all the blame on the foreign country where the rule was enacted or where the judgment was rendered[480], although that foreign country is probably guilty of violating human rights too. If the forum country creates a special provision stipulating that foreign law must not be applied and foreign judgments must not be given effect if the result would violate internationally protected human rights, there is, of course, no need to use the general public policy reservation for that purpose. The same is true if the forum country decides that foreign law cannot be applied if the outcome would be incompatible with civil rights as protected in the forum country's constitution[481]. A stipulation to that effect exists, for

---

[479] Generally about the relationship between human rights, fundamental rights and private international law, see P. Kinsch, *Recueil des cours*, Vol. 318 (2005), pp. 9-332.

[480] See the judgment of the European Court of Human Rights of 20 July 2001 in the case of *Pellegrini* v. *Italy*, application No. 30882/96, where Italy was found guilty of violating Article 6 of the European Human Rights Convention by recognizing a Vatican judgment rendered without a fair trial. The human rights violation must be taken into account even if it is not manifest or grave and probably even if the situation has no or very little connection with the recognizing country.

[481] See, for example, P. Kinsch, *Recueil des cours*, Vol. 318 (2005), pp. 210-212; S. Vrellis, *Recueil des cours*, Vol. 328 (2007), pp. 293-299.

example, in German private international law[482]. Such specification of public policy has the positive effect of making the outcome less unpredictable.

The interference with the applicable foreign law, caused by the use of the public policy exception, should be kept to a minimum necessary for avoiding the conflict with the fundamental legal principles of the *lex fori*[483]. For example, a foreign provision prohibiting marriage between persons of different races can be refused application while the other, acceptable conditions (such as the age required for the conclusion of a marriage) may continue to be governed by the applicable foreign legal system in question[484]. Similarly, even if the court refuses to apply foreign inheritance rules discriminating between sons and daughters, it can examine other issues, such as whether a gift should be treated as an advance on inheritance, under the foreign law in question.

It is important to realize that the use of the forum's public policy reservation does not necessarily imply any moral or other condemnation of or criticism directed against the foreign State or its legal system as such[485]. A foreign rule can be refused application if such application would lead to unacceptable results *in casu*, while the contents of the same foreign rule may

---

[482] See the second sentence in Article 6 of the Introductory Act to the German Civil Code; G. Kegel and K. Schurig, *Internationales Privatrecht*, pp. 530-535; A. Bucher, *Recueil des cours*, Vol. 283 (2000), pp. 62-63.

[483] See, for example, B. Audit, *Droit international privé*, p. 265.

[484] See, for example, M. F. Yasseen, *Recueil des cours*, Vol. 116 (1965), pp. 461-462.

[485] See, for example, *Dicey and Morris on the Conflict of Laws*, pp. 82-83; M. Dogauchi, *Recueil des cours*, Vol. 315 (2005), p. 95; E. Jayme, *Recueil des cours*, Vol. 251 (1995), p. 236; F. Vischer, *Recueil des cours*, Vol. 232 (1992), p. 101.

at the same time be seen as ethically irreproachable *per se*.

For example, a foreign rule imposing maintenance obligations towards a distant relative may be contrary to the fundamental principles of Swedish law, while being totally natural in view of the lack of public social security and the extended family concept prevailing in the foreign country in question. Similarly, a foreign rule allowing an attorney to make a valid contract with his client giving the attorney a certain percentage of the outcome of the dispute *(quota litis)* is considered contrary to the public policy in some countries, while it is absolutely necessary in those other countries, such as the majority of the states within the United States, where an indigent plaintiff has no access to legal aid and can only pay for the services of a lawyer by promising him a portion of the winnings.

Furthermore, a foreign rule whose wording at a superficial glance seems unacceptable may be applied if the results of its application are not shocking in the individual case[486]. For example, a foreign rule setting the minimum age for marrying at ten years may be regarded as shocking *per se* in many countries, but there is no reason to invoke public policy if both parties in the actual case are over eighteen[487]. Or imagine that the Kingdom of Ruritania forbids marriages between persons of different races and considers such marriages to be null and void. At a superficial glance, the Ruritanian law is in this respect manifestly contrary to the public policy and the racial impediment would hopefully be disregarded if two Ruritanians wished

---

[486] See, for example, B. Audit, *Droit international privé*, p. 255; A. Philip, *Recueil des cours*, Vol. 160 (1978), p. 59; G. Parra-Aranguren, *Recueil des cours*, Vol. 210 (1988), p. 89.

[487] See, for example, G. Kegel and K. Schurig, *Internationales Privatrecht*, p. 526.

to marry in, for example, Sweden[488]. However, the automatic nullity of an inter-racial marriage under Ruritanian law would probably not be disregarded if at the time of the marriage both parties were Ruritanian citizens and habitual residents and both of them, relying on their status as unmarried, subsequently married other persons[489].

Another example: assuming that there is a country whose law considers contracts for surrogate motherhood against payment to be enforceable and vests the parental rights and duties in the woman that hired the surrogate mother rather than in the surrogate mother herself, the probable refusal by Swedish courts, on the grounds of Swedish public policy, to enforce the mutual performances by the two women of their obligations under such contract does not necessarily mean that the same contract's consequences regarding parental status would also be denied recognition, because leaving the child without a functioning legal parent may be considered even more contrary to Swedish public policy than surrogate motherhood contracts[490].

The intensity of the connection of the matter with the forum country *(Inlandsbeziehung, lien spatial)* may be of decisive importance when it is to be decided whether the public policy exception should be used or

---

[488] Pursuant to Swedish private international law, the capacity to marry is governed by Swedish law, i.e. the *lex fori*, but the lack of such capacity under foreign law is given certain effects if none of the couple is a Swedish citizen or is domiciled in Sweden, see Chapter 1, Section 1, of the Swedish Act (1904:26) on Some International Marriage and Guardianship Relationships.

[489] Cf. C. M. V. Clarkson and J. Hill, *The Conflict of Laws*, p. 489.

[490] See H. Gaudemet-Tallon, *Recueil des cours*, Vol. 312 (2005), pp. 433-434; H. Lewald, *Recueil des cours*, Vol. 69 (1939), pp. 123-125.

not[491]. For example, the exclusion of "illegitimate" children (children born out of wedlock) from inheritance rights might perhaps be disregarded if the child is a citizen and resident of the forum country, while being tolerated when the child is a foreigner residing abroad. This has to do with the intensity of the impact the application of the foreign rule could have on, or rather the threat it could pose to, the public order of the forum country. Because of similar reasons, the forum will probably show less tolerance when applying foreign law to contemporary events than in relation to events that took place long time ago[492], even though it is in both cases the contemporary public order that is protected (see *infra*). Some of the principles of the *lex fori* may, however, be so fundamental that they will be protected under all circumstances, regardless of the geographical and time aspects. For example, most countries would today treat a contract for the sale of slaves as invalid or at least unenforceable irrespective of whether the contract is recent or 20 years old and regardless of whether the transaction has any connec-

---

[491] See, for example, B. Audit, *Droit international privé*, pp. 261-262; A. Bucher, *Recueil des cours*, Vol. 239 (1993), pp. 47 and 52-56; M. Dogauchi, *Recueil des cours*, Vol. 315 (2005), pp. 95-100; H. Gaudemet-Tallon, *Recueil des cours*, Vol. 312 (2005), p. 424-441; J.-M. Jacquet, *Recueil des cours*, Vol. 292 (2001), pp. 199-202; E. Jayme, *Recueil des cours*, Vol. 251 (1995), pp. 227-228; G. Kegel and K. Schurig, *Internationales Privatrecht*, pp. 521 and 527; P. Mayer, *Recueil des cours*, Vol. 327 (2007), p. 313; G. Parra-Aranguren, *Recueil des cours*, Vol. 210 (1988), pp. 96-97; A. V. M. Struycken, *Recueil des cours*, Vol. 311 (2004), p. 397. Cf. the judgment of the German Federal Court of 20 December 1972, *Entscheidungen des Bundesgerichtshofes in Zivilsachen*, Vol. 60, p. 68, on p. 79.

[492] See, for example, G. Kegel and K. Schurig, *Internationales Privatrecht*, p. 528; M. Dogauchi, *Recueil des cours*, Vol. 315 (2005), pp. 100-102.

tion with the forum country or not. This is in particular
true whenever the application of a foreign rule (or
recognition or enforcement of a foreign judgment)
would make the forum country guilty of violating (or
at least of abetting a violation of) an internationally
protected human right it had pledged itself by treaty
to respect (see *infra*)[493]. It is less clear whether, for
example, the courts of a country forbidding the sale of
human organs, pornography, contraceptives or alcohol
would and should deem such contracts invalid or unenforceable even when they are governed by a legal
system accepting them and their connection with the
forum country is very weak. According to some
authors, the forum should generally extend its own
public policy to protect other countries and societies,
even when these have not enacted equivalent legal protection, but this appears to be a minority view[494].

In view of the flexibility or relativity of public policy, it has also been argued that the forum should be
more tolerant when the foreign law under scrutiny is to
be applied merely within the framework of a preliminary question rather than to the main issue in point[495].
In the words of Allan Philip, it is possible in certain
instances to accept a foreign legal institution, which in
itself is repugnant, as a valid "background institution"
for certain legal effects if it is necessary in order to
reach reasonable results[496]. A common example fre-

---

[493] See, for example, A. Bucher, *Recueil des cours*,
Vol. 239 (1993), pp. 53-54.

[494] Cf. J. Dolinger, *Recueil des cours*, Vol. 283 (2000),
pp. 317-318 and 340.

[495] See, for example, A. Bucher, *Recueil des cours*,
Vol. 239 (1993), p. 55; G. Kegel and K. Schurig, *Internationales Privatrecht*, pp. 527-528; A. Philip, *Recueil des
cours*, Vol. 160 (1978), pp. 59-60.

[496] See A. Philip, *Recueil des cours*, Vol. 160 (1978),
p. 60; H. Batiffol, *Recueil des cours*, Vol. 97 (1959), p. 456;

quently mentioned by legal writers wishing to illustrate this point is that even if it is contrary to the forum's public policy to perform marriage ceremonies creating a polygamous marriage, this should not prevent the use of the forum's rule about presumption of paternity (the *pater est* presumption) to the offspring of such marriages celebrated abroad. It is submitted, however, that public policy can be invoked also in the context of a preliminary question, but it is true that this will happen less frequently than with regard to the main question in dispute, due to the fact that the preliminary question is often less closely connected with the forum country than the main issue or that the application of foreign law to a preliminary question does not amount to actively creating a situation incompatible with the fundamental principles of the *lex fori* (such as a polygamous marriage) but merely to a passive acceptance of its consequences. For the same reason, it can be argued that the public policy of the forum is less sensitive in matters of recognition of foreign judgments than regarding the direct application of foreign law. Such *"effet atténué"* of public policy can be exemplified by reference to a well-known French judgment in the case of *Rivière* v. *Roumiantzeff* from 1953, concerning the recognition in France of a foreign divorce by consensus[497].

Some authors argue that the forum should give effect not merely to its own public policy but even to a "universal" or "real international" public policy *(ordre public universel, ordre public vraiment international)*

G. S. Maridakis, *Recueil des cours*, Vol. 105 (1962), p. 455; M. F. Yasseen, *Recueil des cours*, Vol. 116 (1965), p. 458.

[497] French Cassation Court on 17 April 1953, *Revue critique de droit international privé*, 1953, p. 412, with a note by Batiffol. See also B. Audit, *Droit international privé*, pp. 262-263; A. Bucher, *Recueil des cours*, Vol. 239 (1993), pp. 47-52.

which is shared by the international community of nations and can be characterized as "the common interest of mankind"[498]. It is submitted that such universal public policy does not yet exist, at least not for the purposes of private international law[499]. There are, of course, values that are shared by many countries, such as the internationally protected human rights and freedoms, but from the point of view of private international law they remain basically integral parts of the public policy of the forum or, depending on the forum country's monistic or dualistic approach to international law, may have to be taken into consideration by the forum on account of their status as international legal norms that are binding on the forum country's courts[500]. A truly international public policy can potentially be enacted by binding international legal instruments. An example in that direction is Article 24 of the Commission's proposal, submitted in 2003, for an EC Regulation on the Law Applicable to Non-Contractual Obligations (Rome II), which stipulated that the application of a provision of law awarding non-compensatory damages, such as exemplary of punitive damages, "shall be contrary to Community public policy"[501].

---

[498] See, for example, J. Dolinger, *Recueil des cours*, Vol. 283 (2000), pp. 324-326; A. Mills, *The Confluence of Public and Private International Law*, pp. 274-287.

[499] See, for example, E. Jayme, *Recueil des cours*, Vol. 251 (1995), p. 231; M. Dogauchi, *Recueil des cours*, Vol. 315 (2005), pp. 94-95; A. V. M. Struycken, *Recueil des cours*, Vol. 311 (2004), p. 46.

[500] Another example of the latter situation is an international treaty obligating the forum country to give effects to certain foreign mandatory rules. Cf., for example, Article VIII (2) *(b)* of the Statute of the International Monetary Fund, obligating the Member States to refuse to enforce contracts violating exchange regulations of another Member State.

[501] See COM(2003)427 final.

In the final text of the Regulation there is no reference
of any "Community public policy" and Recital 32
states merely that awarding non-compensatory exemplary or punitive damages of an excessive nature "may,
depending on . . . the legal order of the Member State
of the court seised, be regarded as being contrary to the
public policy *(ordre public)* of the forum". This formula cannot be understood as meaning more than that
in such cases the reliance by the Member State of the
forum on its national public policy must not be held to
be excessive.

4. *Replacement of the Excluded Foreign Rules*

If the application of a foreign rule is excluded due
to the public policy reservation (the so-called "negative
effect" of the reservation), the question may arise what
is to be applied instead. Sometimes there is no need for a
replacement for the excluded foreign rule, for example
a foreign provision prohibiting marriage between
persons of different races can be disregarded without
being replaced by any other rule. This is not always the
case, though. Disregarding the foreign rule may create
a gap which must be filled in one way or another, even
though some authors are of the rather extreme view
that if a court refuses on public policy grounds to apply
the foreign rule designated by the forum's private international law, it should not decide the dispute on its
merits but rather dismiss the whole case "without
prejudice", i.e. without affecting the plaintiff's ability
to sue elsewhere[502].

---

[502] See, for example, Weintraub, 43 *Texas International
Law Journal* 405 and 412 (2008). It is submitted that while
this solution may occasionally be reasonable, it would in
many cases lead to an unacceptable *déni de justice*, in particular if the reprobated foreign rule is relied on by the
defendant. It may, for instance, happen that there is no

If the foreign law governing the capacity to marry allows marriage of children above the age of ten, its application would probably be refused in most countries if the child is really so young, but what age limit should be applied instead of the ten years' limit prescribed by the applicable foreign legal system? According to the prevailing view, considering the *lex fori* as the general residuary law, the unacceptably low age limit of the foreign law is to be replaced with the age limit of the *lex fori*, but this is not self-evident[503].

The task of filling the gaps created by the use of the public policy reservation differs from the corresponding problem arising in purely domestic cases where the forum has to fill gaps in its own substantive law[504]. The last-mentioned problem is very common and presents itself each time the forum has to rule on a point on which there is no clear statutory provision or a precedent. It is hardly controversial to say that such gaps in the *lex fori* should be filled on the basis of the values

---

other jurisdiction the innocent plaintiff can turn to. A dismissal could, furthermore, be very costly, in terms of both time and money, for the plaintiff, who in most European countries would have to pay not only his own but also the defendant's costs. The situation may be somewhat different in the United States, where due to the so-called "American rule" the losing party does not usually have to compensate the winning party for its costs and where due to a contingent fee arrangement the losing party very often does not have to bear its own costs either.

[503] See, for example, H. Batiffol, *Recueil des cours*, Vol. 97 (1959), pp. 457-458; A. Bucher, *Recueil des cours*, Vol. 239 (1993), pp. 29-34; O. Kahn-Freund, *Recueil des cours*, Vol. 143 (1974), p. 429; A. E. von Overbeck, *Recueil des cours*, Vol. 176 (1982), p. 212; G. Parra-Aranguren, *Recueil des cours*, Vol. 210 (1988), p. 100; F. Schwind, *Recueil des cours*, Vol. 187 (1984), pp. 90-91; M. F. Yasseen, *Recueil des cours*, Vol. 116 (1965), pp. 462-463.

[504] Cf. G. S. Maridakis, *Recueil des cours*, Vol. 105 (1962), pp. 457-459.

prevailing in the country of the forum, including the more general principles and analogies found in the *lex fori* itself. Gaps created by the refusal to apply a foreign rule may require a different treatment, as the very fact that the *lex causae* is foreign reflects the view of the forum country's legislator that values and principles other than those of the *lex fori* are conducive to a reasonable solution of the dispute.

A conceivable alternative source of replacement rules could, for example, be the legal system which, apart from the applicable law, has the closest connection with the legal relationship in question, so that an unacceptably low age limit set by the applicable *lex patriae* could be replaced with the age limit stipulated by, for example, the law of the country of habitual residence of the person concerned[505].

In some cases, an unacceptable foreign rule can be replaced with another rule taken from the same foreign legal system. If, for example, the applicable foreign law discriminates against persons belonging to a small ethnic or religious minority and this discrimination is contrary to the public policy of the forum, it might often be more appropriate to apply the rules of the same foreign legal system pertaining to the majority population than mechanically turn to the *lex fori*. Or assume that the foreign law governing a debt stipulates that this particular sort of debts is not subject to prescription or statute of limitations, i.e. the debt continues to exist and remains enforceable for ever. If the court considers this to be incompatible with the forum country's public policy, it has to find and apply some time limits[506]. Again, it may apply the statute of limita-

---

[505] See, for example, A. Philip, *Recueil des cours*, Vol. 160 (1978), pp. 61-62.

[506] See, for example, A. Bucher, *Recueil des cours*, Vol. 239 (1993), p. 31 ; G. Kegel and K. Schurig, *Interna-*

tion of the *lex fori* or apply the general prescription rule of the applicable foreign legal system, i.e. the time limits used for debts that do not belong to the particular category of "eternal" debts[507].

The last-mentioned alternative is undoubtedly appealing and might seem to respect the foreign applicable law to a larger extent that the other solutions, but it may conceivably lead to a more radical interference with that law than the other alternatives, for example if the general prescription rules of the *lex causae* provide for a time limitation that is substantially shorter than the longest prescription period the public policy of the forum can tolerate.

The principle that the interference with the applicable foreign law should be kept at a minimum speaks rather in favour of creating and imposing a tailor-made *ad hoc* time-limit corresponding to the longest prescription period that the public policy of the forum country can accept. Similarly, if the minimum age for marrying pursuant to the law of the forum country is eighteen years but its public policy tolerates sixteen, then sixteen should suffice even in those cases where the applicable legal system has an age limit which is lower than sixteen or imposes no age limit at all[508]. Another example: if the applicable foreign law prescribes excessively high compensation for libel, it can be adjusted to the highest amount the public policy of the forum country can tolerate (it should also be pos-

---

tionales Privatrecht, pp. 538-539; P. Lalive, *Recueil des cours*, Vol. 155 (1977), pp. 247-249.

[507] This method was used by the German *Reichsgericht* in a case decided in 1922 regarding the application of Swiss law, see O. Kahn-Freund, *Recueil des cours*, Vol. 143 (1974), p. 429; P. Lalive, *Recueil des cours*, Vol. 155 (1977), pp. 248.

[508] Cf. M. Dogauchi, *Recueil des cours*, Vol. 315 (2005), pp. 102- 107.

sible to recognize and enforce a foreign judgment
awarding such excessive compensation, but only up to
the amount acceptable to the *ordre public* of the country where the recognition or enforcement is to take
place)[509]. This solution amounts, in fact, to a creation
of a special tailor-made rule of substantive law adapted
to the particular situation at hand[510].

A special situation may arise if the excluded foreign
rule was supposed to be applied on the ground of transmission to a third legal system *(renvoi au second
degré)*[511]. It could be argued that in such a case the
excluded rule should be replaced with the substantive
rules of the primarily applicable foreign law. An
example demonstrating this situation is the Canadian
case of *Vladi* v. *Vladi*, decided by the Nova Scotia
Supreme Court in 1987[512]. The case concerned a matrimonial property dispute and the Nova Scotia conflict
rule referred to the law of the last common habitual
residence of the spouses, which happened to be the law
of Germany. However, German private international law
designated the law of Iran as the law of the country of
the common nationality of the parties. The court was in
principle willing to accept the transmission to Iranian
law but found the application of Iranian law to be
incompatible with the public policy of the forum. The
most interesting feature of the judgment is that the
excluded Iranian rules were not replaced with the substantive rules of the Canadian *lex fori* but with substantive German law, which seems logical in view of the
fact that the private international law of Nova Scotia

---

[509] See, for example, G. Kegel and K. Schurig, *Internationales Privatrecht*, pp. 519 and 530.

[510] See F. Vischer, *Recueil des cours*, Vol. 232 (1992),
p. 104.

[511] See Chapter IX, *supra*.

[512] (1987) 39 DLR (4th) 563 (NSSC); *Dicey and
Morris on the Conflict of Laws*, pp. 75-76.

considered the relationship to be governed by German law in the first place.

5. *Overriding Mandatory Rules of the* Lex Fori

The public policy reservation is normally conceived as a negative (corrective) exception, used for the purpose of excluding some foreign rules that are in principle applicable to the matter at hand, due to the incompatibility *in casu* of their application with the fundamental legal principles of the forum country. It is, however, also possible to imagine a positive (affirmative) construction of *ordre public*, where some of the mandatory rules of the *lex fori* are considered to be so important and sensitive from the viewpoint of public policy that they are intended to be applied, always or at least when the situation is closely connected with the forum country, regardless of whether the issue as such is governed by foreign law and regardless of the contents of that foreign law. Such rules of the *lex fori* can be said to override the usual conflict rules or, rather, to go behind their back. They are therefore often called "overriding mandatory rules", "peremptory norms", "immediately applicable rules" or "super-mandatory rules" (in French *lois d'application immédiate, lois d'ordre public, lois de police, lois internationalement impératives, normes d'application nécessaire, dispositions impératives dérogatoires*, etc.)[513].

---

[513] See, for example, B. Audit, *Droit international privé*, pp. 96-104 and 261 ; H. Batiffol, *Recueil des cours*, Vol. 139 (1973), pp. 136-145 ; A. Bonomi, *Yearbook of Private International Law*, Vol. I (1999), pp. 215-247 ; J. Dolinger, *Recueil des cours*, Vol. 283 (2000), pp. 305-316 ; H. Eek, *Recueil des cours*, Vol. 139 (1973), pp. 1-73 ; H. Gaudemet-Tallon, *Recueil des cours*, Vol. 312 (2005), pp. 256-364 ; J. D. González Campos, *Recueil des cours*, Vol. 287 (2000), pp. 368-376 ; J.-M. Jacquet, *Recueil des*

The existence of such overriding rules of *lex fori* and their legitimacy is confirmed by, for example, Article 9 of the EC Rome I Regulation No. 593/2008 of 17 June 2008 on the Law Applicable to Contractual Obligations[514]. Article 9, point 1, defines overriding mandatory provisions as provisions the respect for which is regarded as crucial by a country for safeguarding its public interests, such as its political, social or economic organization, to such an extent that they are applicable to any situation falling within their scope, irrespective of the law otherwise applicable to the contract. It is clear that this definition does not have in mind all mandatory rules of the *lex fori*, but merely a small minority among them, namely those mandatory rules that are intended to override the usual conflict rules of the forum country[515]. Article 9, point 2, stipulates that the Regulation's conflict rules do not restrict the application of the overriding mandatory provisions of the law of the forum. A similar provision is found, for example, in Article 16, point 2, of the EC Rome II Regulation No. 864/2007 of 11 July 2007 on the Law Applicable to Non-Contractual Obligations[516].

---

cours, Vol. 292 (2001), pp. 208-212; P. Lalive, *Recueil des cours*, Vol. 155 (1977), pp. 120-153; Y. Loussouarn, *Recueil des cours*, Vol. 139 (1973), pp. 317-334; D. McClean, *Recueil des cours*, Vol. 282 (2000), pp. 210-216; G. Parra-Aranguren, *Recueil des cours*, Vol. 210 (1988), pp. 87 and 121; M. Pauknerová, *Czech Yearbook of International Law*, Vol. I (2010), pp. 81-94; A. V. M. Struycken, *Recueil des cours*, Vol. 311 (2004), pp. 33-44 and 406-436; F. Vischer, *Recueil des cours*, Vol. 232 (1992), pp. 153-165; E. Vitta, *Recueil des cours*, Vol. 162 (1979), pp. 118-126.

[514] OJ 2008 L 177, p. 6.

[515] Cf. A. Philip, *Recueil des cours*, Vol. 160 (1978), p. 55.

[516] OJ 2007 L 199, p. 49.

Most overriding mandatory rules of private-law nature are provisions favouring the party considered worthy of special protection, such as children, women, employees or consumers, but more general protective rules are also conceivable. For example, Section 36 of the Swedish Contract Act makes it possible to adjust inappropriate or unfair contractual clauses or even whole contracts. This provision is sometimes considered to be characteristic of the Nordic contracts law and is mandatory in the sense that the parties cannot deviate from it by contract. It could be argued that this possibility of adjustment is so central and important for Swedish law that Swedish courts can and should apply Section 36 even when the contract is otherwise governed by foreign law.

The negative and positive constructions of public policy are closely interrelated and can perhaps be regarded as two sides of the same coin; the statement that a certain provision of the *lex fori* is an overriding mandatory rule is usually just another way of saying that any deviation from that rule would be incompatible with the forum country's *ordre public*[517]. The same idea can be expressed by saying that the public policy of the forum does not consist merely of certain principles but comprises also a number of more precise legal rules[518]. The principal difference between the substance of negative public policy reservation clauses and that of the overriding mandatory rules appears namely to be that the negative reservations normally concern more general legal principles while the overriding mandatory rules are usually much more specific

---

[517] See, for example, J. Dolinger, *Recueil des cours*, Vol. 283 (2000), pp. 312-316; G. Kegel and K. Schurig, *Internationales Privatrecht*, pp. 518 and 520.

[518] See, for example, A. Bucher, *Recueil des cours*, Vol. 239 (1993), p. 26.

and sometimes deal merely with a particular detail; another difference seems to be that the negative clauses are of relevance mainly in the field of family law while overriding mandatory rules are more common in, for example, contractual matters[519]. An additional conceivable difference, related to the previously mentioned ones, seems to be that an overriding mandatory rule can be abolished or modified at any time and with immediate effect by the legislator, whereas the content of the negative reservation, being derived from the general values permeating the society and the legal system of the forum, is normally more difficult to change by a simple legislative action. From a more theoretical viewpoint, it is also worth noting that an overriding mandatory rule of the *lex fori* does not merely exclude the application of a competing foreign rule but provides immediately also for its replacement, so that the problem of filling the gap left by the exclusion of foreign law does not arise[520].

The concept of overriding mandatory rules presupposes that they constitute an exception to the ordinarily applicable law. If the legislator of the forum country decides that an issue is so important and sensitive that it must be governed in its totality and always by the *lex fori*, for example that the capacity to marry is always to be decided by the law of the forum, then the relevant substantive provisions of the *lex fori* become "the applicable *lex causae*" and there is no

---

[519] See, for example, E. Jayme, *Recueil des cours*, Vol. 251 (1995), p. 225. It is, however, possible that the provision in Chapter 6, Section 2a, of the Swedish Children and Parents Code, stipulating that custody of children must be decided in accordance with the best interests of the child, can be considered to be an overriding mandatory rule of Swedish family law.

[520] See A. Bucher, *Recueil des cours*, Vol. 239 (1993), pp. 38-39.

point discussing their overriding mandatory character, simply because there is no foreign applicable law to override.

The borderline between an overriding mandatory rule and a unilateral conflict rule designating the *lex fori* may sometimes be somewhat blurred.

Just like in the case of negative public-policy reservations, the overriding mandatory nature of a legal rule can be relative, i.e. it can depend on the intensity of the connection between the legal relationship in the particular case and the forum country[521]. A rule of labour law of the forum country prohibiting employers to dismiss employees without good cause may, for example, be intended to be applied, irrespective of the legal system governing the employment contract, whenever the employee habitually carries out his work in the forum country, while lacking overriding mandatory character when the work is habitually carried out abroad.

It is also important to note that those overriding mandatory rules that are intended to protect a weaker party are usually mandatory in a unilateral manner only, so that they do not preclude the application of the otherwise applicable legal system if and to the extent it is even more advantageous for the weaker party in

---

[521] See H. Gaudemet-Tallon, *Recueil des cours*, Vol. 312 (2005), p. 260. A different matter is that in the application of some internationally unified or harmonized mandatory rules, all participating countries can sometimes be treated as one single territory. Cf. Article 6, point 2, of the EC Directive No. 93/13 of 5 April 1993 on Unfair Terms in Consumer Contracts, OJ 1993 L 95, p. 29, which obligates the Member States to take the necessary measures to ensure that the consumer does not lose the protection granted by this directive by the virtue of the choice of the law of a non-member country as the law applicable to the contract, "if the latter has a close connection with the territory of the Member States" (thus not necessarily with the territory of the Member State of the forum).

question. The statement above that overriding mandatory rules of the *lex fori* are applied under all circumstances without regard to the contents of the otherwise applicable law might thus be somewhat misleading[522]. Often it is possible to apply the overriding mandatory rule without violating the applicable *lex causae*, for example when the consumer protection rules of both legal systems are mandatory in a one-way manner only and tolerate a more far-reaching protection granted by the other law.

It may occasionally be difficult to establish which legal system is better for the weaker party; when comparing two national systems of labour law it may, for example, easily happen that one of them is more advantageous for the employee in certain respects (such as the protection against groundless dismissal) while being less advantageous in other respects (such as the time limitation for the employee's claims). This is unproblematic as long as the employee is permitted to rely simultaneously on both legal systems by mixing them ("picking cherries out of the cake"), but difficulties may arise if the two legal systems have to be compared in their totality.

Finally, it must be noted that just like the use of the negative public policy reservation, the application of overriding mandatory provisions of the *lex fori*, too, can be restricted by the international commitments of the forum country, such as international treaties or EC law[523].

---

[522] See H. Gaudemet-Tallon, *Recueil des cours*, Vol. 312 (2005), p. 258.

[523] See, for example, the judgment of the EC Court of 19 June 2008 in *Commission* v. *Luxembourg*, case C-319/06, stating that Grand Duchy of Luxembourg has violated EC rules on the freedom to provide services by declaring some of the provisions of its labour law to be mandatory public policy provisions.

6. Public Policy and Overriding Mandatory Rules of Third Countries

Occasionally the question arises whether the forum can and should give effect to the public policy of third countries, i.e. countries that are neither the country of the forum (it is undisputed that the forum can give effect to its own public policy) nor the country whose law governs the relationship (the application of the applicable foreign legal system cannot, by definition, be incompatible with its own public policy). Some authors suggest that the forum should take into due consideration and respect foreign public policy, provided it does not contradict its own local *ordre public*[524].

The problem has sometimes been discussed in connection with *renvoi*, because the countries accepting the doctrine of *renvoi* may find it consistent with that concept to give effect to foreign public policy as part of the private international law of the country of the primarily applicable foreign legal system[525], even though in most cases this would actually amount to refusing to give effect to a substantive rule of the *lex fori*[526]. Accepting the *renvoi* means namely that the *lex*

---

[524] See, for example, J. Dolinger, *Recueil des cours*, Vol. 283 (2000), p. 340.

[525] See Chapter IX, *supra*; G. Parra-Aranguren, *Recueil des cours*, Vol. 210 (1988), p. 101.

[526] An interesting complication arises if the application of a foreign public policy reservation amounts to a violation of the public policy of the forum country, for example if the foreign country would refuse, on the grounds of its *ordre public*, to celebrate an inter-religious marriage while the permissibility of such marriages is part of the fundamental principles of the *lex fori* in the country accepting the *renvoi*. See G. Kegel and K. Schurig, *Internationales Privatrecht*, p. 540, who write that foreign *ordre public* should be given effect within the framework of *renvoi*, but only to the extent it does not violate the *ordre public* of the forum country.

fori becomes applicable after it has gone through the "filter" of the primarily applicable foreign legal system. In the above-mentioned Canadian case of *Vladi* v. *Vladi*[527], involving transmission to a third legal system, the court probably could have refused to apply the discriminatory provisions of Iranian law due to their incompatibility with German public policy, but it chose to rely on the violation of the public policy of the forum instead.

In certain special situations, foreign public policy may even be seen as a fact that is relevant according to the substantive rules of the *lex causae* or of the *lex fori*. In the English case *Lemenda Trading Co.* v. *African Middle East Petroleum Co.*[528], the plaintiffs claimed payment of a commission under a commission contract governed by English law. The commission was a reward for influencing a minister of the State of Qatar. When considering whether the contract should be treated as unenforceable due to its incompatibility with principles of morality, the court held that the English moral principles opposed to corruption could prevail, but merely if the contract was contrary to public policy and unenforceable also under the law of Qatar.

A provision in favour of giving effect to foreign overriding mandatory rules was also found in Article 7, point 1, of the 1980 EC Convention on the Law Applicable to Contractual Obligations[529] (the Rome Convention, now replaced, as far as contracts concluded on or after 17 December 2009 are concerned, by the Rome I Regulation), which provided that

---

[527] (1987) 39 DLR (4th) 563 (NSSC); *Dicey and Morris on the Conflict of Laws*, pp. 75-76.

[528] [1988] QB 448; C. M. V. Clarkson and J. Hill, *The Conflict of Laws*, pp. 488-489; T. C. Hartley, *Recueil des cours*, Vol. 319 (2006), pp. 246-247.

[529] OJ 1998 C 27, p. 36.

"[w]hen applying the law of a country, effect may be given to the mandatory rules of the law of another country with which the situation has a close connection, if and in so far as, under the law of the latter country, those rules must be applied whatever the law applicable to the contract. In considering whether to give effect to these overriding mandatory rules, regard must be had to their nature and purpose and to the consequences of their application or non-application."

This provision, which allowed the court to give effect to overriding mandatory rules of third countries having close relationship with the case, was highly controversial[530], and Article 22 of the Rome Convention gave the contracting States the right to reserve the right not to apply it. Several contracting States, including Germany, Ireland, Luxembourg, Portugal and the United Kingdom, have made such reservations. On the other hand, similar provisions are found in a few Hague conventions[531] and there is of course nothing

---

[530] The "roots" of Article 7 point 1 are supposedly found in the judgment of the Cassation Court of the Netherlands of 13 May 1966 in the case of *Alnati* (*Van Nievelt* v. *Hollandsche Assurantie Societeit*). For a French translation of the text of this judgment, see *Revue critique de droit international privé*, 1967, p. 522, with a note by Struycken.

[531] See Article 16 of the Hague Convention of 14 March 1978 on the Law Applicable to Agency, which stipulates that

"[i]n the application of this Convention, effect may be given to the mandatory rules of any State with which the situation has a significant connection, if and insofar as, under the law of that State, those rules must be applied whatever the law specified by its choice of law rules."

See also Article 16 (2) of the Hague Convention of 1 July

preventing the forum country from using the approach expressed in Article 7, point 1, of the Rome Convention even in those parts of its private international law that are autonomous and not based on any international instrument. The question is rather whether such giving effect to the overriding mandatory rules or the public policy of third countries is appropriate and suitable.

It is submitted, for several reasons, that this is not the case. To begin with, a legal relationship can at the same time have close ties to several countries. The simultaneous taking into account of several legal systems makes the adjudication complicated and the outcome more difficult to foresee. It is usually quite difficult for the court to ascertain what is incompatible with the public policy of a foreign country and which foreign rules are intended to have overridingly mandatory character; as pointed out above, these questions can be very difficult and complicated even in respect of the public policy and mandatory rules of the *lex fori*. A further blow to predictability comes from the non-compulsory nature of Article 7, point 1: even if it is established that a foreign rule is intended to be of an overriding mandatory nature and that there is a close connection between the situation and the country in

---

1985 on the Law Applicable to Trusts and on their Recognition. In national law, see, for example, Article 19 of the Swiss Act on Private International Law of 1987, which stipulates that a mandatory provision of a law other than the one designated by the usual conflict rules may be taken into account "if interests that are according to Swiss views legitimate and clearly overriding so require and the case is closely connected to that law". Whether such a provision should be taken into account "depends on its policy and its consequences for a judgment that is fair according to Swiss views" (the English wording of Article 19 is quoted from P. A. Karrer *et al.*, *Switzerland's Private International Law*, 2nd ed., Boston, Zurich 1994). See also A. E. von Overbeck, *Recueil des cours*, Vol. 176 (1982), pp. 179-182.

question, the court has a considerable discretionary power to ignore it. Furthermore, it must be kept in mind that private international law, just like the rest of the legal system, serves the interests of the forum country and that even the application of foreign law depends on the forum country's conflict rules created to serve that country's interests. Normally there is no reason why the forum should refrain from applying a legal rule, that it considers to be applicable, merely because some other (third) country would find the results of such application objectionable[532].

It is, therefore, satisfactory that there is no provision corresponding to Article 7, point 1, of the Rome Convention in the EC Rome I Regulation No. 593/2008 of 17 June 2008 on the Law Applicable to Contractual Obligations[533], which replaced the Rome Convention. Pursuant to Article 9, point 3, of the Regulation,

> "[e]ffect may be given to the overriding mandatory provisions of the law of the country where the obligations arising out of the contract have to be or have been performed, in so far as those overriding mandatory provisions render the performance of the contract unlawful. In considering whether to give effect to those provisions, regard shall be had to their nature and purpose and to the consequences or their application or non-application."

It is important to note that in contrast to Article 7, point 1, of the Rome Convention, Article 9, point 3, of the Rome I Regulation refers merely to the overriding mandatory rules of the country of performance (thus not any country with which the contract has a close connection) and concerns exclusively those — probably

---

[532] See, however, A. Bucher, *Recueil des cours*, Vol. 239 (1993), pp. 92-101.
[533] OJ 2008 L 177, p. 6.

extremely few — provisions of the *lex loci solutionis* which render the performance unlawful (thus not, for example, most mandatory rules on the protection of consumers or the statute of limitation)[534]. Even though Article 9, point 3, of the Rome I Regulation is by far less problematic than Article 7, point 1, of the Rome Convention, some question marks remain. It is, for example, not quite clear whether "giving effect" is the same as application. The expression seems to imply a choice among effects of various kinds and degrees. They may include a full application (the second sentence of Article 9, point 3, speaks about "application or non-application"), but the court may opt to give the overriding foreign rule less far-reaching effects, for example to discharge a non-performing party of its duty to pay damages while refusing to consider the contract null and void for other purposes. The value of Article 9, point 3, is open to doubt; the unlawfulness of performance under the law of the place where the performance is to take place makes frequently the performance impossible and such impossibility is normally taken into account by the substantive law applicable to the contract, for example under its rules on *force majeure*, quite independently of Article 9, point 3.

7. *The Role of Public Policy in Arbitral Proceedings*

The use of the public policy reservation in arbitration proceedings deserves a few special comments[535].

---

[534] However, some authors understand "unlawful" (*illégal*, *unrechtmässig*, *protiprávní*, *olagligt*, etc.) to include not merely performances that are forbidden but also other cases where the debtor is allowed to refuse to perform due to the local overriding mandatory rules. See, for example, M. Hellner, *Journal of Private International Law*, 2009, pp. 461-462.

[535] See, for example, A. Bucher, *Recueil des cours*, Vol. 341 (2009), pp. 272-276.

According to one view, when the arbitrators apply the private international law of the country where the arbitral tribunal has its seat (which is, incidentally, far from a self-evident choice[536]), it is also the *ordre public* of that country that determines whether a foreign rule must be refused application, whereas if they apply the private international law of another country, the principles of *ordre public* of that other country should be given effect[537]. Some authors argue that arbitrators should take into account or apply any mandatory rules of national origin embodying goals or policies the attainment or advancement of which are essential or of great public importance for the country enacting them, regardless of whether or not such mandatory rules belong to the proper law of the contract chosen by the parties or otherwise established by the Arbitral Tribunal[538].

I find it difficult to agree with these opinions. In my view, the concept of *ordre public*, whose interpretation and contents vary considerably from country to country, should normally not be used at all by arbitrators in international commercial arbitration. As the arbitrators are not instrumentalities of any State, but derive their authority primarily from their mandate given to them by the parties, they cannot be expected to protect the public policy of any particular national community but should rather abide by the common instructions given by the parties[539]. It can, of course, be assumed that the

---

[536] See Chapter V, *supra*.

[537] See, for example, A. Philip, *Recueil des cours*, Vol. 160 (1978), pp. 60-61.

[538] See, for example, H. A. Grigera Naón, *Recueil des cours*, Vol. 289 (2001), p. 375.

[539] See I. Fadlallah, *Recueil des cours*, Vol. 249 (1994), p. 382:

"L'arbitre international, en principe, n'appartient à aucun système. L'on dit qu'il n'a pas de for. Toutes les

arbitrators will normally try to avoid rules whose application *in casu* would lead to grossly unfair results, and to the extent the choice of the applicable law is at their discretion it is possible, or even probable, that they will use their freedom for that purpose. However, if the application of a certain legal system cannot be avoided in this way, for example because that system has been directly or indirectly designated by the parties themselves, it is normally not for the arbitrator to disregard those of its provisions whose application he finds objectionable or even repugnant. I do not share the view of A. V. M. Struycken, who considers the arbitrator to be similar to a physician and points out that a good medical doctor has to stick to the professional ethics prevailing in the legal community in the ambit of which he practises, regardless of what his patient demands[540].

It is a different matter that an arbitrator may resign and thus totally refuse to adjudicate a dispute whose whole object he finds reprehensible, for example if it aims at enforcing a contract promoting slavery, bribery or terrorism[541]. But if the arbitrator chooses not to

---

lois sont, pour lui, étrangères. Il n'a donc pas de système à défendre. Son pouvoir tient de l'investiture des parties. Il s'étend et se limite au cercle des parties. Tout ce qui vient le contraindre est susceptible de le gêner."

[540] See A. V. M. Struycken, *Recueil des cours*, Vol. 311 (2004), pp. 84-85.

[541] Cf. the decision made by Mr. Gunnar Lagergren, a Swedish judge acting as arbitrator in an ICC case concerning a contract the object of which was bribery of high government officials. Mr. Lagergren refused to accept jurisdiction, stating that the parties had forfeited any right to ask for the assistance of the machinery of justice, whether national courts or arbitral tribunals. For more details about this interesting decision, see J. G. Wetter in *Yearbook of the Arbitration Institute of the Stockholm Chamber of Commerce*, 1984, p. 29, note 27.

resign and assumes jurisdiction, he should not try to "correct" the effects of the applicable legal system by imposing his own moral standards that are incompatible with that system[542]. After all, an arbitrator is a paid mandatary of the parties and he has not been engaged to provide them with moral or spiritual guidance. The use of the public policy concept of the country where the proceedings take place is hardly appropriate, especially when the place of the proceedings is fortuitous and unrelated to the dispute as such. Besides, the public policy concept of the country of the proceedings would be extremely difficult for arbitrators from other countries to understand and administer properly. It is, therefore, preferable to put *ordre public* aside. The arbitrator can console himself with the knowledge that his award will be set aside or refused recognition and enforcement by State courts if it is contrary to their public policy[543].

Some authors use the risk of such potential refusal or annulment as an argument against the idea of allowing the arbitral tribunal to disregard considerations of *ordre public*. In their view, the arbitrators should abide by the public policy of the country of arbitration

---

[542] H. A. Grigera Naón, *Recueil des cours*, Vol. 289 (2001), pp. 208-209, suggests, in connection with overriding *lois de police*, that arbitrators take into consideration some legal principles or norms enjoying wide international consensus. A. V. M. Struycken, *Recueil des cours*, Vol. 311 (2004), p. 53, writes that arbitrators, who do not operate in the framework of a State legal order, may be conceived as the spokesmen of a distinct legal civilization with a keen sense of responsibility for order in a world-wide society; they should be aware of being the judiciary of that extra-State community, act as such and show to be aware of its *ordre public*.

[543] See Article V (2) *(b)* of the 1958 New York Convention on the Recognition and Enforcement of Foreign Arbitral Awards.

as well as that of the country (countries?) of enforce-ment[544]. I find it difficult to agree. It is certainly less than appealing to produce knowingly an award that will be refused recognition and enforcement and may even be annulled by a State court. This does not, how-ever, make the award worthless. First of all, the losing party may decide to abide by the award voluntarily, for example in order to protect its reputation in commer-cial circles. Furthermore, thanks to the 1958 New York Convention on the Recognition and Enforcement of Foreign Arbitral Awards, an attempt to have the award enforced can potentially be made in almost any country where the debtor has sequestrable assets and some of them may find the award enforceable.

8. *Concluding Remarks*

A final remark concerning the *ordre public* reserva-tion is that its relevance seems to be decreasing. There are several reasons for this development, one of them being the increased use, in some countries, of very flexible conflict rules, such as those leading to the application of the law of the country most closely con-nected with the legal relationship under scrutiny, the law having most interest in the outcome or simply the law which the forum found to be better as to substance (in fact, some of these methods of determining the applicable law are so flexible that they do not deserve to be called rules at all but should rather be called approaches). Such flexibility enables the forum to avoid undesirable substantive results without having to rely on the public policy exception[545].

---

[544] See, for example, G. C. Moss, *International Com-mercial Arbitration. Party Autonomy and Mandatory Rules*, pp. 301 and 314.

[545] See, for example, A. Bucher, *Recueil des cours*, Vol. 239 (1993), p. 23.

It is also noteworthy that in the common-law countries, which frequently give by various means (for example, by a procedural classification of the issue) priority to the *lex fori*, the exception of public policy plays a less pronounced role than in the private international law of countries with a civil-law system[546]. A unilateral conflict rule, insisting on the application in all situations of the *lex fori*, is in fact usually a reflection of the forum country's public policy and is very similar, in its practical results, to the classification of the substantive *lex fori* provisions concerned as overriding mandatory rules.

Finally, some credit for the decreased use of the public policy reservation can perhaps be given to fragmentation (it may also be called specialization) of the conflict rules[547]. For example, while just a few decades ago one discussed one suitable general conflict rule for non-contractual obligations (torts), today the trend is towards specialized conflict rules for product liability, unfair commercial practices, violations of privacy, environmental damage, infringement of intellectual property rights, etc.[548] With regard to torts, it is also possible to distinguish between the law applicable to the regulation of harmful conduct and the law applicable to the distribution of the resulting loss: it can be argued that the conduct should be governed by the territorial local law, while the loss distribution should depend on the personal laws of the persons involved[549].

---

[546] Bucher, *op. cit.*, pp. 22-23.

[547] See, for example, B. Audit, *Recueil des cours*, Vol. 305 (2003), pp. 343-357.

[548] See, for instance, Articles 4-9 of the EC Regulation No. 864/2007 of 11 July 2007 on the Law Applicable to Non-Contractual Obligations ("Rome II"), OJ 2007 L 199, p. 40.

[549] See, for example, S. C. Symeonides, *Recueil des cours*, Vol. 298 (2002), pp. 154-277. Cf. also Article 17 of

Similarly, in the fields of contracts, previously relatively simple conflict rules covering most categories of
contracts and all types of contractual issues have now
been replaced or modified by special conflict rules for
some contracts (for example weak-party contracts such
as consumer, insurance or employment contracts)[550] or
for certain specific issues[551]. The same trend is noticeable also in the field of family law; Andreas Bucher
speaks in this context about a "morcellement du statut
familial"[552]. Such specialization certainly has its disadvantages, but the specialized conflict rules are
hopefully better adapted to the specific features of

---

the EC Regulation No. 864/2007 of 11 July 2007 on the
Law Applicable to Non-Contractual Obligations ("Rome
II"), OJ 2007 L 199, p. 40, pursuant to which in assessing
the conduct of the person claimed to be liable account
must be taken, as a matter of fact and insofar as is appropriate, of the rules of conduct which were in force at the
place and time of the event giving rise to the liability.

[550] See, for example, Articles 6–8 of the EC Regulation
No. 593/2008 of 17 June 2008 on the Law Applicable to
Contractual Obligations (Rome I), OJ 2008 L 177, p. 6.

[551] See, for example, Article 10, point 2, of the EC
Regulation No. 593/2008 of 17 June 2008 on the Law
Applicable to Contractual Obligations (Rome I), OJ 2008
L 177, p. 6, pursuant to which a party may rely upon the
law of the country in which he has his habitual residence
to establish that he did not consent to the contract if
it appears from the circumstances that it would not be
reasonable to determine the effect of his conduct in
accordance with the law governing the contract. Another
example is Article 13 of the same Regulation, stipulating
that in a contract concluded between persons who are in the
same country, a natural person who would have capacity
under the law of that country may invoke his incapacity
resulting from another law only if the other party to the
contract was aware of this incapacity at the time of the
conclusion of the contract or was not aware thereof as a
result of negligence.

[552] See A. Bucher, *Recueil des cours*, Vol. 283 (2000),
p. 22.

the particular situation and lead to more appropriate results than the — necessarily rather rough — general conflict rules[553]. This should, in turn, mitigate the risk that the *ordre public* reservation must be used in order to avoid inappropriate results[554].

---

[553] It seems that the prophecy of P. Arminjon, *Recueil des cours*, Vol. 21 (1928), p. 509, that private international law will not really exist until it corresponds in size to a code of hundreds or even thousands of articles, may come true within foreseeable future thanks to the current legislative activity within the European Union.

[554] See, for example, A. Bucher, *Recueil des cours*, Vol. 239 (1993), pp. 68-69; J. D. González Campos, *Recueil des cours*, Vol. 287 (2000), pp. 197-201.

CHAPTER XI

ABUSE OF PRIVATE INTERNATIONAL LAW

1. The Problem

In a broad sense, a person can be said to abuse the law if he, without directly violating a specific legal rule, intentionally employs the rule in a way which is incompatible with its purpose and aim (i.e., its *ratio legis*). Such abuse is a general phenomenon which is in no way limited to private international law, but it has a specific meaning and gives rise to rather special problems when the abuse relates to conflict rules or rules on jurisdiction of national courts and recognition/enforcement of foreign judgments. The rules of private international law can potentially be abused to a larger extent than the rules of almost any other branch of the law and this phenomenon, frequently referred to by its French name as *fraude à la loi*[555], deserves a closer discussion.

Assume that a wealthy man, who is a Swedish citizen and resident, wishes to bequeath his assets, all situated in Sweden, to his mistress. Therefore, he wants to be able to dispose of his property by will without

---

[555] The roots of the theory of *fraude à la loi* can be found in the French Cassation Court's judgment, made in 1878, in the case of *Princesse de Bauffremont* v. *Prince de Bauffremont,* where a French national had acquired the citizenship of the Duchy of Sachsen-Altenburg with the sole purpose of escaping French law standing in the way of her remarriage. The Court held that because of this the new marriage would not produce any legal effects in France. See, for example, J. Dolinger, *Recueil des cours*, Vol. 283 (2000), pp. 244-245.

being bound by the rules of the Swedish Inheritance Code on compulsory inheritance share for children. He consults his lawyer who informs him that pursuant to Swedish private international law, the validity of the contents of a will is decided by the law of the country of the testator's citizenship at the time of his death[556]. In order to avoid the Swedish rules on compulsory shares, the testator decides to change his citizenship. This does not necessarily mean that he has to leave Sweden and move abroad or that his property must be transferred from Sweden to a foreign country. There are countries where citizenship can be acquired, if you are sufficiently wealthy, at a distance, and a naturalization in a foreign State enables our hero to request a release from his Swedish citizenship. If read literally, the Swedish conflict rule will after this change of nationality designate the law of the new country of citizenship of the testator to govern the substantive validity of his will, and the mandatory restrictions imposed by the Swedish Inheritance Code will not apply to him any more. In other words, the testator has adapted the facts (his citizenship) to the Swedish conflict rule, so that the determination of the applicable law will suit his purpose. This type of manipulation of the law takes typically the form of an artificial creation of a foreign element, but may as well involve an artificial suppression of a foreign element or an artificial replacement of a foreign element with another foreign element. From a theoretical viewpoint, all such manipulations constitute both an abuse of the conflict rule of the forum and an evasion of the substantive rules that would apply in the absence of manipulation (or will apply if the attempted manipulation fails). The question is whether such

---

[556] See Chapter 1, Section 5, of the Swedish Act (1937:81) on Some International Relationships concerning Estates of Deceased Persons.

manipulations should be tolerated, and thus in fact be rewarded, or should rather be fought and rejected by the courts.

In the example above, the artificial change of citizenship was intended to replace the legal system that would otherwise be applied with another legal system which the testator prefers. The jurisdiction of Swedish courts is not affected; in fact, the scheme presupposes that the validity of the will is to be examined by Swedish courts, which have to abide by the Swedish conflict rules. There is, however, also a different variety of abuse of law related to private international law, where it is the jurisdiction of courts that is manipulated, usually (albeit not always) together with the rules on recognition of foreign judgments. The aim of the manipulation in these cases is to have the matter decided in a certain country, usually in the hope that the resulting judgment (or another public act, such as a celebration of marriage[557]) will be recognized also in the country whose jurisdiction the scheme attempts to avoid[558]. The most notorious example of this kind of abuse of private international law are the so-called "divorce havens", i.e. countries where in exchange for a relatively modest fee even temporary visitors can apply for and obtain a fast and simple divorce. Divorce candidates lacking any significant connection with

---

[557] One might mention the notorious "Gretna Green marriages", celebrated by a duly authorized blacksmith in the Scottish border town of Gretna Green at a time when the minimum age for marriage in Scots law was merely 16 years.

[558] It is important to stress that a certain degree of tactical forum shopping is sometimes quite legitimate, provided the matter has a close and natural connection with more than one country, but the method may become fraudulent if the proceedings are initiated in a country with which the matter has no such connection.

these countries ("divorce tourists") go there for a short visit and buy themselves a divorce[559], probably hoping that it will be valid also in the country of their habitual residence and that they in this way will achieve the same result as if they had obtained a divorce at home, even though divorce proceedings in their own country would be complicated, lengthy, expensive or even totally impossible.

There are many other types of "havens", such as corporate havens (e.g. Delaware in the United States), havens offering flags of convenience for ships (e.g. Panama), wrongful death and personal injury havens (e.g. the United States) and libel havens (e.g. England). The last-mentioned example seems to have given rise to significant "libel tourism"[560]. As English courts tend to apply the *lex fori* in libel cases and English libel law is extraordinarily claimant-friendly (for example, the claimant does not have to prove that the defamatory statement is false or malicious, and the damages awarded are relatively high), foreign claimants prefer to turn to English courts, "as a moth is drawn to the light"[561], even when the situation has merely peripheral connections with England. Even when both parties are foreign, it seems that for the English courts to assume jurisdiction it is sufficient that the defamatory material on the Internet has been downloaded to a computer situated in England or that a defamatory book has been purchased online from England. As most established

---

[559] The almost industrial production of divorces in a notorious divorce haven is illustrated by the American case of *Kugler* v. *Haitian Tours, Inc.* (293 A. 2d 706), decided by a New Jersey Superior Court in 1972. The case concerned a package tour to Haiti, including transportation, accommodation and even a Haitian divorce.

[560] See T. C. Hartley, *International Commercial Litigation*, pp. 277-278.

[561] *Ibid.*, p. 277.

newspapers have today an Internet version and most hard-cover books can be purchased from Internet book-stores such as Amazon, almost any publication any-where can potentially give rise to libel proceedings in England. It is true that in theory the English courts will in such cases deal only with damages resulting from distribution in England, but the amounts awarded are so high that they may achieve a world-wide deterrence effect. In a relatively recent case[562], the Internet orders placed by buyers in England for 23 copies of a book marketed only in the United States and written by an author domiciled in the United States, and the fact that one chapter of the book was available on an American website which was accessible in England, resulted in an English award of damages and costs of almost 115,000 pounds sterling (more than US$200,000) in favour of the claimant, who was a Saudi-Irish busi-nessman apparently living in Saudi Arabia. The risk of having to pay such amounts in England is normally sufficient to deter the defendant from publication any-where. In the same judgment, in addition to damages and costs the court issued an injunction requiring the defendant not to publish the material in England, which in view of the above-said meant *de facto* a world-wide prohibition of publication on or the sale via Internet as a whole. It has been hinted that some claimants, or persons acting on their behalf, have actu-ally ordered books to be delivered in England, or downloaded statements from the Internet to a computer situated in England, for the sole purpose of initiating a libel action in an English court. In many such cases, the dispute will never reach a court of law, because the defendants cannot afford to hire expensive London lawyers and are forced to surrender under the threats of

---

[562] *Bin Mahfouz* v. *Ehrenfeld*, [2005] EWHC 1156 (QB).

litigation. English jurisdictional and conflict rules can thus be used, or rather abused, in order to silence criticism in other countries as well.

An even more notorious example is the concentration of wrongful death and personal injury disputes in American courts. Many foreign plaintiffs prefer to sue there even when the dispute has a relatively weak connection with the United States and they could easily turn to the courts in their own countries. This preference is mainly due to the extremely high damages that American courts (and juries) commonly award plaintiffs in such cases, but there are also other factors making American courts attractive to plaintiffs, for example the contingent fee system used by American attorneys and the fact that American procedural law normally does not require the losing party to pay the winning party's costs. Some counter-balancing is achieved by means of the doctrine of *forum non conveniens*, allowing the American court to refuse, at its discretion, to exercise its jurisdiction if the forum is seriously inconvenient and a more appropriate forum is available elsewhere [563].

It is important to distinguish between typical cases of abuse of law described above and the cases of a pure simulation, where someone attempts to achieve certain advantages by asserting facts that are false, for example if the testator in the introductory example presents forged documents pretending that he has changed his citizenship, without actually having done so. Such falsified facts should naturally be disregarded if their true nature is disclosed [564]. The phenomenon of abuse of the

---

[563] See the leading case of *Gulf Oil Corp.* v. *Gilbert*, 330 US 501 (1947).

[564] See, for example, G. Kegel and K. Schurig, *Internationales Privatrecht*, p. 491. It has even occurred that the whole existence of the foreign country, the laws of

law is more complex and is characterized by the fact that the circumstances relied on by the manipulating party (for example, his acquisition of citizenship or habitual residence in a certain country) do really exist, although they have been created in order to obtain certain advantages of private international law nature. In the cases of a pure simulation there is thus no need to invoke the doctrine of *fraude à la loi*, as it suffices to note that the alleged connecting factor (citizenship, habitual residence, etc.) simply does not exist. A totally different matter is that pursuant to the procedural rules of the forum the court may sometimes be bound by facts on which the parties are in agreement, in particular in those types of disputes that can be resolved by a settlement[565].

It is hardly controversial to state that the abuse of private international law is normally a negative phenomenon, but it is disputed whether and how it should be dealt with. The answer varies from country to country and from legal issue to legal issue[566].

2. Possible Countermeasures

One conceivable approach would be to tolerate the abuse and say that everybody is entitled to use the existing rules for his benefit as long as he does not directly violate them. Such tolerant approach would, in fact, abolish the whole concept of *fraude à la loi*,

---

which were allegedly applicable, was simulated, see Ralf Michaels, "My Own Private Switzerland", *Zeitschrift für europäisches Privatrecht*, 1999, pp. 197-199, about a case concerning the recognition in Germany of a juridical person allegedly incorporated under the laws of the fictitious "Dominion of Melchizedek".

[565] See, for example, Chapter 35, Section 3, of the Swedish Code of Judicial Procedure.

[566] See, for example, R. H. Graveson, *Recueil des cours*, Vol. 109 (1963), pp. 48-58.

which would no longer constitute an abuse (just like the use of a permitted tax deduction does not constitute an abuse of tax law but rather a legitimate tax planning). For example, to the extent the private international law of the forum gives the parties an almost unlimited freedom to agree on the applicable law (see, for example, Article 3 of the EC Rome I Regulation No. 593/2008 of 17 June 2008 on the Law Applicable to Contractual Obligations[567]), it is difficult to see how party autonomy can be "abused" at all.

The opposite approach, based on the principle *fraus omnia corrumpit*, would disregard the artificially created connecting factor. Some partisans of this approach suggest that fraudulent practices should be fought using the public policy reservation[568], but this is hardly a solution suitable for all situations. While public policy is in principle used to avoid negative consequences of the substantive contents of the applicable foreign law, the abuse of the law has more to do with the manner in which the applicable law was designated. In other words, while public policy is used to protect substantive justice, the doctrine of *fraude à la loi* protects the justice on the level of conflicts of law *(internationalprivatrechtliche Gerechtigkeit)*[569]. Besides, public policy cannot be used against the application of the *lex fori* while measures against the abuse of the law are in principle equally called for irrespective of whether the intention of the abuse is to avoid the *lex fori*, to have the *lex fori* applied instead of the foreign law applicable under the conflict rules of the forum, or to have one foreign law applied instead of another foreign law. In all such situations, the manipulation constitutes an

---

[567] OJ 2008 L 177, p. 6.
[568] See Chapter X, *supra*.
[569] See G. Kegel and K. Schurig, *Internationales Privatrecht*, p. 494, and Chapter IV.2, *supra*.

abuse and circumvention of the forum's own conflict rules[570]. The conflict rules reflect the view of the legislator of the forum country that the application of certain foreign law is in some situations more appropriate than the application of the *lex fori*. This means that to evade the applicable foreign law artificially and replace it with the *lex fori* or with another foreign law amounts to circumventing the intentions of the legislator of the forum country and is equally reprehensible as evading the application of the substantive *lex fori*[571]. Similarly, attempts artificially to create jurisdiction of the courts in the forum country should be seen as equally reprehensible as corresponding attempts to avoid the jurisdiction of those courts.

In view of what has just been said, it is clear that the attitude towards evasion of foreign law should not depend on the degree of friendship between the foreign country in question and the country of the forum. Commercial and family relationships between private subjects should not be affected by the current political alliances or sympathies on the governmental level[572]. A strong animosity felt by the forum towards the application of the evaded foreign rule may, on the other hand, be taken into account if the application of that rule would be contrary to the forum's public policy, for example when a couple living in a country where they cannot marry because of racial impediments try to evade those impediments by entering into marriage in another country. Evasion of foreign rules manifestly incompatible with the fundamental principles of law in

---

[570] See, for example, B. Audit, *Droit international privé*, p. 203.

[571] See, for example, G. Parra-Aranguren, *Recueil des cours*, Vol. 210 (1988), p. 108.

[572] Cf. Chapter XII, *infra*, about the laws issued by a non-recognized State or government.

the forum country will usually not be reprobated by the courts and may even be supported by them.

One might ask whether the forum should not take into account the official attitude towards evasion of the law prevailing in the country whose law or jurisdiction has been evaded. For example, if the forum's conflict rules would in the absence of evasion designate the law of country A, but there is an artificially created connection with the country of the forum or a third country B, should the forum accept the evasion if such behaviour is tolerated in country A? This situation is to some extent similar to *renvoi* and it is submitted that it can be treated reasonably in the same manner, i.e. depending on whether the forum country's private international law accepts *renvoi* or not[573]. A somewhat different approach is recommended regarding manipulations with jurisdiction; if the foreign country whose jurisdiction has been avoided tolerates the evasion and is even willing to recognize the judgment made in a third country by a court whose jurisdiction has been created in an artificial manner, then there are no reasons why the forum should not tolerate it as well. If, for example, a couple residing habitually in California has purchased a quick divorce in Haiti, such divorce should be recognized by third countries if it is recognized in California. An over-zealous fight against the evasion of Californian law would in such a case be meaningless and even harmful, as it would increase the number of limping family relationships.

Undoubtedly, the best way of fighting the abuse of private international law is to formulate jurisdictional and conflict rules, as well as the rules on the recognition and enforcement of foreign judgments, in such a way that they are not easy to manipulate, although there are limits to what can be achieved by such pre-

---

[573] See Chapter IX, *supra*.

ventive considerations. The introduction of a general "escape clause" *(clause échappatoire)*, making it possible in a particular case to deviate from the usual conflict rules when they do not lead to the application of the legal system having the closest and most relevant connection to the dispute, is one possible method that can be used to combat the abuse, as an artificially created connecting factor carries hardly much weight in such context[574]. For example, Article 4, point 1, of the EC Regulation No. 864/2007 of 11 July 2007 on the Law Applicable to Non-Contractual Obligations (Rome II)[575] contains a general conflict rule designating the law of the country in which the damage occurs (unless the person claimed to be liable and the person sustaining damage both have their habitual residence in the same country when the damage occurs), but Article 4, point 3, adds that where it is clear from all the circumstances of the case that the tort/delict is manifestly more closely connected with another country, the law of that other country will apply. If the connection with the country in which the damage occurred has been created artificially for the purpose of making the law of that country applicable, this escape clause may be a sufficiently efficient instrument for combating the abuse, so that the special doctrine of *fraude à la loi* need not be used[576]. The same can be said of all those

---

[574] See, for example, E. Jayme, *Recueil des cours*, Vol. 251 (1995), pp. 244-245.

[575] OJ 2007 L 199, p. 40.

[576] As far as potential abuse of jurisdictional rules in concerned, see for example Article 3, point 1, of the EC Regulation No. 1346/2000 of 29 May 2000 on Insolvency Proceedings, OJ 2000 L 160, p. 1, which gives jurisdiction to open insolvency proceedings to the courts of the Member State within the territory of which the centre of the debtor's main interests (his so-called COMI) is situated. This is a jurisdictional criterion which is difficult to

"revolutionary" approaches to private international law
that dislike specific conflict rules and prefer broad formulas allowing the court to avoid undesirable results
without having to rely on any doctrine of abuse[577]. Of
course, the use of such broad formulas and escape
clauses has serious disadvantages, primarily the lack of
predictability.

Some more specific connecting factors, such as the
location of immovable property, cannot be created in a
fraudulent manner at all, and several other factors,
albeit possible to alter by unilateral action of the per-
son(s) concerned, are difficult to abuse. For example, a
real change of one's habitual residence requires usually
a great deal of effort and a certain amount of sacrifice
on the part of the person concerned, and it is doubtful
whether the intolerance towards tactical changes of
habitual residence is always really well founded. If a
person really does change his habitual residence and
moves permanently to a country whose laws he prefers,
it seems quite appropriate to accept it. It is relatively
common and normally considered legitimate that people genuinely change their domicile or even citizenship

---

abuse by the debtor and can even less be abused by a creditor requesting the opening of bankruptcy proceedings. In
the case of a company or legal person, there is, however, a
presumption that the place of the registered office is the
centre of its main interests. This presumption might seem
easy to abuse, but it can be refuted if factors which are
objective and ascertainable by third parties show that an
actual situation exists which is different from that which
locating the centre of the main interests at the registered
office is deemed to reflect, in particular in the cases of
"letterbox companies" not carrying out any business in the
Member States in which the registered office is situated.
See the judgment of the EC Court of Justice in the case of
Eurofood (case C-341/04, decided on 2 May 2006).

[577] See, for example, A. A. Ehrenzweig, *Recueil des
cours*, Vol. 124 (1968), p. 249.

because of tax law, so why should it not be equally legitimate to do so because of private-law rules such as the rules on inheritance, provided naturally that the move is genuine and not merely a simulated one? With regard to real alterations of such connecting factors as habitual residence, it is thus normally appropriate to be generous and tolerant[578].

It can also be argued that a naturalization decision, made by the competent authorities of the forum country, should bind the court even in the context of private international law. If those authorities have granted citizenship of the forum country to a certain person, then it can be assumed that they have examined the legal requirements for naturalization and found them fulfilled and the citizenship thus acquired should be respected and given effect in all parts of the legal system, including private international law. The forum owes no such respect to the naturalization decisions of other countries, but to the extent such decisions are based on the fulfilment of normal requirements such as a residence of several years, they should be respected too, regardless of the motives of the person concerned. The answer may be different if the person concerned has simply purchased a foreign citizenship without there being any real ties between him and the foreign country in question.

On the other hand, there are connecting factors that are very easy to misuse. In many countries there is, for example, a conflict rule stipulating that non-contractual liability (mainly liability for damage caused by a tort) is governed by the law of the country where the harmful act was committed[579]. In these days, when harm can

---

[578] See F. Schwind, *Recueil des cours*, Vol. 187 (1984), p. 93.

[579] This was, for example, the position of Swedish private international law prior to the EC Regulation

often be caused at a distance, for example by uploading defamatory statements on the Internet from a laptop computer or an Internet café anywhere in the world, the application of the law of the place of the harmful act may practically invite wrongdoers to commit torts from a country with substantive tort rules they find advantageous. It is almost equally easy to abuse the principle of *locus regit actum* and make a will or a contract in a certain country in order to avoid the formal requirements imposed by the law of the country whose law would otherwise govern the formal validity of the legal act in question. At the same time, to refrain generally from the use of some of these relatively easily manipulated connecting factors is not a realistic alternative, as they are under normal circumstances very useful and quite appropriate. Abolishing them would frequently lead to unacceptable results detrimental to the legitimate interests and expectations of many innocent parties.

A problematic aspect of the *fraude à la loi* doctrine is the need to prove the intention (which can hardly be other than a direct one, *dolus directus*) of the person(s) concerned to alter the relevant connecting factor in order to achieve certain legal advantages under the rules of private international law. For example, the reasons why the wrongdoer has committed the wrongful act or the testator made his will in a certain country other than his own may be totally unrelated to any fraudulent intention on his part. On the other hand, such intention can sometimes be presumed, for example concerning a quick divorce obtained in a notorious divorce haven after a sojourn of a few days there. The matter may be further complicated by the fact that even

No. 864/2007 of 11 July 2007 on the Law Applicable to Non-Contractual Obligations (Rome II), OJ 2007 L 199, p. 40.

when the fraudulent intent is obvious it may sometimes be uncertain which law has been evaded. If both spouses are citizens of country A and they both reside habitually in country B, it is easy to establish that their purchase of a quick divorce in the notorious divorce haven C was *in fraudem legis*, but it may be more difficult to ascertain the avoided law: did they intend to avoid the law of A, B or both?

This may be of some practical importance, especially if the evaded legal system's attitude towards the abuse is allowed to play a role for the determination of the appropriate counter-reaction by the forum (see *supra*).

It is possible, in order to increase foreseeability, to enact specific rules on certain frequent types of *fraude à la loi*. Thus, a Swedish statutory rule requires in principle for the recognition of foreign (non-European) divorces that the couple had such connection or connections with the country of the judgment that it was "appropriate" for them to obtain a divorce there, albeit even other divorces, including those obtained in a divorce haven, become valid in Sweden if one or both of the spouses subsequently contracted a new marriage[580].

The risk of creating and having to deal with bigamous marriages was obviously considered to be an excessively high price to pay for stopping the abuse of the law in these cases.

Sweden also provides good examples of special statutory regulation intended to prevent the evasion of *foreign* laws. Until 1 May 2009, Swedish law allowed same-sex couples to register a partnership, which had legal effects almost identical to those of a marriage. The procedure and form of such registration, as well as

---

[580] See Chapter 3, Section 7, of the Swedish Act (1904: 26, p. 1) on Some International Marriage and Guardianship Relationships.

its substantive preconditions (impediments, etc.), were determined in accordance with Swedish law[581]. It was feared that this general application of the Swedish *lex loci celebrationis* could lead to the rise of "registration tourism", i.e. attract same-sex couples from countries without registered partnerships to come to Sweden for a short-time visit in order to register their partnership there. It was, therefore, considered inappropriate to follow the same approach as that used regarding the celebrations of marriages and open the possibility to register a partnership even when none of the parties had a permanent and close relation to Sweden. In order to avoid the risk of Sweden becoming a "registration haven", and in order to prevent the creation of a large number of limping partnership registrations (i.e. Swedish registrations that would be refused recognition abroad), Chapter 1, Section 2, of the Registered Partnership Act provided that a Swedish registration could take place only if at least one of the partners was habitually resident in Sweden since at least two years, *or* if at least one of the partners was a Swedish citizen with habitual residence in Sweden. On 1 May 2009, the Registered Partnership Act was repealed and same-sex couples were at the same time permitted to enter into regular marriages, subject to the same rules as the traditional, heterosexual marriages, for which there is, as has just been mentioned, no requirement of a similar connection with Sweden, so that even foreign couples on a short-time visit can enter into marriage there[582]. A

---

[581] See Chapter 1, Section 3, para. 4, and Section 9 of the Swedish Registered Partnership Act (1994:1117).

[582] In a judgment of 17 April 2007, the Court of First Instance of Hasselt (Belgium) found that the exception of *fraude à la loi* did not apply when a man from India and a woman from the Netherlands married in Sweden without having any natural connection with Sweden at all. The Belgian city to which they moved refused to recognize the

relatively new Swedish conflict rule, enacted in 2004, requires, however, that if none of the couple to be married is a Swedish citizen or habitual resident, then in addition to complying with Swedish law each of them must show that he or she has the capacity to marry under the law of his/her country of nationality or his/her country of habitual residence[583]. This makes it difficult to use Sweden as a "marriage haven", even though an escape clause makes it possible, when the circumstances in the individual case provide "special reasons" for an exception, to celebrate the marriage in Sweden even if the couple (or one of them) has capacity to marry under Swedish law only.

In some branches of business activity, artificially created connections with a certain country (and thereby with its legal system) are widely used and generally accepted, for example in respect of the registrations ("flags") of convenience for commercial ships. Even when the ship has manifestly no natural relation whatsoever to the country of its registration (often Panama or Liberia), it appears to be almost universally recognized that it is, in principle, the law of that country that governs legal relationships on board the ship[584].

Swedish marriage on the basis of *fraude à la loi*, arguing that the couple should have married in the Netherlands or in Belgium, and only went to Sweden because of the less stringent legal requirements there. The court found that the marriage should be recognized, mentioning that this was not a simulated marriage. This footnote is based on a short report of the case posted on 16 May 2007 by Thalia Kruger on www.conflictoflaws.net.

[583] Chapter 1, Section 1, of the Swedish Act (1904:26) on Some International Marriage and Guardianship Relationships (as amended in 2004).

[584] See, for example, the decision of the Swedish Supreme Court in *Nytt Juridiskt Arkiv*, 1987, p. 885, regarding the validity of collective agreements and individual employment contracts pertaining to the ship's crew.

Similarly, the rules creating an integrated common market, consisting of a number of Member or Contracting States and characterized by a free movement of persons, goods, services and capital, may, regarding certain matters, intentionally provide for the right of businesses and other economic actors to choose freely the most advantageous among the legal systems of all the participating countries. For example, the EU rules on the freedom of establishment offer businessmen the possibility of avoiding the company law of the Member State where they wish to do business by using a company registered in another Member State with a more advantageous company legislation, irrespective of the fact that the company in question will do no business at all in the country of its registration, where it exists as a mere "letter-box" company, and regardless of the fact that it has been created there exclusively for the purpose of carrying out its business in another Member State[585]. Another example is the so-called "Italian torpedo", i.e. the abuse of the *lis pendens* rule in Article 27 of the EC Brussels I Regulation No. 44/2001 of 22 December 2000 on Jurisdiction and the Recognition and Enforcement of Judgments in Civil and Commercial Matters[586]. As a consequence of the ECJ judgment in the case of *Gasser* v.

---

[585] See the judgments of the EC Court in the cases of *Centros* v. *Erhvervs- og Selskabsstyrelsen* (case C-212/97, decided on 9 March 1999), *Überseering* v. *NCC* (case C-208/00, decided on 5 November 2002), and *Kamer van Koophandel* v. *Inspire Art Ltd.* (case C-167/01, decided on 30 September 2003). At the same time, the EC Regulation No. 1346/2000 of 29 May 2000 on Insolvency Proceedings, OJ 2000 L 160, p. 1, does not accept such "letter-box" company address as a basis for bankruptcy jurisdiction, see Article 3, point 1, of the Regulation and point 35 in the EC Court's judgment in the case of *Eurofood* (case C-341/04, decided on 2 May 2006).

[586] OJ 2001 L 12, p. 1.

MISAT[587], proceedings pending in a Member State prevent initiation of new proceedings, involving the same
cause of action and between the same parties, in
another Member State even if the first-mentioned
Member State manifestly lacks jurisdiction and the
case was brought there solely because, due to the slow
working pace of the courts of that Member State, it
will take a long time before they dismiss the case and
the other party can start legitimate proceedings in a
Member State having jurisdiction. On the other hand,
the ECJ has on other occasions declared that EU law
must in no case be extended to cover abuses, that is to
say, activities which are not carried out in the context
of normal commercial transactions but only with the
aim of circumventing the EU rules. Thus, when the law
applicable to manning of ships performing maritime
cabotage transport between ports in the same State
depended, pursuant to an EC regulation, on whether
the voyage followed or preceded a voyage to or from
another State, the EC Court held that such following or
preceding international voyage must not be taken into
account when its sole purpose was to make the law of
the ship's flag applicable instead of the law of the State
where the cabotage transport was performed[588].

It follows from what has been said that the whole
issue of abuse of private international law is complicated and not suitable for simple and general solutions.
It is submitted that the courts should have the authority
to take countermeasures against flagrant abuses of private international law, although they should take such
measures only when they find that it is appropriate to

---

[587] Case C-116/02, decided on 9 December 2003. See
M. Bogdan, *Scandinavian Studies in Law*, Vol. 51 (2007),
pp. 89-97.
[588] See *Agip* v. *Capitaneria di porto di Siracusa* (case
C-456/04, decided on 6 April 2006).

do so having regard to the circumstances in the individual case and the potential consequences of refusing to give effect to the artificially created connection[589]. Such flexibility will make it possible to take into consideration such factors as, for example, the nature and importance of the evaded substantive rules, the potential effects on the legitimate interests of third parties who had acted in good faith, the time that has passed since the fraudulent connection was created, or whether the party invoking the fraud was itself actively involved in it[590].

---

[589] See, for example, M. Bogdan, *Svensk internationell privat- och processrätt*, pp. 95-99; P. A. Nielsen, *International privat- og procesret*, pp. 75-80.

[590] See, for example, B. Audit, *Droit international privé*, pp. 202 and 204.

CHAPTER XII

FOREIGN RULES MADE BY NON-STATE
OR UNRECOGNIZED ENTITIES

1. Non-State Rules

While conflict rules are normally understood as referring to "law", defined as rules upheld by State power (including rules recognized by territorial subdivisions of a State such as provinces or municipalities), it happens occasionally that the parties agree, or are assumed to agree, on the application of non-State rules, for example by subjecting their commercial contract to the Unidroit Principles of International Commercial Contracts, the Lando Commission's Principles of European Contract Law, the Common Frame of Reference of European Private Law, *"lex mercatoria"*, etc.[591] As these and other similar private or semi-private sets of rules usually are not sufficiently comprehensive to regulate all potential problems that may arise, there is a substantial role left to be played by legal rules, but sometimes the parties seem to attempt to exclude all legal systems and agree to subject their contract exclusively to its own provisions (so-called self-regulating contracts, such as when the contract stipulates that "the law between the parties is the contract itself") or provide that all disputes arising out of the contract should be resolved pursuant to "natural law", "natural justice", "the holy Sharia", "Roman law"[592] etc. Various combi-

---

[591] See, for example, A. Bucher, *Recueil des cours*, Vol. 341 (2009), pp. 85-92 and 140-157.

[592] Roman law used, of course, to be a regular valid legal system, but is today perceived as an ideal, non-State set of rules.

nations of legal and non-State rules are also possible, for example a choice-of-law clause saying that "Subject to the principles of the Glorious Sharia, this Agreement shall be governed by and construed in accordance with the laws of England."[593] The validity and legal effects of such choices of non-State rules have been much discussed and are not uncontroversial.

To begin with, it is important to differentiate between contracts that are intended to be legally binding and those that are mere gentle-men's agreements, expected to be complied with voluntarily or under the pressure of moral or religious rather than legal rules. The demarcation line between these two types of agreements is procedural rather than depending on the rules governing the substantive rights and duties of the parties. What is decisive is whether the parties intended to enter into an agreement which can ultimately, after judicial, arbitral or other similar proceedings, be enforced by the machinery of the State. There is, of course, nothing forbidding the parties to make purely moral agreements renouncing all involvement of the State power, but such agreements are beyond the scope of this presentation and will not be dealt with here. Instead, I shall focus on references to non-State rules in those contracts that are intended to be legally binding and enforceable as such.

Today it is the prevailing view that every contract that is intended to be legally binding must be subject to an existing national legal system governing its contents and material validity. There are exceptions though; there seems to be an increasing support in the legal literature for the opinion favouring the right of the parties to choose freely among both State and private sets of rules, including their right to subject the contract

---

[593] See the English case of *Beximco* v. *Shamil Bank*, [2004] 1 WLR 1784 (Court of Appeal).

exclusively to "self-standing" or "floating" rules independent of all national legal systems.

This matter was discussed extensively in connection with the enactment of the EC Regulation No. 593/2008 of 17 June 2008 on the Law Applicable to Contractual Obligations (Rome I)[594]. The Commission's proposal allowed the parties to choose as the applicable law "the principles and rules of the substantive law of contract recognised internationally or in the Community"[595], but even this limited possibility to choose non-State sets of rules, excluding obscure private codifications and imprecise concepts such as the *lex mercatoria*, was at the end of the day abandoned in the final wording of the Regulation, whose Article 3, dealing with the freedom of the parties to choose the law governing the contract, continues to be interpreted as excluding the choice of non-State bodies of law. It is true that Recital 13 points out that the Regulation does not preclude the parties from incorporating by reference into their contract non-State rules or international conventions, but it appears to have in mind merely those situations where such incorporation replaces non-mandatory provisions of the legal system governing the contract pursuant to the Regulation's conflict rules.

The last-mentioned situations, where the chosen non-State rules in question deal only with matters that are, in the legal system governing the contract, regulated by non-mandatory substantive legal rules, are relatively unproblematic. In such cases, the reference to these non-State rules simply incorporates them as contractual terms validly agreed on within the framework of the freedom of contract enjoyed by the parties pursuant to the applicable legal system. To the extent the

---

[594] See A. V. M. Struycken, *Recueil des cours*, Vol. 311 (2004), pp. 390-394.
[595] COM(2005)650, p. 5.

non-State rules are incompatible with mandatory provisions of the governing legal system, that system prevails though. However, within foreseeable future this may change, at least in the EU Member States. Pursuant to Recital 14 of the Rome I Regulation, future EU legal instruments, adopting rules of substantive contract law including standard terms and conditions, "may provide that the parties may choose to apply those rules". This seems to imply that such future substantive rules of EU law may be chosen by the parties even if they are incompatible with mandatory provisions of the national legal system otherwise governing the contract in question.

2. Rules Issued by Unrecognized States or Governments

As pointed out at the outset, when a conflict rule of the forum country refers to a foreign legal system, it has in principle in mind only those rules that fall within the definition of "law", and not other rules such as decrees issued by a group of private persons, regardless of whether the persons in question consider themselves to be the rightful Government of the foreign country or even pretend to represent a new, independent country of their own. It is not quite easy to define which rules deserve in this respect to be called "law", but in order to belong to that category they should normally be upheld by an organized apparatus having a relatively stable and effective control of the foreign territory in question.

A similar problem may arise in connection with the recognition and enforcement of foreign judgments, where it may sometimes be disputed whether the foreign decision was made by a court created or at least accepted as such by an entity that can be considered to be a foreign State.

Occasionally it may be difficult for the forum to obtain a reliable and complete picture of the situation in a distant foreign country, for example when a civil war makes it uncertain which is the real and legitimate Government there (similar questions may arise when a border dispute between two foreign countries gives rise to doubts as to which of them is to be considered the legitimate sovereign over a certain territory). The court cannot normally refuse to adjudicate the dispute or stay the proceedings until the situation in the foreign country becomes sufficiently clear[596]; it would be equally wrong to treat the foreign country as a legal vacuum where there is no law at all. In such situations, it might seem natural that the court seeks and relies on information and guidance provided by the forum country's Ministry of Foreign Affairs or some other similar body. This entails, however, a certain danger that instead of forming its own opinion the forum might, even in the context of private international law, blindly follow the official policy of the forum country's Government, as expressed by its diplomatic recognition or non-recognition of the foreign State or Government in question. Some countries adhere openly to the so-called "recognition doctrine", pursuant to which the forum should in principle be bound by the official position taken by the Government of the forum State towards the foreign entity whose laws or judicial decisions are to be applied or recognized/enforced.

The United Kingdom seems to be the country where the recognition doctrine used to play the most important role. Until 1980, British courts did not officially recognize a law or act of a foreign Government unless it was a law or act either of a foreign Government recognized by Her Majesty's Government in the United Kingdom or of a subordinate body set up by such a for-

---

[596] Cf. the similar reasoning in Chapter VII.3, *supra*.

eign Government to act on its behalf[597], even though
the British courts were conscious of the fact that a rigid
adherence to the recognition doctrine could often lead
to unacceptable results which needed to be avoided in
some manner. Perhaps the most notorious case on
point is *Carl Zeiss Stiftung* v. *Rayner and Keeler Ltd.*
from 1967[598], where a juridical person incorporated
under the laws of East Germany (German Democratic
Republic) initiated an action in English courts in order
to prevent the use by the defendants of the "Carl Zeiss"
name. The defendants demanded that the action be dismissed on the ground that the representatives of the
plaintiff, albeit entitled to represent it under East
German law, were not to be considered its lawful representatives in England as they had been set up by a
decree of the (at that time) unrecognized Government
of the German Democratic Republic. The defendants
argued that the English courts had to ignore the decrees
of that unrecognized body which had to be considered
a nullity in the eyes of English law. When the case
reached the House of Lords, it was held by that court
that although the German Democratic Republic was
not recognized by Her Majesty's Government, its acts
could and should be recognized by the English courts
as acts done by a subordinate body which the true sovereign — the recognized Soviet Union — set up to act
on its behalf!

Today, such rather artificial constructions enabling
the English courts to avoid impractical results while
formally respecting the recognition doctrine are no
longer needed, as the British Government, instead of
issuing certificates as to whether a foreign regime is

---

[597] See *Dicey and Morris on the Conflict of Laws*,
p. 997.
[598] [1967] AC 853 (House of Lords), 43 *International
Law Reports* 23.

recognized, limits itself nowadays to assisting the courts by providing information about the situation in the country in question[599]. On the European Continent, the recognition doctrine has never become popular, even though some traces of it can sometimes be found in older judicial practice[600].

The forum State's policy of granting or refusing a *de jure* or *de facto* recognition to foreign States and regimes can most frequently be assumed to correspond to a realistic evaluation of the situation in the foreign country, but this is not always the case. Due to various, more-or-less legitimate political reasons, the forum State may choose to recognize political entities or Governments that are mere fictions or, on the other hand, decide not to recognize political entities or Governments in spite of their undisputed factual existence. For example, some countries continued to recognize officially the Baltic republics of Estonia, Latvia and Lithuania as independent sovereign States even during the more than four decades of Soviet annexation, although their Governments in exile had no control of what was going on in their respective territories, while most countries today refuse to recognize the Republic of China even though for all practical purposes it certainly functions as an independent country as far as the island of Taiwan is concerned.

The recognition or non-recognition policy of the forum State may be guided by the most respectable intentions, but it should not, as such, be decisive for the application of foreign law or recognition and enforcement of foreign judgments in civil disputes, where the effective and stable control of the foreign territory

---

[599] See *Dicey and Morris on the Conflict of Laws*, pp. 997-998.

[600] See, for example, the Swedish Svea Court of Appeal in *Nytt Juridiskt Arkiv*, 1929, p. 471.

and its population should alone be decisive[601]. The application of laws enacted by a foreign entity, or the recognition or enforcement of judgments made by a foreign entity, has never been considered to imply any recognition in the sense of public international law. It can thus hardly be said that a court applying the law of a non-recognized State or Government, or recognizing or enforcing a judgment emanating from such an entity, contradicts the policy of the executive branch of the Government of the country of the forum.

Most importantly, it must be recalled that the application of foreign law is not a service rendered to the foreign State as such. Private international law concerns the everyday life of natural and juridical persons regarding family matters, succession, contracts, torts, property, etc.

The recognition of marriages celebrated in Taiwan by Taiwanese officials in accordance with Taiwanese law should not depend on whether the forum State likes or dislikes the regime there, but rather on whether the Taiwanese authorities have a stable and effective control of the territory and its inhabitants, so that they can enforce their laws there.

Couples living in Taiwan can probably marry and divorce there only in accordance with Taiwanese law and using Taiwanese officials and courts, so that their marriages and divorces should be recognized in other countries regardless of the lack of diplomatic recognition as such, provided of course that all the other conditions for applying foreign law or recognizing foreign

---

[601] See, for example, B. Audit, *Droit international privé*, pp. 245-246; E. Jayme, *Recueil des cours*, Vol. 251 (1995), p. 623; G. Kegel and K. Schurig, *Internationales Privatrecht*, p. 21; K. Lipstein, *Recueil des cours*, Vol. 135 (1972), pp. 187-188; G. Parra-Aranguren, *Recueil des cours*, Vol. 210 (1988), pp. 71-72; J. Verhoeven, *Recueil des cours*, Vol. 192 (1985), p. 180.

decisions have been fulfilled. Similarly, there is no reason to refuse to apply Taiwanese law on contracts,
companies or other private-law matters, provided
Taiwanese law is applicable under the conflict rules of
the forum country.

CHAPTER XIII

LEGAL PHENOMENA UNKNOWN
TO THE *LEX FORI*

The conflict rules of the forum deal usually with legal relationships and legal problems known in the substantive private law of the forum country. They speak about the conclusion, dissolution and effect of marriages, validity of wills and contracts, maintenance obligations towards children, etc. There are normally no established conflict rules on legal phenomena unknown to the *lex fori*. It is, for example, rare that non-Islamic countries enact conflict rules on such matters as the Islamic *mahr* (a kind of bride price to be paid by the bridegroom). Does this mean that foreign substantive provisions concerning legal phenomena unknown in the *lex fori* cannot be applied and that they consequently cannot be given any effect in the forum country?

It should be recalled that one of the main purposes of private international law is to ensure that private-law relationships are governed by the legal system with which they are most closely and significantly connected. If a situation is so connected with a foreign country, it is normally appropriate to apply even those rules of that country that have no counterpart in the *lex fori*, provided of course that their application does not violate the public policy of the forum. The lack of a corresponding legal institution in the *lex fori* does not necessarily mean that the foreign institution is incompatible with the forum's public policy[602]. In Sweden,

---

[602] See, for example, A. Bucher, *Recueil des cours*, Vol. 239 (1993), p. 23.

for example, the duty of children to pay maintenance to their needy parents was abolished more than a quarter of a century ago, not because the Swedish legislator had any moral or other objections against the children helping their needy parents but rather because such maintenance was not considered necessary any more due to the Swedish public social insurance system which provides for pensions or at least guarantees basic welfare benefits for all individuals residing in the country. The existence of such guarantees under the Swedish welfare system does not, of course, constitute a reasonable ground for refusing maintenance payments to a parent living in a foreign country without similar social security protection, who initiates proceedings in a Swedish court against his children living in Sweden. The fact that there is today[603] no statutory or other established Swedish conflict rule regarding the duty of children to support their needy parents is not an insurmountable obstacle. In Sweden, like in many other countries (including numerous countries with codified legal systems of the Romano-Germanic continental type), the statutory conflict rules are not exhaustive and leave substantial gaps to be filled by the creative activities of the courts.

It is also quite common that an existing conflict rule is formulated or can at least be interpreted in such a general manner that it covers even certain legal phenomena not existing in the forum country's substantive private law. A conflict rule providing that "maintenance obligations arising out of a family relationship

---

[603] This situation will change when the Hague Protocol of 23 November 2007 on the Law Applicable to Maintenance Obligations becomes applicable in the EU, see Article 15 of the EC Regulation No. 4/2009 of 18 December 2008 on Jurisdiction, Applicable Law, Recognition and Enforcement of Decisions and Cooperation in Matters Relating to Maintenance Obligations, OJ 2009 L 7, p. 1.

are governed by the law of the country of the maintenance creditor's habitual residence" would obviously also cover maintenance obligations towards parents irrespective of whether such obligations exist under the substantive law of the forum country or not. This example also illustrates that the answer to the question about whether a particular legal relationship is really unknown in the *lex fori* may depend on the level of generalization. Maintenance obligation towards parents may be seen in Sweden as a phenomenon unknown in Swedish law, but it can instead be considered to be merely a special type of the well-known concept of maintenance obligations based on family ties. Similarly, it is an open question whether the same-sex marriages existing today in some countries such as Belgium, Netherlands, Spain and Sweden, would in the eyes of the courts in other countries constitute a phenomenon unknown in their law or just a variety of the well-known concepts of marriage or registered partnership.

It is submitted that the concepts used in the forum country's conflict rules should be interpreted generously as comprising even foreign legal institutions not corresponding exactly to but closely related to their counterparts in the forum country's law[604]. True, the classification or reclassification of some unknown legal phenomena in order to make them fit into the existing conflict rules of the forum country is not always simple. It may even happen that different aspects of the same foreign legal phenomenon fall within the scope of different conflict rules of the forum. For example, in at least one Swedish judgment the above-mentioned *mahr* of Islamic law was subjected to the Swedish conflict rule on maintenance

---

[604] Cf. the discussion of the classification problem in Chapter VIII.5, *supra*.

obligations between ex-spouses, whereas another
Swedish court concluded that it was an issue pertaining
to the matrimonial property regime[605]. Both these classifications can be defended, as the purpose of *mahr* is
to contribute to the ex-wife's maintenance and, at the
same time, to achieve a certain re-distribution of the
property of the spouses. Speaking for Swedish private
international law, I submit that it should be admitted
openly that the established Swedish conflict rules have
not been formulated with *mahr* in mind and are applicable to *mahr* merely by a very extensive interpretation
or by analogy. The choice between the two alternative
Swedish conflict rules (the conflict rule on maintenance and the conflict rule on matrimonial property
regime) should be made taking into account the circumstances of the spouses in the individual case under
scrutiny. Is the *mahr* in an individual case presumably
intended mainly to provide the (ex-)wife with the
everyday necessities of life, such as when it is payable
upon the dissolution of marriage following the repudi-
ation of the wife by the husband, it seems natural to
consider it to be a kind of lump-sum maintenance,
while conflict rules on the division of matrimonial
property are closer at hand if the *mahr* appears to
have more to do with the equalization of the property
situation of the spouses, such as when it is payable at
the beginning of the marriage. Such distinctions are,
naturally, not always easy to make.

---

[605] See Chapter VIII.4, *supra*.

CHAPTER XIV

PRELIMINARY QUESTIONS

1. The Problem

It happens that the court, in order to be able to decide the disputed issue, must first decide a preliminary question concerning another matter, which is subject to a different conflict rule than the main question. For example, in a dispute on the duty of a spouse to pay alimonies to the other spouse, the court may be compelled to deal even with the maintenance debtor's objection that the marriage is null and void because it was not concluded in a proper form. The decision of the court on such "preliminary" or "incidental" question (in France called *question préalable*, and in Germany known as *Vorfrage*) may be decisive for the answer to the main question, but in most countries it has normally no binding force outside of the proceedings where it was made, so that the judicial statement on the validity of a marriage made in a maintenance dispute does not bind other courts in the same country when they a couple of years later have to adjudicate on the validity of the same marriage in a dispute about, for example, inheritance. Those cases where the validity of a marriage is examined as a preliminary issue must thus be distinguished from the cases where the same question arises as the main issue in the proceedings, for example in a case where the plaintiff asks for a judicial declaration that the marriage is null and void.

Preliminary questions of the above-described type may, of course, arise also in purely domestic cases without any cross-border dimensions, but in situations involving private international law they create complications of a special kind. This is in particular true in connection with "limping" relationships, i.e. relationships that are valid in the country of the forum but invalid in the country of the applicable foreign law *(lex causae)* or vice versa[606]. The relationship may be limping due to differences in conflict rules (for example, when the validity of a marriage is in the forum country considered to be governed by a law different from the law applied in the country of the *lex causae*) or differences in rules on recognition of foreign decisions (for example, a divorce judgment valid in the forum country may be refused recognition in the country of the *lex causae* or vice versa).

Assume that a childless Ruritanian national habitually residing in Sweden dies intestate and a dispute about the distribution of his estate arises in a Swedish court. Pursuant to current Swedish private international law, the distribution is governed by Ruritanian law as the last *lex patriae* of the deceased[607]. Assume also that Ruritanian substantive succession law gives the whole estate of a childless person to his surviving spouse and, if the deceased was not married and his parents are dead, to his siblings. It turns out that some time before his death, the deceased married in Germany and that this marriage is valid in Sweden pursuant to the rules of Swedish private international law. The same marriage is, however, because of some reason pertaining to form not valid in Ruritania, i.e. the country whose law is to be applied to the distribution of the estate. Assume finally that a brother of the deceased claims the estate for himself, relying on the invalidity of the

<hr>

[606] See, for example, T. Svenné Schmidt, *Recueil des cours*, Vol. 233 (1992), pp. 319-320.

[607] See Chapter 1, Section 1, of the Swedish Act (1937:81) on Some International Relationships concerning Estates of Deceased Persons.

marriage. His lawyer argues that the term "surviving spouse" in the Ruritanian succession rule must be interpreted loyally, i.e. in the Ruritanian way, so that only marriages that are valid in the eyes of Ruritania can be taken into account. As could be expected, the lawyer representing the widow is of a different opinion. In his view, Ruritanian law should be applied merely to issues of inheritance law, and the validity of the deceased's marriage is not one of them. The widow's lawyer argues that even when examined within the framework of application of Ruritanian inheritance law, the question whether the deceased was married and to whom is a separate issue, where the applicable law must be determined by Swedish conflict rules on marriages and not indirectly by Swedish conflict rules on inheritance.

2. *The Two Possible Approaches*

The two opposing views in the described example illustrate the two fundamental alternative methods of dealing with preliminary questions in private international law. The first method, which is usually denoted "the *lex causae* approach", is based on the theory that the preliminary question should be answered in the same way as it would be answered in the country of the applicable law. In the example above, this method leads to the result that the widow will lose her right to inherit her husband, as her marriage is not valid in Ruritania. i.e. the country whose law governs, pursuant to the Swedish conflict rules, the distribution of her husband's estate. The fact that the same marriage is valid in Sweden for other purposes (such as maintenance or presumption of paternity that are governed by Swedish law or by the law of a third country recognizing the marriage) is according to this approach of no importance.

The other, alternative method is usually called "the *lex fori* approach"[608], because it makes the *lex fori*, including the conflict rules of the forum country, decisive for answering the preliminary question; the answer to the preliminary question should, according to this method, be the same as if that question were examined in the forum country as the main question in separate proceedings. As the marriage in the example above would be considered valid if examined as the main issue in Swedish separate proceedings, this approach means that it must be considered valid even when dealt with as a preliminary issue for the purposes of Ruritanian inheritance law. The *lex fori* approach would thus give the widow in the example above the right to inherit.

The choice between the two methods is, naturally, relevant only if they lead to different answers to the main question[609]. The fundamental precondition of this happening is that the main question is governed by foreign law, i.e. the *lex causae* and the *lex fori* must not be the same legal system[610]. Further, the preliminary issue must be an issue of law and not of a mere fact[611].

---

[608] In Germany it is called *"selbständliche Anknüpfung"*, see T. Svenné Schmidt, *Recueil des cours*, Vol. 233 (1992), pp. 320-321.

[609] See, for example, T. Svenné Schmidt, *Recueil des cours*, Vol. 233 (1992), p. 317.

[610] Cf., however, the decision of the German Constitutional Court dated 30 November 1982, where on the basis of Article 6 (1) of the German Constitution (protection of marriage and family) the widow of a limping marriage invalid in Germany but valid in the country of the citizenship of the spouses was held to be entitled to certain financial benefits granted to widows by German welfare law (the *lex fori*!), see *IPRax*, 1984, p. 88, and E. Jayme, *Recueil des cours*, Vol. 251 (1995), pp. 100-101.

[611] This is not always self-evident. For example, in a dispute about inheritance there may be a preliminary question regarding the time of death of the deceased. This is

Finally, the preliminary issue must not, under the private international law of the forum, be subjected to the same conflict rule as the main question, although the two conflict rules may lead to the application of the same legal system. The last-mentioned condition may sometimes be problematic because the delimitation of issues covered by various conflict rules is not always clear, as has already been pointed out in connection with the classification problem[612]. For example, when dealing with a contract of sale which is subject to a foreign legal system containing special provisions for sales between merchants, the question whether the parties *in casu* are merchants cannot be seen as a preliminary issue if it is considered to be a problem of the law of sales and subject to the same conflict rule that pertains to the rest of the sales contract. If it is, instead, considered to be a separate problem covered by a separate conflict rule (for example a rule leading to the application of the law of the country of the respective party's seat or habitual residence), it may arise as a preliminary issue in a contractual dispute, where it can be discussed whether the merchant status should be decided as if it arose independently in separate proceedings (the *lex fori* approach) or in accordance with the law applicable to the contract including its rules on private international law[613] (the *lex causae* approach).

---

usually a question of fact, but in the case of a presumption or declaration of death of a missing person it must be considered to be rather a question of law, cf. M. Bogdan, *Liber Memorialis Petar Šarčević*, pp. 25-33.

[612] See Chapter VIII, *supra*.

[613] The taking into account of the conflict rules of the country of the *lex causae* makes the *lex causae* approach to incidental questions in some respects similar to *renvoi*, see E. Vitta, *Recueil des cours*, Vol. 162 (1979), p. 70. This similarily is, however, merely superficial, see H. Lewald, *Recueil des cours*, Vol. 69 (1939), pp. 65-66; G. S. Maridakis, *Recueil des cours*, Vol. 105 (1962), p. 446.

In most countries, there is no legislation prescribing which of the two alternative approaches to preliminary questions should be used. It is, of course, possible to enact statutory rules on the treatment of some specific preliminary questions. For example, pursuant to Section 50 of the English Family Law Act of 1986, the non-recognition in a foreign country of a divorce or marriage annulment granted by an English court or recognized in England will not preclude re-marriage in England[614]. This means that even though the capacity to marry of a person domiciled abroad may be governed by foreign law, the preliminary question of whether that person is already married will in these cases be decided by the *lex fori* (including English rules on the recognition of foreign divorces and marriage annulments).

It is also possible to mention Article 12 of the Hague Convention of 14 March 1978 on Celebration and Recognition of the Validity of Marriages, which opts for the *lex fori* approach by stipulating that the rules of the Convention will apply even where the recognition of the validity of a marriage is to be dealt with as an incidental question in the context of another question (unless that other question, under the choice of law rules of the forum, is governed by the law of a non-contracting State).

3. *The Choice of the Best Approach*

It seems that the *lex fori* approach prevails in France[615], where the Cassation Court in a case concerning succession made it clear that while it was for the foreign law governing succession issues to decide

---

[614] See *Dicey and Morris on the Conflict or Laws*, p. 50.
[615] See B. Audit, *Droit international privé*, pp. 212-215.

whether the surviving spouse was entitled to inheritance, it was not for that law to decide whether a particular person was the spouse of the deceased[616]. There are, however, French writers favouring the *lex causae* approach as the main principle[617]. The views of German authors are also divided[618]. The same can be said about most common-law jurisdictions[619] and Scandinavia[620]. The Swedish Supreme Court has within an interval of about one year rendered two judgments which dealt with preliminary questions in opposite ways. In the first case, the preliminary question (the validity of a divorce in a maintenance dispute) was decided in the same manner as if it were examined independently[621], while in the second case the preliminary issue was considered to be governed by the law applicable to the main issue (the preliminary question concerned the lawfulness of an industrial action in a Swedish workplace and arose in a dispute concerning the validity of the resulting contracts governed by foreign law)[622].

---

[616] The case of *Djenangi* v. *Djenangi*, Cassation Court on 22 April 1986, *Journal du droit international (Clunet)* 1986, p. 1025, with a note by Sinay-Cytermann; *Revue critique de droit international privé*, 1988, p. 302 (where the same judgment is dated 11 March 1986) with a note by Bischoff.

[617] The most prominent among them is Paul Lagarde, see *Revue critique de droit international privé*, 1960, pp. 459-484.

[618] See the survey by T. Svenné Schmidt, *Recueil des cours*, Vol. 233 (1992), pp. 350-354.

[619] *Ibid.*, pp. 363-365.

[620] *Ibid.*, pp. 366-367 and 383.

[621] *Nytt Juridiskt Arkiv*, 1986, p. 615.

[622] *Nytt Juridiskt Arkiv*, 1987, p. 885. It deserves to be noticed that in this case the Supreme Court decided the preliminary question by applying the substantive rules of the legal system governing the main issue, without taking into account the conflict rules of that system.

Just like the other general problems of private international law, the special complications associated with the treatment of preliminary questions often remain unnoticed by the courts and the parties, probably because they do not realize the potential importance of such problems for the outcome of the dispute.

It is not settled which of the two methods of dealing with preliminary questions is generally preferable. Each of the two approaches certainly has its advantages and its disadvantages. The *lex causae* approach is conducive to an improved international harmony between the treatment of the preliminary question and the treatment of the main issue (for example, Ruritanian law will decide who is to be considered a spouse at the application of Ruritanian inheritance law), while the *lex fori* approach attempts to achieve or maintain internal consistency between the treatment of a legal issue when it arises as a preliminary question and the treatment of the same issue in other contexts. The *lex fori* approach means namely that the forum country can consider the marriage as either valid or invalid, but the answer must be the same regardless of what the dispute *in casu* is about (for example, if a marriage is valid in Sweden it will be treated as valid for all purposes, including for the purpose of inheritance governed by Ruritanian law)[623].

In support of the *lex causae* approach, it can be argued that foreign law applicable to the main question

---

[623] See, for example, F. Schwind, *Recueil des cours*, Vol. 187 (1984), p. 69, who confronts *"harmonie internationale"* with *"harmonie intérieure"*. A. Bucher, *Recueil des cours*, Vol. 341 (2009), p. 245, uses the terms *"harmonie internationale des solutions"* and *"harmonie matérielle"*, while E. Vitta, *Recueil des cours*, Vol. 162 (1979), p. 69, speaks about *"solution conjointe"* and *"solution disjointe"*. Cf. also F. K. Juenger, *Recueil des cours*, Vol. 193 (1985), pp. 195-196.

is to be applied loyally, i.e. as it would be applied in its own country, and that the Ruritanian law in my example, when stipulating that inheritance should go to the surviving spouse, has probably in mind exclusively those persons who are recognized as spouses in Ruritania. Besides, the *lex causae* approach can be said to enhance the uniformity of decisions[624], because in theory it would make the Swedish court to arrive at the same conclusion as Ruritanian courts.

4. Concluding Remarks

It is submitted, nevertheless, that the *lex fori* approach is normally to be preferred, at least as a general guiding principle that must give way whenever the *lex causae* approach is believed to lead to a more reasonable result[625]. It is normally not appropriate to consider the same relationship, for example the same marriage, to be valid for some purposes (for example maintenance) while considering it invalid for other purposes (for example inheritance), depending on which legal system applies to the main question (maintenance, inheritance, etc.). The *lex causae* approach could, in fact, lead to the absurd and almost schizophrenic[626] result that the same marriage would be valid with regard to the husband's right to inherit his wife while being invalid with regard to the wife's right to inherit her husband, provided that the inheritance after

---

[624] See, for example, T. Svenné Schmidt, *Recueil des cours*, Vol. 233 (1992), p. 368; E. Vitta, *Recueil des cours*, Vol. 162 (1979), p. 69.

[625] See, for example, B. Audit, *Droit international privé*, pp. 215-216; C. M. V. Clarkson and J. Hill, *The Conflict of Laws*, p. 481; G. Kegel and K. Schurig, *Internationales Privatrecht*, pp. 378-381.

[626] See R. De Nova, *Recueil des cours*, Vol. 118 (1966), p. 569.

the husband and after the wife were governed by different legal systems (due to, for example, their different citizenships). If the *lex causae* approach were applied consistently, it would mean that not even a marriage celebrated by a competent official of the forum country, or a final divorce judgment made by a court in the forum country in accordance with its law and perfectly valid there, would be given effect when the main question, for instance inheritance, were governed by the law of a foreign country which does not recognize that marriage or divorce[627]. The argument that foreign law is to be applied loyally does not really support the *lex causae* approach. It is true that the Ruritanian inheritance rule in the example above is to be interpreted in the same way as it is interpreted in Ruritania, but the validity of a marriage does not concern the interpretation of a rule about inheritance. The whole problem concerns rather the interpretation of the forum country's conflict rules[628]. It is hardly the intention of the conflict rule on inheritance to deal with the validity of marriages, not even when such validity is examined as a preliminary question in a dispute about inheritance. It cannot, however, be excluded that sometimes a particular conflict rule must, in view of its purpose, be understood as to mean that it is the *lex causae* approach to preliminary questions that corresponds best to the intentions of the legislator of the forum

---

[627] It seems that even some authors normally supporting the *lex causae* approach are willing to make an exception for those cases where the preliminary question concerns the validity of a legal relationship created by the authorities of the forum country, for example when a marriage has been celebrated by an official of the forum country or a divorce has been pronounced by a court there. See P. Lagarde, *Revue critique de droit international privé*, 1960, pp. 479-483.

[628] See P. Lalive, *Recueil des cours*, Vol. 155 (1977), p. 300.

country[629]. As it was put by Andreas Bucher, private international law cannot be expected to achieve the impossible, such as a perfectly homogeneous solution for a situation connected with several mutually hetero-geneous legal systems[630].

A possible special case mentioned in the literature is that if the forum has to decide whether a person is a citizen of a foreign country and this citizenship depends on a certain family status such as marriage or paternity, then the validity of that status must be judged in accordance with the opinion of the foreign country in question[631]. It would certainly be erroneous to consider a person to be a national of a foreign coun-try if he is not considered as such by the country in question or to deny the existence of his foreign nation-ality when the foreign country considers him as its national. In order to avoid this kind of problems, it is submitted that questions regarding foreign nationality should normally be answered by the presentation of documents issued by the foreign country in question (such as a passport or a certificate of naturalization) rather than by attempts to apply directly foreign rules about the acquisition or loss of citizenship.

---

[629] See, for example, A. A. Ehrenzweig, *Recueil des cours*, Vol. 124 (1968), pp. 244-245.

[630] See A. Bucher, *Recueil des cours*, Vol. 341 (2009), p. 248:

> "On constatera à cette occasion que la résolution du conflit de lois ne peut réaliser l'impossible, à savoir l'homogénéité parfaite d'une situation juridique qui dispose d'un potentiel d'hétérogénéité du fait de ses liens avec plusieurs ordres juridiques."

[631] See, for example, B. Audit, *Droit international privé*, p. 215; G. Kegel and K. Schurig, *Internationales Privatrecht*, p. 382; F. Rigaux, *Recueil des cours*, Vol. 213 (1989), p. 165; T. Svenné Schmidt, *Recueil des cours*, Vol. 233 (1992), p. 382.

Finally, it should be noted that preliminary questions may have their own preliminary questions. Assume that in a dispute between a child and a man concerning the maintenance obligation of the latter, the conflict rules of the forum designate the law of country A, which says that the child can claim alimonies from its father. This gives rise to the preliminary question of whether the man is the father and the answer to that question is assumed to depend on the *"pater est"* presumption, for which the forum has a different conflict rule, designating the law of country B. That law makes the presumption depend on the validity of the marriage between the man in question and the child's mother, which thus is a preliminary issue in relation to the issue of paternity. The validity of the marriage in question may pursuant to the forum's conflict rules depend on the law of country C. The law of country C may consider the marriage invalid if the previous marriage of one of the spouses has not been validly dissolved, which may in the eyes of the forum depend on the law of the country D, etc. A consistent use of the *lex causae* approach would in such a situation become extremely complicated, requiring, *inter alia*, the taking into account of the approach to preliminary questions prevailing in countries B and C.

CHAPTER XV

THE PROBLEM OF EQUIVALENCE

It is not uncommon that a legal status, for example paternity or adoption, is created pursuant to one legal system while its legal effects have to be determined in accordance with another legal system. It may, for instance, happen that paternity regarding a child born out of wedlock was established under the law of the country of the citizenship or habitual residence of the child, whereas the child's right to inherit his father is governed by the law of the country of the last citizenship or the last habitual residence of the father. This may cause problems, because in most countries the substantive rules on the creation of a legal status (such as the determination of paternity) and on its legal consequences (such as the child's inheritance rights) are co-ordinated, so that they take each other into account.

If, as is the case in Sweden, a man is not judicially declared to be the father of a child unless it is practically certain that he really is the biological father, it is natural to give such paternity far-reaching effects regarding maintenance, custody, visitation, surname, inheritance, etc. Similarly, if paternity is given such far-reaching consequences, it is natural to expect that it is not judicially confirmed unless the biological tie is certain or almost certain.

Some countries have chosen a different approach in their substantive family law: paternity can be imposed on a man even though the probability of his biological fatherhood is not very high, but the legal effects of such paternity are limited to certain maintenance payments, excluding other consequences such as custody, inheritance and surname. The classical example of such paternity is the former German so-called *Zahl-*

vaterschaft[632]. It can be assumed that in view of such
limited effects, many German men used to acknow-
ledge paternity rather than risking the costs and publicity of court proceedings, even though they were far
from certain about their biological relationship with the
child (this was before the development of the DNA
technology making it possible to establish biological
fatherhood with the probability of almost one hundred
per cent).

The question arising in this context is whether it is
appropriate to give a paternity determined under such
rules the dramatically more far-reaching legal effects
pursuant to another legal system which assumes that
the legal father is identical to the biological one. This
is the so-called "equivalence problem" or "substitution
problem", which in essence poses the question whether
a legal relationship created under a certain legal system
(e.g. the former German *Zahlvaterschaft*, irrespective
of whether established in Germany or in another country pursuant to German law) is qualitatively equivalent
to and can substitute corresponding or similar relationships at the application of another legal system (e.g.
when distributing inheritance pursuant to Swedish
inheritance law)[633].

---

[632] See the former Article 1589, para. 2, of the German
Civil Code, according to which a child born out of wedlock and its father were not even considered to be related
to one another: "Ein uneheliches Kind und dessen Vater
gelten nicht als verwandt." The provision was abolished in
1969.

[633] There is at least one French judgment where the
German *Zahlvaterschaft* was denied effects in respect of
succession rights governed by French law, see the case of
Ulrich Bidlingmaier v. *Veuve Chambon*, Tribunal de
grande instance de la Seine, 1 March 1967, *Journal du
droit international (Clunet)*, 1968, p. 358, with a comment
by Ph. K. See also B. Audit, *Droit international privé*,
pp. 266-268.

Similar problems may arise even when the disputed effects of the foreign legal relationship under the law creating it are comparable to those stipulated in the substantive law governing its effects, if the whole nature of the two relationships in the two legal systems is fundamentally different.

For example, according to the customary law of some tribes in Africa, when a childless man dies his tribe designates a boy, normally a relative, who will be subsequently considered to be the son of the deceased and, as such, preserve his lineage for the future. Even if some of the effects of such relationship are similar to those of a Swedish adoption (for example, the boy inherits the property of the deceased), it is dubious whether the boy can be considered to be a "descendant" if Swedish law is applicable to the distribution of the deceased man's estate.

The purpose of an adoption in Swedish law is namely to establish a parent-child relationship between living persons and not to preserve the lineage for deceased ancestors. Or, does a marriage concluded for a short period of time determined in advance (such marriages exist in, for example, Iranian law) constitute a marriage for the purposes of Swedish family and succession law when Swedish law is applicable to the effects of the marriage? The recognition of such foreign legal relationships may sometimes be contrary to the forum's public policy, but the general problems, arising out of the need to assimilate legal relationships created pursuant to the law of one country into the substantive rules of another country, are not limited to such situations.

It seems that the answer is in principle to be sought and found in a reasonable interpretation of the substantive rules governing the various legal effects of the status relationship in question, irrespective of whether these rules belong to the *lex fori* or to some foreign law[634]. It is, for example, for the applicable Swedish substantive inheritance law to decide whether its references to the "spouse" or "descendants" of the deceased can be understood to comprise even legal relationships which, even though perhaps carrying the same name as marriage or paternity under Swedish law, are fundamentally different as to their creation, function and legal consequences. A comparison must thus be made between the law governing the effects of the legal relationship, for example Swedish inheritance law if the deceased was a Swedish national and habitual resident, and the law pursuant to which the relevant relationship, such as paternity or adoption, was created. Clearly, many differences in these respects must be accepted, but if they become too great then there is no equivalence and substitution would be inappropriate. Drawing the line is not easy, but it can be said that the substantive and functional contents of the legal relationship should be given more weight than outward appearances such as how a certain relationship is called. The name of a legal relationship is to large extent a mere empty frame *(Rahmenbegriff)*, whose legal contents in different legal systems may be totally different[635]. The solution necessitates comparisons between institutions of various legal systems in order to find out whether an institution taken from one legal system can be "integrated" into another[636]. Comparative legal science can

---

[634] See, for example, Article 4 of the Resolution of the Institute of International Law on substitution and principle of equivalence in private international law, *Annuaire de l'Institut de droit international,* Vol. 72, 2007 (session of Santiago de Chile), p. 73.

[635] See, for example, T. Svenné Schmidt, *Recueil des cours*, Vol. 233 (1992), p. 336; W. Wengler, *Rabels Zeitschrift*, 1934, pp. 152 and 154.

[636] See G. van Hecke, *Recueil des cours*, Vol. 126 (1969), pp. 501-505; H. Lewald, *Recueil des cours*,

be of great help when it comes to identifying, for the purposes of private international law, the similarities and differences between seemingly corresponding legal institutions and concepts in various legal systems[637]. It may, even though it is less frequent, also happen that two legal institutions or concepts, carrying different names and seemingly far apart, turn out, at a closer look, to be related to one another to such a degree that they can be treated as corresponding and equivalent for the purposes of private international law.

As the answer to the question of equivalence normally depends on the interpretation and presumed aims of the substantive rules applicable to the legal effects of the legal relationship concerned, it may occur that equivalence can be confirmed for some purposes (effects) while denied for other[638]. The former German *Zahlvaterschaft* could, for example, be acceptable for the application of Swedish substantive rules on maintenance, while possibly being refused effects under Swedish rules on custody, succession or surname.

The equivalence problem does not necessarily always concern the equivalence of a foreign legal relationship at the application of the substantive rules of the *lex fori*. The opposite situation may also arise, where the question is whether a legal relationship created under the *lex fori* can be given much more far-reaching legal effects due to the application of foreign law. It may even happen that the court faces the question whether a legal relationship created under one for-

---

Vol. 69 (1939), pp. 130-136; K. Lipstein, *Recueil des cours*, Vol. 135 (1972), pp. 208-209.

[637] The comparison may sometimes result in the conclusion that the foreign legal relationship is a legal phenomenon totally unknown to the *lex fori*, see Chapter XIII, *supra*.

[638] See, for example, T. Svenné Schmidt, *Recueil des cours*, Vol. 233 (1992), p. 336.

eign legal system can be given effects according to another foreign legal system. It is submitted that the answer in all these situations should not depend on the legal terminology used but should rather be sought by a comparative study of the applicable substantive rules regulating the legal effects in question, and that those legal relationships that have been created by the application of the *lex fori* should not be given any preferential treatment in this respect.

CHAPTER XVI

ADJUSTMENT

Private international law leads often to a situation
where two or more legal systems are applied to different aspects of the same dispute. Thus, procedural matters are normally governed by the rules of the *lex fori*
even when the substance of the dispute is governed by
foreign law; preliminary questions may be governed
by other law than that governing the main issue; the
existence of a legal relationship or status may be governed by another legal system than its effects; a surviving spouse's right to a share of the deceased spouse's
assets may partly be governed by the legal system
applicable to inheritance and partly by the legal system
governing the matrimonial property regime, etc. This is
occasionally problematic, because, as Allan Philip has
put it, a legal system is normally a coherent system in
the way that the rules of different parts of it are
expected to fit well together and result in an even balance between various interested parties [639]. The result
of combining rules of various legal systems may be
that this balance is lost, causing hardships and material
injustice [640].

This has been described using the metaphor of an
attempt to assemble a puzzle using bits belonging
to different sets; even though there is nothing wrong
with the various individual bits as such, they do not fit
together and may need reshaping (François Rigaux

---

[639] A. Philip, *Recueil des cours*, Vol. 160 (1978), p. 37.
[640] See K. Lipstein, *Recueil des cours*, Vol. 135 (1972),
p. 209.

speaks about "redécouper les contours")[641]. After all, the co-ordination between legal systems is often said to be the very purpose and essence of private international law[642].

Assume that after the death of a married person the court has to divide the matrimonial property and distribute the inheritance. Assume also that according to the private international law of the forum the matrimonial property division is governed by the law of the country where the spouses took habitual residence at the time of the wedding, whereas inheritance is to be distributed pursuant to the law of the country where the deceased habitually resided at the time of his death.

Assume further that the substantive laws of both these countries give the surviving spouse approximately the same total benefits, but they use different legal vehicles to achieve this result. The law of the country where the couple took residence at the time of their wedding gives the surviving spouse no rights at the matrimonial property division, but compensates this by giving the surviving spouse extensive inheritance rights. At the same time, the law of the country where the deceased habitually resided at the time of his death gives the surviving spouse no right to inherit but compensates this by providing for a generous share at the division of the matrimonial property. The peculiar result of a mechanical application of the described rules will be that the surviving spouse receives nothing at all. If the couple had moved in the opposite direc-

---

[641] See F. Rigaux, *Recueil des cours*, Vol. 213 (1989), p. 167. I prefer the metaphor of the construction of a car using spare parts that are faultless as such but need to be adjusted to each other because they are of different models.

[642] See P. Mayer, *Recueil des cours*, Vol. 327 (2007), p. 23.

tion, the surviving spouse would, on the other hand, be entitled to receive the benefit of both legal systems, i.e. both a share of the matrimonial assets and a share at the distribution of inheritance. Both results are clearly incompatible with the intentions of each of the two legal systems involved, and should be reasonably and appropriately adjusted. The adjustment can be made on the level of conflict rules, for example by subjecting spousal inheritance to the same law that governs the matrimonial property division [643], alternatively by subjecting the matrimonial property division to the law governing spousal inheritance [644]. A solution may be sought also on the level of substantive law, for example by avoiding the double benefits of the surviving spouse by deducting from the inheritance the amount he or she has already received as a result of the matrimonial property division or vice versa.

Another type of adjustment problems can be exemplified by a situation where the legal system applicable to the maintenance obligations between ex-spouses after a divorce (often the law of the country of the habitual residence of the maintenance creditor) stipulates that such maintenance is due only to an ex-spouse who in the divorce judgment was declared to be innocent of the breakdown of the marriage. This requirement is in principle impossible to fulfil if the divorce took place in Sweden, because in Swedish divorce proceedings the courts are not allowed to pass judgment on which of the spouses is to blame; in fact they are not even allowed to enquire into the reasons of the divorce petition. It would, however, be inappropriate if an ex-spouse were deprived of maintenance solely

---

[643] See, for example, G. van Hecke, *Recueil des cours*, Vol. 126 (1969), pp. 509-513.

[644] See, for example, A. Bucher, *Recueil des cours*, Vol. 341 (2009), p. 243.

because the divorce had taken place in Sweden. The problem can be solved by a reasonable adjustment of the applicable substantive rule on maintenance, for example by replacing the requirement of judicial declaration of innocence in the divorce judgment with an examination, within the framework of the maintenance dispute, of whether during the marriage the ex-spouse claiming maintenance had in some way behaved improperly towards the other ex-spouse.

Yet another conceivable candidate for adjustment is the situation of an adopted child whose right to inherit his biological and adoptive parents is governed by different legal systems. This is not unusual, as such rights normally depend on the nationality or habitual residence of the respective parent. While in some countries the adoptive child inherits the adoptive parents but not the biological ones, the law of other countries stipulates the opposite. Even though the laws of both countries are based on the idea that the adopted child should be entitled to inherit either its biological or its adoptive parents, the conflict rules can result in that the child falls between two stools and inherits nobody or receives double inheritance.

Finally, consider the example of a a traffic accident where a married woman drives her car against a tree and injures her husband. Neither the parties' home State law nor the law of the State of the accident entitle the husband to damages, although because of different reasons: the home State law considers the husband guilty of contributory negligence because he did not wear a seatbelt, while the *lex loci delicti* recognizes inter-spousal tort immunity. If the private international law of the forum subjects questions of negligence to the *lex loci delicti* and inter-spousal immunity to the *lex domicilii* of the couple, the husband will suddenly become entitled to compensation even though he has no such right under any of the two systems involved.

As asked by Juenger[645], is it proper to combine the two legal systems in this way and allow the plaintiff to put together half a donkey and half a camel, and then ride to victory on the synthetic hybrid? The answer is far from self-evident.

It is very difficult to formulate a general rule on how exactly the adjustment *(adaptation, Angleichung)* should be achieved. As illustrated in the examples above, there may be great differences between the various situations and different types of solutions may be required. The judge should be given the authority to intervene and make an adjustment, i.e. to correct the result if he feels that the conflict rules lead to an outcome which in fact is incompatible with the aims of the substantive rules of the applicable legal system or systems[646]. The adjustment should in any case be as limited as possible and should be compatible with the intentions of the applicable law or laws rather than with those of the *lex fori*. It can be added that adjustments of the *lex fori* should be possible to the same extent as those of foreign law.

---

[645] See F. K. Juenger, *Recueil des cours*, Vol. 193 (1985), p. 196 with reference to B. Currie.

[646] See, for example, B. Audit, *Droit international privé*, pp. 268-271; G. Cansacchi, *Recueil des cours*, Vol. 83 (1953), pp. 111-119 and 144-155; G. A. L. Droz, *Recueil des cours*, Vol. 229 (1991), pp. 368-370; G. Kegel and K. Schurig, *Internationales Privatrecht*, pp. 358-365; E. Vitta, *Recueil des cours*, Vol. 162 (1979), pp. 71-72. Some authors suggest that the problem of adjustment can be reduced "clearly and simply to a question of interpretation of the applicable rule", see A. A. Ehrenzweig, *Recueil des cours*, Vol. 124 (1968), p. 253; H. Lewald, *Recueil des cours*, Vol. 69 (1939), pp. 140-142.

CHAPTER XVII

FOREIGN PUBLIC LAW

1. The Problem

As indicated by the word "private" in "private international law", this branch of the law deals with relationships and disputes of private-law nature, such as matters of family, successions, contracts, property, torts, etc. Matters of public law, for example criminal, fiscal and administrative matters, are not included[647]. This does not mean, however, that rules of public law are without interest from private international law viewpoint, as such rules may have direct impact on private-law relationships too. A party to a contract may, for example, assert that it cannot fulfil its contractual duty because the performance would violate currency exchange regulations or a trade embargo imposed by a certain foreign State; another example is a debtor who refuses to pay his debt on the ground that he has already discharged it by paying abroad to a foreign State which had confiscated the creditor's claim.

There seems to be consensus in the private international law of most countries that foreign rules of public law are not to be treated in all respects in the same manner as foreign private-law rules, even though it is sometimes difficult to differentiate between the two

---

[647] Problems of jurisdiction and, to some minor extent, applicable law may, however, arise even in connection with public law, for example in respect of jurisdiction to deal with crimes committed abroad or the self-imposed territorial limits of administrative licensing requirements.

categories[648]. As an approximate "rule of thumb", it can be said that foreign private law regulates relationships between individual natural or juridical persons and serves primarily their interests, while public law serves primarily the *direct* public interests of the enacting foreign State as such and focuses on the relations between the State and an individual[649]. This definition is far from exact, as all rules, including those belonging to classical private law (family law, contracts, torts, etc.), serve to some extent the interests of the State by creating an indispensable legal framework for a well-functioning family life and commerce. Nevertheless, this general and indirect interest of the State in the well-being of the society as a whole is shared by practically all States, which cannot be said of the direct and immediate State interests represented by typical rules of public law such as tax laws, currency restrictions,

---

[648] Some authors try to avoid the term "public law". For example, J. D. González Campos, *Recueil des cours*, Vol. 287 (2000), pp. 371-376, divides overriding mandatory rules into *"règles de protection"* (such as rules protecting the weaker party in a legal relationship) and *"règles de direction"*. The definition on page 374 of the latter category seems practically identical to the category of mandatory rules of public law:

> "Les 'règles de direction' ont un caractère que l'on peut appeler 'ordopolitique', car elles imposent les principes ordonnateurs de la vie économique et sociale d'un Etat, en configurant ainsi son modèle social et économique. Il s'agit, par conséquent, de règles dont l'objet porte sur des biens ou des intérêts à portée générale, autrement dit, des biens ou intérêts qui n'appartiennent pas aux titulaires du contrat, mais qui se trouvent 'en dehors' du contrat."

Cf. T. Gihl, *Recueil des cours*, Vol. 83 (1953), pp. 163-254, who preferred to speak about *"lois politiques"*.

[649] Cf., for example, H. Eek, *Recueil des cours*, Vol. 139 (1973), p. 27; T. Gihl, *Recueil des cours*, Vol. 83 (1953), p. 12; M. Hellner, *Internationell konkurrensrätt*, pp. 90-94.

export prohibitions or confiscations. Such rules serve exclusively the interests of the State that has enacted them. It is also typical of these rules that they are intended, by the State that enacted them, to be applied or not to be applied regardless of whether they belong to the legal system applicable pursuant to the conflict rules used with regard to private law. It is, for example, normally clear that export prohibitions are intended for all transactions involving exports from the enacting country irrespective of the law governing the contracts involved, while they are normally not intended to stop exports from other countries, not even if the individual contract happens to be governed by the law of the country of the prohibition. The courts are naturally bound by the public-law rules of the *lex fori* and have to apply them in accordance with the intentions of the forum country's legislator, irrespective of the law governing the private-law aspects of the relationship pursuant to the conflict rules of the forum[650]. The matter is somewhat more complicated as far as foreign public-law rules are concerned. As will be shown in the following, they are invoked in various situations requiring various treatments[651].

2. Non-Enforcement of Claims Based on Foreign Public Law

The prevailing view[652], that foreign public-law rules need not and should not be treated in all respects in the

---

[650] See, for example, G. Kegel and K. Schurig, *Internationales Privatrecht*, pp. 152-153.

[651] See, for example, G. van Hecke, *Recueil des cours*, Vol. 126 (1969), pp. 484-498.

[652] See, for example, the survey of the attitude towards foreign revenue claims in a number of European countries in J. Basedow *et al.*, *Yearbook of Private International Law*, Vol. VI (2004), pp. 1-70.

same manner as foreign rules of private-law nature, is based on the idea that public interests of foreign States do not normally deserve to be *enforced* by courts, unless there is some kind of international commitment to the contrary, either agreed in the form of an international treaty or enacted in the form of a legally binding instrument by an international organization (e.g. an EU Regulation).

The main reason behind this negative attitude is that private international law rules have in principle been enacted and foreign laws are applied in the interest of the forum country. The forum State is interested in achieving stability and good functioning of international commerce and cross-border family relations, and this requires that foreign law be applied in some situations.

On the other hand, in the absence of an international commitment to the contrary, the forum State normally has no interest to spend its taxpayers' money on actively promoting the interests of foreign States in respect of the collecting of taxes, enforcing confiscations, upholding currency exchange regulations or securing that the laws forbidding trade with enemy nationals are respected[653]. This is a matter of interpretation of the forum country's private international law.

The usual conflict rules of the forum country normally cannot reasonably be interpreted as intending to

---

[653] See, for example, B. Audit, *Droit international privé*, pp. 92 and 242-243; C. M. V. Clarkson and J. Hill, *The Conflict of Laws*, pp. 490-493; *Dicey and Morris on the Conflict of Laws*, pp. 89-100; G. Kegel and K. Schurig, *Internationales Privatrecht*, pp. 1092-1093; E. F. Scoles *et al.*, *Conflict of Laws*, pp. 147-148; A. V. M. Struycken, *Recueil des cours*, Vol. 311 (2004), pp. 432-436; F. Vischer, *Recueil des cours*, Vol. 232 (1992), pp. 186-198.

include these types of foreign provisions to the same extent as provisions of a private-law nature[654].

The restrictive attitude towards the enforcement of foreign public-law claims is thus not primarily an expression of the forum country's *ordre public*, but rather a matter of defining the task of the forum: it is not the role and purpose of the court of one country to act as an extended arm of foreign States in serving their public interests which are not shared by the forum State. Thus, foreign tax claims are unenforceable even when they are fully compatible with the fundamental principles of the *lex fori*, for example even when they are of the same type and much lower than corresponding taxes in the country of the forum. Some authors and judges are of the view that the enforcement of foreign tax claims would constitute an impermissible assertion of the foreign State's sovereign authority within the territory of the forum country[655], but there seems to be no rule of public international law forbidding one State's attempt to obtain a voluntary assistance of another State's courts regarding the enforcement of tax claims. It is submitted here that it is rather the indifference on the part of the forum country towards foreign public-law claims that is the reason of why the courts of one country will normally be passive and refuse to enforce public laws of another country. From the practical viewpoint, it is less important whether this passive attitude leads to the dismissal of the foreign State's claim because of the lack of jurisdiction to entertain the action or because the forum after an examination of the merits found the foreign claim to be unenforceable.

---

[654] See T. Gihl, *Recueil des cours*, Vol. 83 (1953), pp. 244-249.

[655] See, for example, Lort Keith of Avonholm in *Government of India* v. *Taylor*, [1955] AC 491, on p. 511.

The problem can be illustrated using the decision of the Swedish Supreme Court of 21 March 1961 in the case of *Bulgaria* v. *Takvorian*[656]. In this case, the Bulgarian State sued Mr. Takvorian for certain sums of money deposited with a Swedish public authority. Bulgaria did not dispute that the money belonged to Mr. Takvorian as payment for tobacco exported by him from Bulgaria to Sweden, but claimed the right to dispose of the money on the basis of Bulgarian foreign exchange regulations, as well as on the basis of Mr. Takvorian's promises, made in connection with his application for a Bulgarian export licence, to accept payment in accordance with those regulations. The Svea Court of Appeal found that the claims of the Bulgarian State were based to such an extent on the exchange control measures carried out by the Bulgarian State in order to supply the country with foreign currency that this action must be regarded as predominantly of a public-law character. The Court of Appeal concluded, therefore, that the action brought by the Bulgarian State could not be considered on its merits by a Swedish court and had to be dismissed. Bulgaria appealed to the Supreme Court which agreed with the Court of Appeal that Bulgaria's claim was predominantly of a public-law nature and that the action, as relating

---

[656] See *Nytt Juridiskt Arkiv*, 1961, p. 145; 47 *International Law Reports* 40. From the French case law, it is possible to mention the judgment of the Cassation Court rendered in 1990 in the case of *Guatemala* v. *SINCAFC,* where it was confirmed in principle that claims of foreign States linked to the exercise of their public power and based on public law "ne peuvent être portées devant les jurisdictions françaises", see Cassation Court on 2 May 1990, *Journal du droit international (Clunet)*, 1991, p. 137. Similarly, English courts have no jurisdiction to entertain an action for the enforcement, either directly or indirectly, of a penal, revenue or other public law of a foreign State, see *Dicey and Morris on the Conflict of Laws*, p. 89.

mainly to a foreign interest of a public-law character, should not be considered on its merits. The decision of the Court of Appeal was, consequently, affirmed[657].

What has just been said does not mean that foreign public-law claims should generally be regarded as invalid or null and void. It is more appropriate to see them rather as claims that are unenforceable in the forum country. To the extent the foreign State is successful in enforcing its public-law claims by its own efforts, the resulting fait accompli should normally be recognized as legitimate, unless the recognition would be contrary to the forum's public policy (e.g. confiscations of property belonging to persons of a certain race). For example, if a foreign State's tax claim has been collected from the tax debtor's assets situated in that foreign State or has been satisfied voluntarily by a tax debtor residing in the forum country, the forum will not help the debtor to recover the tax money, not even by a set-off. As the power of the foreign State is normally limited to its own territory, this principle of unenforceability leads usually to the same results as the so-called "principle of territoriality", which is frequently invoked in connection with foreign expropriations and is supposed to mean that such measures will only be given effect regarding property situated in the foreign expropriating State and not as to property situated outside of it[658]. The two principles do slightly dif-

---

[657] One of the Supreme Court Justices dissented on the ground that Mr. Takvorian's promise to accept payment through clearing in accordance with Bulgarian exchange control rules may have given Bulgaria's claim a real private-law (probably contractual) character.

[658] See, for example, M. Bogdan, *Expropriation in Private International Law*, pp. 50-52; *Dicey and Morris on the Conflict of Laws*, p. 99; G. Kegel and K. Schurig, *Internationales Privatrecht*, pp. 156 and 1097-1108, with further references.

fer however, as is demonstrated by their treatment of property that at the time of the expropriation was in fact located in the expropriating foreign State but was removed from there by its original owner before the expropriating State succeeded in taking over the possession[659].

3. Foreign Public Law in Private Disputes

The public-law interests of a foreign State can be at stake even in some private-law disputes between private parties, where foreign public law is relied on by a party who is not identical to the foreign State in question. If that party acts as an instrumentality of the foreign state, which uses it in order to enforce its public-law claim, there are no reasons to treat it differently than the foreign State itself. This may happen, for instance, when a foreign State assigns ("sells") a tax claim to a private debt collection agency which then sues, in its own name, the tax debtor in the forum country, or if the action is brought by a foreign bankruptcy administrator acting in insolvency proceedings where the foreign State is the sole creditor[660].

---

[659] See, for example, M. Bogdan, *Expropriation in Private International Law*, pp. 52-54; C. M. V. Clarkson and J. Hill, *The Conflict of Laws*, pp. 491-492; *Dicey and Morris on the Conflict of Laws*, p. 99.

[660] See, for example, the English case of *QRS1* v. *Frandsen*, [1999] 1 WLR 2169 (CA), where a claim presented by a liquidator of a Danish company was held to be unenforceable because the Danish tax authorities were the only creditor. It is less certain how English courts would treat a foreign administrator if there were other (private) creditors as well. C. M. V. Clarkson and J. Hill, *The Conflict of Laws*, p. 492, seem to assume that the principle of unenforceability of foreign revenue claims will not apply if there are such additional creditors, but it is possible that the court will take account of the proportions between the

The situation is somewhat different when the foreign public-law rule is relied on by a private party whose interests are separate from, but happen to coincide with, those of the foreign State. For example, a party may attempt to escape its own obligation to pay a contractual debt on the ground that the currency exchange regulations or the trading-with-the-enemy laws of a foreign State make the payment illegal. Some authors are of the view that such payment prohibitions and other similar rules should be given effect if they have been enacted by the country whose law governs the contract, i.e. that the foreign public law should in this situation be subjected to the same conflict rules as private law. This solution seems to prevail in England[661], but it has some support even elsewhere[662].

---

different claims. It can be added that Article 39 of the EC Regulation No. 1346/2000 of 29 May 2000 on Insolvency Proceedings, OJ 2000 L 160, p. 1, entitles all creditors with habitual residence, domicile or registered office in a Member State other than the State of the opening of bankruptcy, "including the tax authorities and social security authorities of Member States" to lodge their claims, and the rights of the liquidator to dispose of and distribute the assets will pursuant to Article 18 of the same Regulation in principle be recognized in all Member States (except Denmark) regardless of the private-law or public-law nature of the claims of the participating creditors.

[661] See, for example, *Kleinwort* v. *Ungarische Baumwolle Industrie*, [1939] 2 KB 678; C. M. V. Clarkson and J. Hill, *The Conflict of Laws*, p. 492; T. C. Hartley, *Recueil des cours*, Vol. 319 (2006), pp. 273-274.

[662] See, for example, O. Lando, *Recueil des cours*, Vol. 189 (1985), p. 403: "It is submitted here that the court should apply the economic legislation and other public law rules of the proper law of the contract." Similarly A. Bucher, *Recueil des cours*, Vol. 239 (1993), p. 81, writing about foreign economic measures such as embargoes:

"Dans l'hypothèse où la loi applicable est celle d'un Etat étranger connais-sant des dispositions impératives

In my opinion, this is not a reasonable approach. The usual conflict rules, ordering courts to apply foreign law to contractual and other private-law relationships, are based on considerations which do not warrant the upholding of public-law interests of foreign States. Recognizing the nullifying effect of a foreign embargo or foreign exchange regulation would amount to assisting the foreign State in achieving its political aims, usually at the expense of some other State. It is submitted that the forum should not normally make itself an instrument for enforcing foreign public-law prohibitions and other similar rules, irrespec-tive of whether they are part of the applicable *lex causae* or not. Public-law rules are simply to be treated as a category of their own, and their treatment should in essence depend on the power, in the individual case, of the foreign State to enforce its own rules. This power is normally unrelated to whether the law of that foreign State governs the relationship in question pursuant to the conflict rules of the forum, and the applicability of foreign public-law rules should, therefore, be independent of those conflict rules *(Sonderanknüpfung)*[663]. As it was put by Frank Vischer, it is difficult to explain why, in the case of a sales contract governed by the law of the seller, the export ban imposed by the seller's

---

de cette nature, le tribunal respectera celles-ci, sous réserve de l'ordre public de l'Etat du for ; il n'y a pas lieu, à cet égard, de se retrancher derrière le principe révolu de la non-applicabilité du droit public étranger."

About foreign embargoes and similar measures see also F. Rigaux, *Recueil des cours*, Vol. 213 (1989), pp. 314-317.

[663] See, for example, G. Kegel and K. Schurig, *Internationales Privatrecht*, pp. 155-157, 324-325 and 1115 ; A. Bucher, *Recueil des cours*, Vol. 239 (1993), pp. 88-92 ; F. Vischer, *Recueil des cours*, Vol. 232 (1992), pp. 151 and 165-186.

country should be respected while the import ban enacted by the buyer's country should be ignored[664].

Finally, it must be stressed that the *de facto* effects of foreign public-law rules cannot be ignored if and to the extent such effects are relevant pursuant to the law governing the affected private-law relationship. This can be illustrated using a judgment made by the Court of Appeal for Western Sweden on 2 November 2001[665]. A Swedish shipping company (the carrier) undertook to carry certain American-manufactured equipment from Canada to Libya via Germany. Because of the US embargo against Libya, the carrier refused to deliver the equipment in Germany to the holder of the original bill of lading, who sued the carrier in Sweden demanding delivery. The bill of lading contained a choice-of-law clause in favour of Swedish law. The District Court, whose judgment was affirmed by the Court of Appeal, stated that Swedish courts do not, in principle, take into account demands based on foreign public law and that the American legislation could not, as such, be given direct effect in Sweden. However, due to the severe US sanctions threatening the carrier in case of embargo violation, the court concluded that under the circumstances the carrier was entitled to refuse delivery. The action was, therefore, dismissed. It is worth noting that in this case it was not the foreign State or its stooge that turned to Swedish courts with demands based on its public law. It was the defendant who relied on foreign public law, using it as a shield, not as a sword. The US embargo law was not "applied" as law,

---

[664] See F. Vischer, 232 *Recueil des cours*, Vol. 232 (1992), p. 166.

[665] *Nordiske domme i sjøfartsanliggender*, 2001, p. 36. The decision affirmed a Göteborg District Court judgment published in *Nordiske domme i sjøfartsanliggender*, 2000, p. 24.

but the threat of American sanctions seems to have been taken into consideration as a fact, the negative consequences of which had to be distributed between the parties, obviously in accordance with the principles of Swedish substantive law.

Similarly, if the performance under a contract has become impossible due to a foreign export prohibition, this impossibility is a fact which may constitute a *force majeure* or be given other effects under the law governing the contract in question. The impossibility to perform is real regardless of whether the export prohibition is part of the legal system governing the contract or not, but the legal consequences of the impossibility should reasonably be decided by the proper law of the contract. Again, this manner of taking into account of the impossibility created by foreign public law does not mean that the foreign law is "applied", but rather that it is dealt with as a fact whose harmful consequences have to be appropriately distributed between the parties [666]. This loss partition is a matter of substantive law rather than of private international law, and the law governing the relationship (usually the proper law of the contract [667]) will probably distribute the loss taking into account all relevant circumstances, for example that in the contract one of the parties has assumed the responsibility for obtaining the export permit or that the export prohibition was caused by the improper behaviour of one of the parties. It may also be argued that the seller, who is probably a national and resident of the exporting country, should carry the loss resulting from the prohibition enacted by it. In any case, it should not be relevant whether the prohibi-

---

[666] Cf. G. Kegel and K. Schurig, *Internationales Privatrecht*, p. 1108.

[667] See, for example, A. Bucher, *Recueil des cours*, Vol. 239 (1993), p. 83.

tion is part of the legal system governing the contract or not[668].

4. Concluding Remarks

The negative attitude towards the enforcement of foreign public law may be changing, at least in some fields. States are becoming increasingly aware of their common interests and do not see themselves as isolated islands indifferent to the interests of their neighbours[669]. As early as in 1945, Article VIII (2) *(b)* of the International Monetary Fund Agreement provided that exchange contracts involving the currency of any Member State and contrary to the exchange-control regulations of any Member State maintained or imposed consistently with the IMF agreement "shall be unenforceable in the territories of any member". These developments are reflected in the changing attitudes among legal scholars as well, even though the changes are somewhat hesitant. In its resolution on the application of foreign public law, the Institut de droit international concluded in 1975 that the public-law character attributed to a provison of foreign law, which is desig-

---

[668] It is doubtful whether Article 9, pont 3, of the EC Regulation on the Law Applicable to Contractual Obligations (Rome I) adds much to what has just been said. Pursuant to this Article, effect may be given to the overriding mandatory provisions of the law of the country where the obligations arising out of the contract have to be or have been performed, in so far as those overriding mandatory provisions render the performance of the contract unlawful. It is submitted that it is the impossibility of performance, resulting from this unlawfulness, that is to be given effect rather than the foreign provision itself. Cf. Chapter X.6, *supra*.

[669] See, for example, C. M. V. Clarkson and J. Hill, *The Conflict of Laws*, p. 490; A. V. M. Struycken, *Recueil des cours*, Vol. 311 (2004), p. 421.

nated by the rule of conflict of laws, should not prevent the application of that provision and that this should apply even with regard to provisions which do not concern the protection of private interests but primarily serve the interests of the State[670], but the same Institut concluded two years later that claims based on the exercise of governmental power by foreign States should in principle be inadmissible unless justified by reason of the subject matter of the claim, the needs of international co-operation or the interests of the States concerned[671]. A resolution adopted in 1988 at the 63rd Conference of the International Law Association[672] stated that the legal, social, economic and political development of national States had reached a point where the general presumption in private international law should be that foreign public laws ought not *per se* to be accorded special treatment when considering their entitlement to recognition or enforcement, even though the resolution added that it was not concerned with the recognition and enforcement of foreign expropriatory laws and that a forum may limit its recognition of, or totally decline to enforce, foreign penal laws and foreign revenue laws.

It is submitted that the 1975 resolution of the Institut de droit international and the 1988 resolution of the International Law Association have gone too far if and to the extent they propose that foreign public law be treated in all respects in the same manner and be subjected to the same conflict rules as foreign private law. It is certainly true that the efforts to combat

---

[670] See *Annuaire de l'Institut de droit international*, Vol. 56 (1975), pp. 550-553.

[671] See *Annuaire de l'Institut de droit international*, Vol. 57 (1977), tome II, pp. 2-35 and 328-331.

[672] See *International Law Association. Report of the 63rd Conference*, Warsaw, 1988, pp. 29-30.

tax fraud, corruption, smuggling and all kinds of organized crime have led to an increased international co-operation in the fields of penal and fiscal law. Sometimes it may also happen that the interests protected and enhanced by a foreign public-law rule are identical to those of the country of the forum, such as when an allied country requisitions certain assets for warfare purposes[673] or when a foreign trade embargo is part of a concerted international action in which the forum country participates as well[674]. Under such circumstances it is natural to give effect to the foreign provision[675], but even then this should happen irrespective of whether it belongs to the *lex causae* or not. An interesting illustration of this is the decision of the German Federal Court of 22 June 1972[676], concerning certain pieces of Nigerian indigenous art, whose exportation had been forbidden by the Nigerian Government. The court held that a contract violating the Nigerian export prohibition was invalid as being immoral, even though the contract as such was governed by German and not Nigerian law. As the immorality of the contract

---

[673] See, for example, the English case of *Lorentzen* v. *Lydden*, [1942] 2 KB 202, concerning the validity of a decree made by the Norwegian Government in exile requisitioning all Norwegian ships; M. Bogdan, *Expropriation in Private International Law*, p. 56.

[674] See, for example, G. Kegel and K. Schurig, *Internationales Privatrecht*, pp. 1096-1097 and 1122; F. Vischer, *Recueil des cours*, Vol. 232 (1992), p. 175.

[675] See the decision of the French Cassation Court of 2 May 1990 in the case of *Guatemala* v. *SINCAFC*, *Journal du droit international (Clunet)*, 1991, p. 137, where the Court stated that the principle of non-admissibility of foreign public-law demands can be set aside if in the opinion of the forum the requirements of international solidarity or the convergence of interests justify it.

[676] See *Entscheidungen des Bundesgerichtshofes in Zivilsachen*, Vol. 59, p. 83; G. Kegel and K. Schurig, *Internationales Privatrecht*, pp. 156 and 1147.

resulted merely from its violating Nigerian law (a similar contract concerning exports from a country not forbidding the transaction would certainly have been upheld), this decision amounted in fact to giving effect to the Nigerian legislation.

Furthermore, the application of the conflict rules of the forum country is sometimes impossible without considering or even applying foreign public law. To the extent the conflict rules of the forum use citizenship as a connecting factor for natural persons, foreign citizenship laws may have to be taken into account. The question whether a foreign State instrumentality or municipality was properly represented at the conclusion of a contract can usually be answered only on the basis of foreign administrative law, etc. In these and similar situations, foreign public law is taken into account in the interest of reaching a reasonable solution for a dispute of private-law nature rather than in the interest of the foreign State in question.

BIBLIOGRAPHY

Ago, R., "Règles générales des conflits de lois", *Recueil des cours*, Vol. 58 (1936), pp. 243-469.

Arminjon, P., "L'objet et la méthode du droit international privé", *Recueil des cours,* Vol. 21 (1928), pp. 429-512.

Audit, B., "Le caractère fonctionnel de la règle de conflit (Sur la "crise" des conflits de lois)", *Recueil des cours*, Vol. 186 (1984), pp. 219-397.

—, "Le droit international privé en quête d'universalité", *Recueil des cours*, Vol. 305 (2003), pp. 9-487.

—, *Droit international privé*, 4th ed., Paris, 2006.

Barile, G., "La fonction historique du droit international privé", *Recueil des cours*, Vol. 116 (1965), pp. 301-381.

Bartin, E., "La doctrine des qualifications et ses rapports avec le caractère national du conflit des lois", *Recueil des cours*, Vol. 31 (1930), pp. 561-621.

Basedow, J., J. von Hein, D. Janzen and H.-J. Puttfarken, "Foreign Revenue Claims in European Courts", *Yearbook of Private International Law*, Vol. VI (2004), pp. 1-70.

Batiffol, H., "Principes de droit international privé", *Recueil des cours*, Vol. 97 (1959), pp. 431-573.

—, "Le pluralisme des méthodes en droit international privé", *Recueil des cours,* Vol. 139 (1973), pp. 75-147.

Beaumont, P. R., "Reflections on the Relevance of Public International Law to Private International Law Treaty Making", *Recueil des cours,* Vol. 340 (2009), pp. 9-61.

Boele-Woelki, K., and R. H. van Ooik, "The Communitarization of Private International Law", *Yearbook of Private International Law*, Vol. IV (2002), pp. 1-36.

de Boer, Th., "Facultative Choice of Law: The Procedural Status of Choice-of-Law Rules and Foreign Law", *Recueil des cours*, Vol. 257 (1996), pp. 223-427.

Bogdan, M., *Expropriation in Private International Law*, Lund, 1975.

—, *Comparative Law*, Stockholm, 1994.

—, *Svensk internationell privat- och processrätt*, 7th ed., Stockholm, 2008.

—, *Concise Introduction to EU Private International Law*, Groningen, 2006.

—, "Dead or Alive? The Status of Missing Disaster Victims in Swedish Substantive and Private International Law", in

Liber Memorialis Petar Šarčević, Munich, 2006, pp. 25-33.

—, "The Brussels/Lugano Lis Pendens Rule and the 'Italian Torpedo'", *Scandinavian Studies in Law*, Vol. 51 (2007), pp. 89-97.

Bonomi, A., "Mandatory Rules in Private International Law. The Quest for Uniformity of Decisions in a Global Environment", *Yearbook of Private International Law*, Vol. I (1999), pp. 215-247.

Borrás, A., "Le droit international privé communautaire : réalités, problèmes et perspectives d'avenir", *Recueil des cours*, Vol. 317 (2005), pp. 313-536.

Brilmayer, L., "The Role of Substantive and Choice of Law Policies in the Formation and Application of Choice of Law Rules", *Recueil des* cours, Vol. 252 (1995), pp. 9-111.

Brown, J. R., "44.1 Ways to Prove Foreign Law", 9 *The Maritime Lawyer* 179-196 (1984).

Bucher, A., "L'ordre public et le but social des lois en droit international privé", *Recueil des cours*, Vol. 239 (1993), pp. 9-116.

—, "La famille en droit international privé", *Recueil des cours*, Vol. 283 (2000), pp. 9-186.

—, "La dimension sociale du droit international privé", *Recueil des cours*, Vol. 341 (2009), pp. 9-526.

Calvo Caravaca, A.-L., and J. Carrascosa González, "The Proof of Foreign Law in the New Spanish Civil Procedure Code 1/2000", *IPRax*, 2005, pp. 170-174.

Cansacchi, G., "Le choix et l'adaptation de la règle étrangère dans le conflit de lois", *Recueil des cours*, Vol. 83 (1953), pp. 79-162.

Cavers, D. F., "A Critique of the Choice-of-Law Problem", 47 *Harvard Law Review* 173-208 (1933-1934).

—, "Contemporary Conflicts Law in American Perspective", *Recueil des cours*, Vol. 131 (1970), pp. 75-308.

Charfi, M., "L'influence de la religion dans le droit international privé des pays musulmans", *Recueil des cours*, Vol. 203 (1987), pp. 321-454.

Cheatham, E. E., "Problems and Methods in Conflict of Laws", *Recueil des cours*, Vol. 99 (1960), pp. 233-355.

Clarkson, C. M. V., and J. Hill, *The Conflict of Laws*, 3rd ed., Oxford, 2006.

Currie, B., *Selected Essays on the Conflict of Laws*, Durham, 1963.

Davies, D. J. L., "Règles générales des conflits de lois", *Recueil des* cours, Vol. 62 (1937), pp. 423-546.

De Nova, R., "Historical and Comparative Introduction to Conflict of Laws", *Recueil des cours*, Vol. 118 (1966), pp. 435-621.

Dicey and Morris on the Conflict of Laws (13th ed. under the general editorship of L. Collins), London, 2000.

Dogauchi, M., "Four-Step Analysis of Private International Law", *Recueil des cours*, Vol. 315 (2005), pp. 9-140.

Dolinger, J., "Evolution of Principles for Resolving Conflicts in the Field of Contracts and Torts", *Recueil des cours*, Vol. 283 (2000), pp. 187-512.

Droz, G. A. L., "Regards sur le droit international privé comparé. Cours général de droit international privé", *Recueil des cours*, Vol. 229 (1991), pp. 9-424.

Dutoit, B., *Droit international privé suisse*, Basel, 2005.

Eek, H., "Peremptory Norms and Private International Law", *Recueil des cours*, Vol. 139 (1973), pp. 1-73.

Ehrenzweig, A. A., "Specific Principles of Private Transnational Law", *Recueil des cours*, Vol. 124 (1968), pp. 167-366.

Eichel, F., "Die Revisibilität ausländischen Rechts nach der Neufassung von § 545 Abs. 1 ZPO", *IPRax*, 2009, pp. 389-393.

Einhorn, T., "The Ascertainment and Application of Foreign Law in Israeli Courts — Getting the Facts and Fallacies Straight", in *International Cooperation through Private International Law. Essays in Memory of Peter E. Nygh* (edited by T. Einhorn and K. Siehr), The Hague, 2004, pp. 107-118.

Evrigenis, D. J., "Tendances doctrinales actuelles en droit international privé", *Recueil des cours*, Vol. 118 (1966), pp. 313-433.

Fadlallah, I., "L'ordre public dans les sentences arbitrales", *Recueil des cours*, Vol. 249 (1994), pp. 369-430.

Fallon, M., and J. Meeusen, "Private International Law in the European Union and the Exception of Mutual Recognition", *Yearbook of Private International Law*, Vol. IV (2002), pp. 37-66.

Fauvarque-Cosson, B., "Foreign Law before the French Courts: The Conflicts of Law Perspective", in *Comparative Law before the Courts* (edited by G. Canivet *et al.*), London, 2004, pp. 3-12.

Fentiman, R. G., "Foreign Law in National Courts", in *Comparative Law before the Courts* (edited by G. Canivet *et al.*), London, 2004, pp. 13-31.

Flessner, A., "Fakultatives Kollisionsrecht", *Rabels Zeit-*

schrift für ausländisches und internationales Privatrecht, 1970, pp. 547-584.

Gaudemet-Tallon, H., "Le pluralisme en droit international privé: richesses et faiblesses (Le funambule et l'arc-en-ciel). Cours général", *Recueil des cours*, Vol. 312 (2005), pp. 1-489.

Gihl, T., *Den internationella privaträttens historia och allmänna principer*, Stockholm, 1951.

—, "Lois politiques et droit international privé", *Recueil des cours*, Vol. 83 (1953), pp. 163-254.

Girsberger, D., *et al.*, *Zürcher Kommentar zum IPRG. Komentar zum Bundesgesetz über das Internationale Privatrechts (IPRG) vom 18. Dezember 1987*, 2nd ed., Zurich, 2004.

González Campos, J. D., "Diversification, spécialisation, flexibilisation et matérialisation des règles de droit international privé", *Recueil des cours*, Vol. 287 (2000), pp. 9-436.

Gottwald, P., "Zur Revisibilität ausländischen Rechts", *IPRax*, 1988, pp. 210-212.

Graveson, R. H., "Comparative Aspects of the General Principles of Private International Law", *Recueil des cours*, Vol. 109 (1963), pp. 1-164.

Grigera Naón, H. A., "Choice-of-Law Problems in International Commercial Arbitration", *Recueil des cours*, Vol. 289 (2001), pp. 9-395.

Gruber, U. P., and I. Bach, "The Application of Foreign Law. A Progress Report on a New European Project", *Yearbook of Private International Law*, Vol. XI (2009), pp. 157-169.

Hambro, E., "The Relations between International Law and Conflict Law", *Recueil des cours*, Vol. 105 (1962), pp. 1-68.

Hartley, T. C., "Pleading and Proof of Foreign Law: The Major European Systems Compared", 45 *International and Comparative Law Quarterly* 271-292 (1996).

—, "The Modern Approach to Private International Law. International Litigation and Transactions from a Common Law Perspective", *Recueil des cours*, Vol. 319 (2006), pp. 11-324.

—, *International Commercial Litigation. Text, Cases and Materials on Private International Law*, Cambridge, 2009.

Hausmann, R., "Pleading and Proof of Foreign Law — a Comparative Analysis", *European Legal Forum*, 2008, pp. I-1-I-13.

Hay, P., "Flexibility versus Predictability and Uniformity in Choice of Law. Reflections on Current European and

United States Conflicts Law", *Recueil des cours*, Vol. 226 (1991), pp. 281-412.

van Hecke, G., "Principes et méthodes de solution des conflits de lois", *Recueil des cours*, Vol. 126 (1969), pp. 399-569.

Hellner, M., *Internationell konkurrensrätt. Om främmande konkurrensrätts tillämplighet i svensk domstol*, Uppsala, 2000.

—, "Third Country Overriding Mandatory Rules in the Rome I Regulation: Old Wine in New Bottles?", *Journal of Private International Law*, 2009, pp. 447-470.

Hood, K. J., "Drawing Inspiration? Reconsidering the Procedural Treatment of Foreign Law", 2 *Journal of Private International Law* 181-193 (2006).

Jacquet, J.-M., "La fonction supranationale de la règle de conflit de lois", *Recueil des cours*, Vol. 292 (2001), pp. 147-248.

Jänterä-Jareborg, M., "Foreign Law in National Courts. A Comparative Perspective", *Recueil des cours*, Vol. 304 (2003), pp. 181-385.

Jayme, E., "Identité culturelle et intégration: le droit international privé postmoderne", *Recueil des cours*, Vol. 251 (1995), pp. 9-267.

Jessurun d'Oliveira, H. U., "The Non-Election Rule and Procedural Treatment of Foreign Law: Some Observations", *Revue hellénique de droit international*, 2008, pp. 499-520.

Juenger, F. K., "General Course on Private International Law (1983)", *Recueil des cours*, Vol. 193 (1985), pp. 119-387.

Kahn-Freund, O., "General Problems of Private International Law", *Recueil des cours*, Vol. 143 (1974), pp. 139-474.

Kay, H. H., "A Defense of Currie's Governmental Interest Analysis", *Recueil des cours*, Vol. 215 (1989), pp. 9-204.

Kegel, G., "The Crisis of Conflict of Laws", *Recueil des cours*, Vol. 112 (1964), pp. 91-268.

Kegel, G., and K. Schurig, *Internationales Privatrecht*, 9th ed., Munich, 2004.

Kessedjian, C., "Codification du droit commercial international et droit international privé. De la gouvernance normative pour les relations économiques transnationales", *Recueil des cours*, Vol. 300 (2002), pp. 79-308.

Kinsch, P., "Droits de l'homme, droits fondamentaux et droit international privé", *Recueil des cours*, Vol. 318 (2005), pp. 9-332.

Kohler, C., "Verständigungsschwierigkeiten zwischen europäischem Gemeinschaftsrecht und internationalem Privatrecht", *Festschrift für Erik Jayme*, Munich, 2004, pp. 445-459.

Kreuzer. K., "Clash of Civilizations and Conflict of Laws", *Revue hellénique de droit international*, 2009, pp. 629-694.

Lagarde, P., "La règle de conflit applicable aux questions préalables", *Revue critique de droit international privé*, 1960, pp. 459-484.

—, "Le principe de proximité dans le droit international privé contemporain", *Recueil des cours*, Vol. 196 (1986), pp. 9-237.

Lalive, P., "Tendances et méthodes en droit international privé. Cours général", *Recueil des cours*, Vol. 155 (1977), pp. 1-424.

Lando, O., "The Conflict of Laws of Contracts: General Principles", *Recueil des cours*, Vol. 189 (1985), pp. 225-447.

Leflar, R. A., *American Conflicts Law*, 2nd ed., Indianapolis-Kansas City-New York, 1968.

Lewald, H., "Règles générales des conflits de lois. Contribution à la technique du droit international privé", *Recueil des cours*, Vol. 69 (1939), pp. 1-147.

Lipstein, K., "The General Principles of Private International Law", *Recueil des cours*, Vol. 135 (1972), pp. 97-229.

Van Loon, H., "The Hague Conference — Its Origin, Organization and Achievements", *Svensk Juristtidning*, 1993, pp. 293-307.

Loussouarn, Y., "Cours général de droit international privé", *Recueil des cours*, Vol. 139 (1973), pp. 271-385.

Lowenfeld, A. F., "International Litigation and the Quest for Reasonableness. General Course on Private International Law", *Recueil des cours*, Vol. 245 (1994), pp. 9-319.

Mann, F. A., *Foreign Affairs in English Courts*, Oxford, 1986.

—, "The Doctrine of International Jurisdiction Revisited after Twenty Years", *Recueil des cours*, Vol. 186 (1984), pp. 9-115.

Maridakis, G. S., "Introduction au droit international privé", *Recueil des cours*, Vol. 105 (1962), pp. 375-515.

Maury, J., "Règles générales des conflits de lois", *Recueil des cours*, Vol. 57 (1936), pp. 325-570.

Mayer, P., "Le phénomène de la coordination des ordres juridiques étatiques en droit privé", *Recueil des cours*, Vol. 327 (2007), pp. 9-378.

McClean, D., "De conflictu legum. Perspectives on Private Internatinal Law at the Turn of the Century", *Recueil des cours*, Vol. 282 (2000), pp. 41-227.

von Mehren, A. T., "Theory and Practice of Adjudicatory Authority in Private International Law: A Comparative Study of the Doctrine, Policies and Practices of Common- and Civil-Law Systems", *Recueil des cours*, Vol. 295 (2002), pp. 9-431.

Michaels, R., "After the Revolution — Decline and Return of U.S. Conflict of Laws", *Yearbook of Private International Law*, Vol. XI (2009), pp. 11-30.

Mills, A., *The Confluence of Public and Private International Law. Justice, Pluralism and Subsidiarity in the International Constitutional Ordering of Private Law*, Cambridge, 2009.

Moss, G. C., *International Commercial Arbitration. Party Autonomy and Mandatory Rules*, Oslo, 1999.

Mostermans, P. M. M., "Optional (Facultative) Choice of Law? Reflections from a Dutch Perspective", *Netherlands International Law Review*, 2004, pp. 393-410.

Moura Ramos, R. M., "Public Policy in the Framework of the Brussels Convention. Remarks on Two Recent Decisions of the European Court of Justice", *Yearbook of Private International Law*, Vol. II (2000), pp. 25-39.

Muir Watt, H., "Aspects économiques du droit international privé", *Recueil des cours*, Vol. 307 (2004), pp. 25-383.

Neuhaus, P. H., "Abschied von Savigny?", *Rabels Zeitschrift für ausländisches und internationales Privatrecht*, 1982, pp. 4-25.

Niboyet, J.-P., *Traité de droit international privé français*, tome I, Paris, 1938.

Nielsen, P. A., *International privat- og procesret*, Copenhagen, 1997.

North, P. M., "Reform but Not Revolution. General Course on Private International Law", *Recueil des cours*, Vol. 220 (1989), pp. 9-288.

Oppetit, B., "Le droit international privé, droit savant", *Recueil des cours*, Vol. 234 (1992), pp. 331-433.

von Overbeck, A. E., "Les questions générales du droit international privé à la lumière des codifications et projets récents. Cours général de droit international privé", *Recueil des cours*, Vol. 176 (1982), pp. 9-258.

Pamboukis, C. P., "Droit international privé holistique: droit uniforme et droit international privé", *Recueil des cours*, Vol. 330 (2007), pp. 9-474.

Parra-Aranguren, G., "General Course of Private International Law: Selected Problems", *Recueil des cours*, Vol. 210 (1988), pp. 9-223.

Pauknerová, M., "Overriding Mandatory Rules and Czech Law", *Czech Yearbook of International Law*, Vol. 1 (2010), pp. 81-94.

Philip, A., "General Course on Private International Law", *Recueil des cours*, Vol. 160 (1978), pp. 1-73.

Picone, P., "Les méthodes de coordination entre ordres juridiques en droit international privé", *Recueil des cours*, Vol. 276 (1999), pp. 9-296.

Pillet, A., "Théorie continentale des conflits de lois", *Recueil des cours*, Vol. 2 (1924), pp. 447-484.

Pocar, F., "La protection de la partie faible en droit international privé", *Recueil des cours*, Vol. 188 (1984), pp. 339-417.

Qingjiang Kong and Hu Minfei, "The Chinese Practice of Private International Law", 3 *Melbourne Journal of International Law* 414-435 (2002).

Rabel, E., "Das Problem der Qualifikation", *Zeitschrift für ausländisches und internationales Privatrecht*, 1931, pp. 240-288.

Reese, W., "Discussion of Major Areas of Choice of Law", *Recueil des cours*, Vol. 111 (1964), pp. 311-417.

Reese, W. L. M., "General Course on Private International Law", *Recueil des cours*, Vol. 150 (1976), pp. 1-193.

Restatement of the Law. Second. Conflict of Laws 2nd, St. Paul, 1971.

Rheinstein, M., "Comparative Law — Its Functions, Methods and Uses", in Rotondi (ed.), *Inchieste di diritto comparato 2. Buts et méthodes du droit comparé*, Padua-New York, 1973, p. 553.

Rigaux, F. "Les situations juridiques individuelles dans un système de relativité générale. Cours général de droit international privé", *Recueil des cours*, Vol. 213 (1989), pp. 9-407.

Romano, G. P., "La bilatéralité éclipsée par l'autorité. Développements récents en matière d'état des personnes", *Revue critique de droit international privé*, 2006, pp. 457-519.

Schwind, F., "Aspects et sens du droit international privé. Cours général de droit international privé", *Recueil des cours*, Vol. 187 (1984), pp. 9-144.

Scoles, E. F., P. Hay, P. J. Borchers and S. C. Symeonides, *Conflict of Laws*, 4th ed., St. Paul, 2004.

Siehr, K., "General Problems of Private International Law in Modern Codifications", *Yearbook of Private International Law*, Vol. VII (2005), pp. 17-61.

Sperduti, G., "Théorie du droit international privé", *Recueil des cours*, Vol. 122 (1967), pp. 173-336.

Story, J., *Commentaries on the Conflict of Laws, Foreign and Domestic*, 2nd ed., Boston, 1865.

Strömholm, S., *Torts in the Conflict of Laws. A Comparative Study*, Stockholm, 1961.

Struycken, A. V. M., "Co-ordination and Co-operation in Respectful Disagreement. General Course on Private International Law", *Recueil des cours*, Vol. 311 (2004), pp. 9-551.

Svenné Schmidt, T., "The Incidental Question in Private International Law", *Recueil des cours*, Vol. 233 (1992), pp. 305-415.

Symeonides, S. C., "The American Choice-of-Law Revolution in the Courts: Today and Tomorrow", *Recueil des cours*, Vol. 298 (2002), pp. 9-448.

—, "The American Revolution and the European Evolution in Choice of Law: Reciprocal Lessons", 82 *Tulane Law Review* 1741-1799 (2008).

Takahashi, K., "Foreign Law in Japanese Courts — A Comparison with the English Approach: Idealism versus Pragmatism", [2002] *Singapore Journal of Legal Studies* 489-496.

Thue, H., *Internasjonal privatrett. Personrett, familierett og arverett. Alminnelige prinsipper og de enkelte reguleringer*, Oslo, 2002.

Trias de Bes, J. M., "Règles générales des conflits de lois", *Recueil des cours*, Vol. 62 (1937), pp. 1-93.

Trooboff, P. D., "Proving Foreign Law", 9/18/2006 *The National Law Journal* 13 (Col. 1).

Valladão, H., "Développement et intégration du droit international privé, notamment dans les rapports de famille. Cours général de droit international privé", *Recueil des cours*, Vol. 133 (1971), pp. 413-528.

Vallindas, P. G., "La structure de la règle de conflit", *Recueil des cours*, Vol. 101 (1960), pp. 327-380.

Verhoeven, J., "Relations internationales de droit privé en l'absence de reconnaissance d'un Etat, d'un gouvernement ou d'une situation", *Recueil des cours*, Vol. 192 (1985), pp. 9-232.

Vischer, F., "General Course on Private International Law", *Recueil des cours*, Vol. 232 (1992), pp. 9-255.

Vitta, E., "Cours général de droit international privé", *Recueil des cours*, Vol. 162 (1979), pp. 9-243.

—, "The Impact in Europe of the American 'Conflicts Revolution'", 30 *American Journal of Comparative Law* 1-18 (1982).

Vrellis, S., "Conflit ou coordination de valeurs en droit international privé. A la recherche de la justice", *Recueil des cours*, Vol. 328 (2007), pp. 177-485.

Weintraub, R. J., "The Choice-of-Law Rules of the European Community Regulation on the Law Applicable to Non-Contractual Obligations: Simple and Predictable, Consequence-Based, or Neither?", 43 *Texas International Law Journal* 401-426 (2008).

Wengler, W., "Die Vorfrage im Kollisionsrecht", *Rabels Zeitschrift für ausländisches und internationales Privatrecht* 1934, pp. 148-251.

—, "The General Principles of Private International Law", *Recueil des cours*, Vol. 104 (1961), pp. 273-469.

Wolff, M., *Private International Law*, 2nd ed., Oxford, 1950.

Wortley, B. A., "The General Principles of Private International Law", *Recueil des cours*, Vol. 94 (1958), pp. 85-260.

Yasseen, M. F., "Principes généraux de droit international privé", *Recueil des cours*, Vol. 116 (1965), pp. 383-467.

Yates, G. T., "Foreign Law before Domestic Tribunals", 18 *Virginia Journal of International Law* 725-751 (1977-1978).

Zweigert, K., "Zur Armut des internationalen Privatrechts an sozialen Werten", *Rabels Zeitschrift für ausländisches und internationales Privatrecht*, 1973, pp. 435-452.

ABOUT THE AUTHOR

Biographical Note

Michael Bogdan, born in 1946 in Banská Bystrica in former Czechoslovakia.

JUDr. (Prague, 1969), B.A. (Lund), LL.M. (Lund) and Juris Doctor (Lund).

Since 1968 has been living in Sweden and is, since 1995, Professor of Comparative and Private International Law in the Law Faculty of the University of Lund. Previous positions: Professor of Private Law and International Trade Law (1985-1995), Associate Professor of International Law (1978-1984), Assistant Professor of Law (1976-1978), Research Assistant (1975-1976), all at the University of Lund.

Member and former President of GEDIP (Groupe européen de droit international privé), member of the International Academy of Comparative Law and associated member of the Institut de droit international.

Author of 12 books and more than 400 articles and reviews on various legal subjects.

The preparation of these lectures has been supported by the Institute for Research in Legal Science (Institutet för rättsvetenskaplig forskning) in Stockholm.

Principal Publications

Books and Other Major Works

Expropriation in Private International Law, Lund, 1975.

Travel Agency in Comparative and Private International Law, Lund, 1976.

Internationell konkurs- och ackordsrätt, Stockholm, 1984 (*International Insolvency Law*, in Swedish).

Äganderätten som folkrättsligt skyddad mänsklig rättighet, Lund, 1986 (*Right to Property as an Internationally Protected Human Right*, in Swedish).

"Aircraft Accidents in the Conflict of Laws", *Recueil des cours*, Vol. 208 (1988), pp. 9-168.

Comparative Law, Deventer, 1994.

Utrikeshandelns civilrättsliga grundproblem, 2nd ed., Stockholm, 1994 (*Fundamental Private-Law Questions of International Trade*, in Swedish).

The Brussels Jurisdiction and Enforcement Convention — An EC Court Casebook, Stockholm, 1996.

Lagkonflikter i utrikeshandeln, Stockholm 1996 (*Conflict of Laws in International Trade*, in Swedish).

Sveriges och EU:s internationella insolvensrätt, Stockholm, 1997 (*Sweden's and EU's Law of International Insolvency*, in Swedish).

Swedish Law in the New Millennium, Stockholm, 2000 (editor).

Komparativ rättskunskap, 2nd ed., Stockholm, 2003 (*Comparative Legal Science*, in Swedish).

Internationellt privaträttsliga rättsfall, 3rd ed., Lund, 2006 (*Private International Law Casebook*, in Swedish).

EU Private International Law : An EC Court Casebook, Groningen, 2006 (together with U. Maunsbach).

Concise Introduction to EU Private International Law, Groningen, 2006.

Svensk internationell privat- och processrätt, 7th ed., Stockholm, 2008 (*Swedish Private International Law*, in Swedish).

"Sweden", *International Encyclopaedia of Laws : Private International Law*, Kluwer, 2008.

Swedish Legal System, Stockholm, 2010 (editor).

Selected Articles in Chronological Order

"Några anteckningar till svensk internationell namnrätt", *Tidskrift för Sveriges Advokatsamfund*, 1977, pp. 43-54.

"Admission of Foreign Tourists and the Law of Nations", *Zeitschrift für ausländisches öffentliches Recht und Völkerrecht*, 1977, pp. 87-106.

"Psykofarmaka och cannabis i internationell rätt", *Tidsskrift for Rettsvitenskap*, 1977, pp. 70-90.

"Erkännande och verkningar i Sverige av i utlandet fastställt faderskap", *Svensk Juristtidning*, 1977, pp. 161-178.

"Något om Helsingforsdokumentets folkrättsliga betydelse", *Svensk Juristtidning*, 1977, pp. 303-311.

"Något om internationellt-privaträttsliga frågor i kyrkobokföringen", *Förvaltningsrättslig Tidskrift*, 1977, pp. 40-53.

"General Principles of Law and the Problem of Lacunae in the Law of Nations", *Nordic Journal of International Law*, 1977, pp. 37-53.

"Some Reflections concerning Unregistered Treaties", *Revue de droit international*, 1977, pp. 114-134.

"Free Movement of Tourists within the E.E.C.?", 11 *Journal of World Trade Law*, 468-475 (1977).

"Restrictions Limiting the Right of Foreigners to Acquire Real Property in Sweden", *Rabels Zeitschrift für ausländisches und internationales Privatrecht*, 1977, pp. 536-548.

"Réflexions sur certaines dispositions juridiques internationales et suédoises concer-nant les infractions en matière de drogue", *Bulletin des stupéfiants*, 1977, No. 3, pp. 1-20 (together with Per Falk).

"Traveller's Cheques and Credit Cards in Private International Law", *Scandinavian Studies in Law* 1977, pp. 23-61.

"Transkei — ett nytt folkrättssubjekt?", *Svensk Juristtidninig*, 1977, pp. 741-745.

"Rättsställning i Sverige av invandrarnas polygamiska äktenskap", *Tidskrift för Sveriges Advokatsamfund*, 1978, pp. 135-142.

"Familjerättsligt underhåll i svensk internationell privaträtt", *Svensk Juristtidning* 1978, pp. 161-186.

"Application of Foreign Rules on Non-Possessory Security Interests in Swedish Private International Law", *Nordic Journal of International Law*, 1978, pp. 14-29.

"Different Economic Systems and Comparative Law", 2 *Comparative Law Yearbook* 89-115 (1978).

"Den svenska internationella arbetsrättens grunder", *Svensk Juristtidning*, 1979, pp. 81-121.

"The International Legal Status of Governing Political Parties in One-Party States", *German Yearbook of International Law*, 1979, pp. 335-351.

"Svensk internationell konkursrätt", *Svensk Juristtidning*, 1980, pp. 321-345.

"Katja of Sweden-målet och svensk internationell konkursrätt", *Svensk Juristtidning* 1980, pp. 710-712.

"Patent och varumärke i den svenska internationella privat- och processrätten", *Nordiskt Immateriellt Rättsskydd*, 1980, pp. 269-286.

"Om svensk exekutionsbehörighet", *Svensk Juristtidning*, 1981, pp. 401-426.

"Obeståndsbegreppet och gäldenärens tillgångar i utlandet", *Svensk Juristtidning*, 1981, pp. 500-518.

"Internationella barnarov ur svensk rätts synvinkel", *Tidskrift, utgiven av Juridiska föreningen i Finland*, 1982, pp. 97-139.

"1980 års EG-konvention om tillämplig lag på kontraktsrättsliga förpliktelser — synpunkter beträffande den svenska inställningen", *Tidsskrift for Rettsvitenskap*, 1982, pp. 1-49.

"Labor Relations in the Swedish Conflict of Laws", *Nordic Journal of International Law*, 1982, pp. 211-222.

"Europarådets konkurskonventionsutkast", *Advokaten*, 1984, pp. 177-183.

"International Bankruptcy Law in Scandinavia", 34 *International and Comparative Law Quarterly* 49-86 (1985).

"The Recognition in Sweden of Money Judgments in Civil and Commercial Matters", *Nordic Journal of International Law*, 1985, pp. 85-87.

"Några internationellt privaträttsliga problem rörande passagerarbefordran med flyg", in *Festskrift till Sveriges Advokatsamfund*, 1987, pp. 145-171.

"Flygbiljettpriserna och EG:s konkurrensrätt", *Svensk Juristtidning*, 1987, pp. 77-94.

"Befinner sig den internationella konkursrätten i konkurs?", *Tidsskrift for Rettsvitenskap* 1987, pp. 361-383.

"Bekvämlighetsflagg och svensk internationell privaträtt", *Lag & Avtal*, 1988, No. 1, pp. 29-31.

"Conflict of Laws in Air Crash Cases: Remarks from a European's Perspective", 54 *Journal of Air Law and Commerce* 303-348 (1988).

"Letters of Comfort i ett internationellt perspektiv", in *Letters of Comfort. Handelsrättslig skriftserie utgiven av Institutionen för handelsrätt vid Lunds universitet*, No. 1, 1989, pp. 9-23.

"Nationality as a Connecting Factor in Swedish Private International Law", in *Liber Memorialis François Laurent*, Brussels, 1989, pp. 679-693.

"Den gemensamma advokatmarknaden i EG", *Advokaten*, 1989, pp. 180-186.

"Marriage in Swedish Private International Law", in U. Blaurock, ed., *Entwicklungen im Recht der Familie und der ausserehelichen Lebensgemeinschaften*, Frankfurt a.M., 1989, pp. 117-129.

"The 'Common Market' for Judgments: The Extension of the E.E.C. Jurisdiction and Enforcement Treaty to Nonmember States", 9 *St. Louis University Public Law Review* 113-129 (1990).

"Samboende utan äktenskap och svensk internationell privaträtt", in *Festskrift till Lars Hjerner*, 1990, pp. 35-61.

"Some Arbitration-Related Problems of Swedish Private

International Law", *Swedish and International Arbitration*, 1990, pp. 70-79.

"Cross-Border Insolvency", in I. F. Fletcher, ed., *Cross-Border Insolvency: Comparative Dimensions*, UK National Committee of Comparative Law, 1990, pp. 109-118 and 175-176.

"Cross-Border Insolvency", *Swedish National Reports to the XIIIth International Congress of Comparative Law*, Uppsala, 1990, pp. 157-169.

"Ein neues schwedisches IPR-Gesetz zum Ehegüterrecht", *IPRax*, 1991, pp. 70-72.

"Intermediaries in Shipping: Choice of Forum and Choice of Law", in K. Grönfors, ed., *Intermediaries in Shipping*, Göteborg, 1991, pp. 205-217.

"Något om EG-reglerna avseende offentlig upphandling", *Förvaltningsrättslig Tidskrift* 1991, pp. 86-96.

"Om lovligheten av i svensk hamn vidtagna fackliga blockader mot främmande fartyg", in *Festskrift till Kurt Grönfors*, Göteborg, 1991, pp. 65-81.

"Något om gränsöverskridande barnkidnappningar", in *Festskrift till Ulla Jacobsson*, Stockholm, 1991, pp. 17-29.

"Luganokonventionen", *Tidsskrift for Rettsvitenskap*, 1991, pp. 387-411.

"Nordisk internationell konsumenträtt", *Nord*, 1992:31.

"Article 6", in A. Eide *et al.*, eds., *The Universal Declaration of Human Rights. A Commentary*, Oslo, 1992, pp. 111-113.

"Trans-Border Abductions of Children: The Swedish Legal View", *Scandinavian Studies in Law*, 1992, pp. 59-75.

"The Lugano Convention and Its Extension: The Swedish Point of View", in E. Jayme, ed., *Ein internationales Zivilverfahrensrecht für Gesamteuropa*, Heidelberg, 1992, pp. 263-271.

"Ordre public och tvingande rättsregler i Haagkonventionerna om internationell privat- och processrätt", *Svensk Juristtidning*, 1993, pp. 308-318.

"Tillämplig lag på handelsagentur", *Juridisk Tidskrift*, 1992-1993, pp. 912-916.

"Islamisk brudpenning (mahr) inför svensk domstol", *Svensk Juristtidning*, 1993, pp. 597-600.

"Custody and Visitation Rights in Swedish Private International Law", in L. Frost, ed., *International Family Law: A Scandinavian Approach*, Århus universitet, 1994, pp. 91-97.

"Den nya skuldsaneringslagens tillämpning i internationella förhållanden", *Juridisk Tidskrift*, 1993-1994, pp. 676-686.

"The Czech-Slovak Customs Union", in *Current International Law Issues. Essays in Honour of J. Sztucki*, 1994, pp. 11-23.

"Marknadsföringslagens tillämplighet i EES-rättslig belysning", *Svensk Juristtidning*, 1994, pp. 277-288.

"Registrerat partnerskap och svensk internationell privaträtt", *Svensk Juristtidning*, 1994, pp. 773-784.

"The Nordic Bankruptcy Convention: A Healthy Sexagenarian?", in *Comparability and Evaluation, Essays in Honour of Dimitra Kokkini-Iatridou*, Dordrecht, 1994, pp. 27-36.

"The Nordic Bankruptcy Convention", in J. S. Ziegel, ed., *Current Developments in International and Comparative Corporate Insolvency Law*, Oxford, 1994, pp. 700-708.

"Application of Public International Law by Swedish Courts", *Nordic Journal of International Law*, 1994, pp. 3-16.

"IPR-Aspekte der schwedischen eingetragenen Partnerschaft für Homosexuelle", *IPRax*, 1995, pp. 56-57.

"Fastighetsmäklare och svensk internationell konsumenträtt", *Svensk Juristtidning*, 1995, pp. 1-6.

"Oskäliga avtalsvillkor i gränsöverskridande konsumentavtal", *Svensk Juristtidning*, 1995, pp. 189-206.

"Kollektiva konsumentintressen i den internationella processrätten", *Juridisk Tidskrift*, 1994-1995, pp. 905-916.

"Swedish Report", in J. J. Fawcett, ed., *Declining Jurisdiction in Private International Law. Reports to the XIVth Congress of the International Academy of Comparative Law*, Oxford, 1995, pp. 371-379.

"What Has Been Done and What Is Proposed: Sweden", 4 *International Insolvency Review (Special Conference Issue)* 72-76 (1995).

"Marriage in Swedish Family Law and Swedish Conflicts of Law", 29 *Family Law Quarterly* 675-684 (1995) (together with Eva Ryrstedt).

"Justice and Cross-Border Consumer Contracts in the Common Market", in U. Bernitz and P. Hallström, eds., *Principles of Justice and the European Union*, Stockholm, 1995, pp. 103-109.

"Om konsten att implementera konsumentavtalsvillkorsdirektivets art. 6 (2)", *Svensk Juristtidning* 1996, pp. 37-41.

"Tillämplighet av avtalslagen 36 § i internationella förhållanden", *Lov og Rett*, 1996, pp. 114-122.

"International Bankruptcy Law in Europe", in B. Dahl and R. Nielsen, eds., *New Directions in Business Law Research*, Copenhagen, 1996, pp. 249-260.

"Trans-Border Abductions of Children: Swedish Report", in N. Lowe and G. Douglas, eds., *Families across Frontiers*, The Hague/Boston/London, 1996, pp. 693-703.

"Klippanmålet och internationell skadeståndsrätt", *Juridisk Tidskrift*, 1996-1997, pp. 782-787.

"Misleading Cross-Border TV Advertising in the EU", in G. Melander, ed., *Modern Issues in European Law: Nordic Perspectives. Essays in Honour of Lennart Pålsson*, Stockholm, 1997, pp. 1-15.

"Den nya EU-konkurskonventionen", in *Festskrift till Stig Strömholm*, Uppsala, 1997, pp. 173-189.

"Injunctions for the Protection of Cross-Border Consumer Interests: Comments on a Proposed E.C. Directive from a Nordic Viewpoint", in *Injunctions for the Protection of Cross-Border Consumer Interests, TemaNord*, 1997:556, pp. 15-30.

"Common Law versus Civil Law in International Development Aid", in *Festskrift til Ole Lando*, Copenhagen, 1997, pp. 69-81.

"Den komparativa rättens betydelse för utbildningen i internationell rätt och EG-rätt", in *Ånd og rett. Festskrift til Birger Stuevold Lassen*, Oslo, 1997, pp. 203-208.

"The EU Bankruptcy Convention", 6 *International Insolvency Review* 114-126 (1997).

"Consumer Interests and the New E.U. Bankruptcy Convention", [1997] *Consumer Law Journal* 141-143.

"Faillites internationales en Europe", in *16ᵉ Congrès de l'Union internationale des huissiers de justice et officiers judiciaires*, Stockholm, 1997, pp. 103-107.

"Svensk behörighet att verkställa förpliktelse som inte avser betalningsskyldighet", *Juridisk Tidskrift*, 1997-1998, pp. 485-488.

"Private International Labour Law", in *International Encyclopedia of Laws, Labour Law (Sweden)*, Suppl. 199, September 1997, Kluwer, 1998, pp. 58-62.

"Gränsöverskridande förtal i Cyberspace", *Svensk Juristtidning*, 1998, pp. 1-15.

"EU-direktivet om förbudsföreläggande för att skydda konsumenternas intressen", *Svensk Juristtidning*, 1998, pp. 533-543.

"Security Interests in International Bankruptcies in Sweden", *Nordic Journal of International Law*, 1998, pp. 289-297.

"Kan en Internethemsida utgöra ett driftställe vid bedömningen av svensk domsrätt och tillämplig lag?", *Svensk Juristtidning*, 1998, pp. 825-836.

"Some Reflections Regarding the New EU Directive on Injunctions for the Protection of Consumers' Interests", [1998] *Consumer Law Journal* 369-375.

"Utländsk konfiskation av upphovsrätt i Sverige", *Juridisk Tidskrift*, 1998-1999, pp. 640-644.

"Svensk yttrandefrihet och erkännande av utländsk förtalsdom", *Juridisk Tidskrift*, 1998-1999, pp. 644-649.

"Jurisdiktions- och lagvalsfrågor på Internet", *Ny Juridik*, 1999, No. 4, pp. 7-26.

"Internationell familjerätt i en internationaliserad värld", *Svensk Juristtidning*, 2000, pp. 299-305.

"Ursprungslands- och effektlandsprincipen i den europeiska kollektiva konsumenträtten", *TemaNord*, 2001:511.

"Cross-border Transactions on the Internet", in G. Hohloch, ed., *Recht und Internet, Arbeiten zur Rechtsvergleichung nr 197*, Baden-Baden, 2001, pp. 59-69.

"Gränsöverskridande marknadsföring via Internet", *Juridisk Tidskrift*, 2000-2001, pp. 621-625.

"Ordre public, internationellt tvingande rättsregler och kringgåendeläran i EG-domstolens praxis rörande internationell privaträtt", *Svensk Juristtidning*, 2001, pp. 329-346.

"Amendment of Swedish Private International Law Regarding Registered Partnerships", *IPRax*, 2001, pp. 353-354.

"Electronic Commerce: Problems of Jurisdiction and Applicable Law", in J. Fejø *et al.*, eds., *Legal Aspects of Electronic Commerce*, Copenhagen, 2001, pp. 75-88.

"Registrerat partnerskap inför EG-domstolen", *Juridisk Tidskrift*, 2001-2002, pp. 97-103.

"Individuella anställningsförhållanden i Sveriges nya internationella privaträtt — en översikt", *Svensk Juristtidning*, 2001, pp. 845-860.

"Chapter 24: Sweden", in R. Potok, ed., *Cross Border Collateral: Legal Risk and the Conflict of Laws*, Butterworths, 2002, pp. 551-567 (together with Dan Hanqvist and Mikael Sedolin).

"Något om lagvalsregler vid pantsättning av dokumentlösa finansiella instrument", *Juridisk Tidskrift*, 2001-2002, pp. 517-528 (together with Lars Afrell).

"Fastställande av avtalsorten vid tillämpning av regeln om kontraktsforum i rättegångsbalkens 10 kap. 4 §", *Juridisk Tidskrift*, 2001-2002, pp. 622-624.

"Internationellt privaträttsliga aspekter av äggdonation och surrogatmoderskap", *Svensk Juristtidning*, 2002, pp. 745-747.

"Internationale Aspekte der schwedischen Gesetzesnovelle über die Adoption von Kindern durch eingetragene Lebenspartner", *IPRax*, 2002, pp. 534-535.

"Amsterdamfördraget och medborgarskapets roll inom den svenska internationella privaträtten", in *Festskrift till Gösta Walin*, Stockholm, 2002, pp. 61-74.

"Om Bryssel/Luganoreglernas tillämpning i marknadsrättsliga mål", *Juridisk Tidskrift*, 2002-2003, pp. 410-416.

"The E.C. Law of International Insolvency", *Revue des affaires européennes*, 2001-2002, pp. 452-459.

"Erkännande och verkställighet av med den europeiska människorättskonventionen oförenlig utländsk dom", *Svensk Juristtidning*, 2003, pp. 18-29.

"Registered Partnerships and EC Law", in K. Boele-Woelki and A. Fuchs, eds., *Legal Recognition of Same-Sex Couples in Europe*, Antwerp-Oxford-New York, 2003, pp. 171-177.

"EG-fördragets direkta inverkan på medlemsstaternas internationella namnrätt: några funderingar kring EG-domstolens Avello-dom", *Svensk Juristtidning*, 2003, pp. 1057-1068.

"Les aperçus de l'évolution des règles de conflits de lois dans les pays nordiques", *Travaux du Comité français de droit international privé, 2000-2003*, Paris, 2004, pp. 195-220.

"Convergence and Divergence between Brussels I and Rome I with Regard to Contracts Regulating Matters of Family Law", in J. Meeusen *et al.*, eds., *Enforcement of International Contracts in the European Union: Convergence and Divergence between Brussels I and Rome I*, Antwerp-Oxford-New York, 2004, pp. 211-223.

"Some Reflections on the Treatment of Dutch Same-Sex Marriages in European and Private International Law", in T. Einhorn and K. Siehr, eds., *International Cooperation through Private International Law. Essays in Memory of Peter E. Nygh*, The Hague, 2004, pp. 25-35.

"EG-rättsliga synpunkter på användning av medborgarskapet som anknytningsmoment i den internationella familjerätten", in M. Holdgaard and A. López-Rodríguez, eds., *Globalisering og familieret*, Copenhagen, 2004, pp. 85-96.

"Den italienska litispendenstorpeden", *Ny Juridik*, 2004, No. 3, pp. 53-62.

"Die Reform des schwedischen IPR zur Vermeidung von Kinder- und Zwangsehen", *IPRax*, 2004, pp. 546-549.

"Private International Law of Registered Partnerships in the Nordic Countries", in *Aspects de droit international privé des partenariats enregistrés en Europe, Publications de l'Institut suisse de droit comparé*, No. 49, 2004, pp. 61-69.

"Marshallöarnas atomansvarighetsdomstol: en följd av bombnedslag i Bikini", in *Festskrift till Hans Ragnemalm*, Lund, 2005, pp. 49-62.

"Användning av allmänt förmögenhetsforum med avseende på papperslösa aktier i svenska aktiebolag", *Juridisk Tidskrift*, 2004-2005, pp. 674-679.

"Jurisdiction and Applicable Law on the Internet", in *Cyberspace 2004: Normative Framework. Acta Universitatis Masarykianae Brunensis Iuridica*, No. 288, Brno, 2005, pp. 37-43.

"The Impact of the E.C. Treaty on the Surnames of Migrating European Citizens", in *Obra homenaje al professor Julio D. González Campos*, Madrid, 2005, Vol. II, pp. 1277-1286.

"Private International Law Aspects of Trans-Border Invasion of Personality Rights by the Media", in A. Beater and S. Habermeier, eds., *Verletzungen von Persönlichkeitsrechten durch die Medien*, Tübingen, 2005, pp. 138-149.

"Is There a Curricular Core for the Transnational Lawyer?", 55 *Journal of Legal Education* 484-487 (2005).

"General Aspects of the Future Regulation", in A. Malatesta, ed., *The Unification of Choice of Law Rules on Torts and Other Non-Contractual Obligations in Europe*, Milan, 2006, pp. 33-44.

"Chronique de jurisprudence suédoise (1996-2004)", *Journal du droit international*, 2006, pp. 719-752 (together with K. Hobér).

"Dead or Alive? — The Status of Missing Disaster Victims in Swedish Substantive and Private International Law", in *Liber Memorialis Petar Sarčević*, Munich, 2006, pp. 25-33.

"Refugees in Swedish Private International Law", in J. Grimheden and R. Ring, eds., *Human Rights Law: From Dissemination to Application. Essays in Honour of Göran Melander*, Leiden/Boston, 2006, pp. 311-320.

"International Development Aid in the Legal Field as a Vehicle for Globalization of Law", in R. Blanpain and B. Flodgren, eds., *Corporate and Employment Perspec-*

tives in a Global Business Environment, Kluwer, 2006, pp. 35-41.

"Web-sites, Establishment and Private International Law", (2006) *King's College Law Journal* 97-104.

"Hotar EU:s nya internationella privat- och processrätt den svenska tryck- och yttrandefriheten?", in *Festskrift till Rune Lavin*, Lund, 2006, pp. 23-32.

"Svensk rättspraxis: internationell privat- och processrätt 2001-2005", *Svensk Juristtidning*, 2006, pp. 601-644.

"Herkunftslandprinzip und Familienrecht", in G. Reichelt, ed., *Das Herkunftslandprinzip im Europäischen Gemeinschaftsrecht*, Vienna, 2006, pp. 63-69.

"Can a Web-site Constitute an Establishment for the Purposes of Jurisdiction and Applicable Law?", in *Cyberspace 2005, Acta Universitatis Masarykianae Brunensis Iuridica*, No. 302, Brno, 2006, pp. 27-33.

"The EC Treaty and the Use of Nationality and Habitual Residence as Connnecting Factors in International Family Law", in J. Meeusen *et al.*, eds., *International Family Law for the European Union*, Antwerp, 2007, pp. 303-317.

"The Brussels/Lugano Lis Pendens Rule and the 'Italian Torpedo'", *Scandinavian Studies in Law*, 2007, pp. 89-97.

"Internet and Private International Law", in R. Polčák *et al.*, *Introduction to ICT Law (Selected Issues)*, Brno, 2007, pp. 21-42.

"Något om den kollisionsrättsliga behandlingen av islamisk morgongåva (mahr)", in *Rett og toleranse. Festskift til Helge Johan Thue*, Oslo, 2007, pp. 175-185.

"Conflict of Laws Regarding Liability Allocation between Insureres in Cases of Double Insurance", in R. Cranston *et al.*, eds., *Commercial Law Challenges in the 21st Century. Jan Hellner in Memoriam*, Stockholm, 2007, pp. 1-10.

"Den nya Rom II-förordningen om tillämplig lag för utomobligatoriska förpliktelser", *Svensk Juristtidning*, 2007, pp. 929-941.

"Den EG-rättsliga ursprungslandsprincipen och svensk internationell sakrätt", in *Vänbok till Axel Adlerceutz*, Lund, 2007, pp. 59-71.

"EG-kommissionens förslag till förordning om tillämplig lag för avtalsförpliktelser", in *Festskrift till Lars Gorton*, Lund, 2007, pp. 47-61.

"Om svenskt äktenskapsförords rättsverkan efter att svensk rätt slutat vara tillämplig på makarnas förmögenhetsförhållanden", *Svensk Juristtidning*, 2008, pp. 122-124.

"Uteslutning av offentlig rätt från Bryssel I-förordningens tillämpningsområde", in *Festskrift till Hans-Heinrich Vogel*, Lund, 2008, pp. 47-59.

"Behandling av miljöskador i EG:s Rom II-förordning", *Juridisk Tidskrift*, 2007-2008, pp. 575-584.

"Foreign Public Law and Article 7 (1) of the Rome Convention: Some Reflections from Sweden", in *Mélanges en l'honneur de Hélène Gaudemet-Tallon*, Paris, 2008, pp. 671-682.

"Nya EG-regler om indrivning av obestridda fordringar och småfordringar på privaträttens område", in *Festskrift till Lars Heuman*, Stockholm, 2008, pp. 89-103.

"Torts in Cyberspace: The Impact of the New Regulation 'Rome II'", *Masaryk University Journal of Law and Technology*, 2008, pp. 1-10.

"Market Economy as a Precondition for Human Rights", in *Metamorfózy práva ve střední Evrope*, Prague-Pilsen, 2008, pp. 81-84.

"Den nya Rom I-förordningen om tillämplig lag för avtalsförpliktelser", *Tidsskrift for Rettsvitenskap*, 2008, pp. 442-465.

"The New EC Rules on Summary Proceedings in Civil and Commercial Matters", *Revue hellénique de droit international*, 2008, pp. 55-69.

"Some Reflections Regarding Environmental Damage and the Rome II Regulation", in *Nuovi Strumenti del diritto internazionale privato. Liber Fausto Pocar*, Milan, 2009, pp. 95-105.

"The EC Treaty and International Family Law" in *Európska únia — právo a skutočnosť. Medzinárodné symposium 6.-7. apríl 2009*, Bratislava, 2009, pp. 7-18.

"Individuella anställningsavtal i den nya Rom I-förordningen", *Europarättslig tidskrift*, 2009, pp. 13-24.

"Efternamns fria rörlighet inom EU", *Juridisk Tidskrift*, 2008-2009, pp. 647-653.

"The Treatment of Environmental Damage in Regulation Rome II", in J. Ahern and W. Binchy, eds., *The Rome II Regulation on the Law Applicable to Non-Contractual Obligations*, Leiden, 2009, pp. 219-230.

"Domain Names as Jurisdiction-Creating Property in Sweden", *Masaryk University Journal of Law and Technology*, 2009, pp. 175-182 (together with Ulf Maunsbach).

"Private International Law Aspects of the Introduction of Same-Sex Marriages in Sweden", *Nordic Journal of International Law*, 2009, pp. 253-261.

"Contracts in Cyberspace and the New Regulation 'Rome I'",
Masaryk University Journal of Law and Technology,
2009, pp. 219-225.

"Cooperation between Legal Systems: The Nordic Model",
in E. Cashin Ritaine, ed., *Legal Engineering and Comparative Law. Rapports du Colloque du 25ᵉ anniversaire de
l'Institut suisse de droit comparé du 29 août 2008 à
Lausanne*, Vol. 2, Schulthess, 2009, pp. 59-68.

"The Rome I Regulation on the Law Applicable to
Contractual Obligations and the Choice of Law by the
Parties", *Nederlands Internationaal Privaatrecht*, 2009,
pp. 407-410.

"Promoting Market Economy and Human Rights by Means
of Development Assistance in the Field of Law", in
P. Bergling *et al.*, eds., *Rule of Law Promotion: Global
Perspectives, Local Applications*, Uppsala, 2009, pp. 317-
324.

"EG-domstolens och svensk rättspraxis i internationell
privat- och processrätt 2006-2008", *Svensk Juristtidning*,
2010, pp. 33-77.

"Private International Law", in M. Bogdan, ed., *Swedish
Legal System*, Stockholm, 2010, pp. 509-529.

"Some Reflections on Contracts and Torts in Cyberspace in
View of Regulations Rome I and Rome II", in K. Boele-
Woelki *et al.*, eds., *Convergence and Divergence in
Private International Law. Liber Amicorum Kurt Siehr*,
Zurich, 2010, pp. 375-387.

"Cyberspace Pirates Walk the Plank: Some Comments on
the Swedish Judgment in the Pirate Bay Case", *Masaryk
University Journal of Law and Technology*, 2010, pp. 113-
126.

"Gränsöverskridande personlighetskränkningar och svensk
internationell privaträtt", in *Festskrift till Gertrud
Lennander*, Stockholm, 2010, pp. 27-37.

"Development Assistance in the Field of Legal Education",
in M. Hiscock and W. van Caenegem, eds., *The Interna-
tionalisation of Law. Legislating, Decision-Making,
Practice and Education*, Elgar, Cheltenham, 2010,
pp. 105-116.

"EG/EU-domstolens praxis på den internationella insolven-
srättens område", in *Festskrift till Torkel Gregow*,
Norstedts Juridik, 2010, pp. 27-45.

PUBLICATIONS
OF THE HAGUE ACADEMY
OF INTERNATIONAL LAW

COLLECTED COURSES

Since 1923 the top names in international law have taught at the Hague Academy of International Law. All the volumes of the *Collected Courses* which have been published since 1923 are available, as, since the very first volume, they are reprinted regularly in their original format. There is a complete and detailed catalogue.

Since 2008, certain courses have been the subject of a pocketbook edition (see below).

In addition, the total collection now exists in electronic form. All works already published have been put "on line" and can be consulted under one of the proposed subscription methods, which offer a range of tariffs and possibilities.

WORKSHOPS

The Academy publishes the discussions from the Workshops which it organizes. The latest title of the Workshops already published is as follows : *Topicality of the 1907 Hague Conference, the Second Peace Conference* (2007).

CENTRE FOR STUDIES AND RESEARCH

The scientific works of the Centre for Studies and Research in International Law and International Relations of the Hague Academy of International Law, the subjects of which are chosen by the Curatorium of the Academy, have been published, since the Centre's 1985 session, in a publication in which the Directors of Studies reported on the state of research of the Centre under their direction. This series has been discontinued and the title of the latest booklet published is as follows: *Rules and Institutions of International Humanitarian Law Put to the Test of Recent Armed Conflicts*. Nevertheless, when the work of the Centre has been of particular interest and originality, the reports of the Directors of Studies together with the articles by the researchers form the subject of a collection published in the series The Law Books of the Academy. (See below.)

THE LAW BOOKS OF THE ACADEMY

(By chronological order of publication)

Dupuy, R.-J. (dir. publ./ed.) : Manuel sur les organisations internationales/A Handbook on International Organizations. (1988, 714 pages.)

(ISBN 978-90-247-3658-4)

Dupuy, R.-J., and D. Vignes (eds.) : A Handbook on the New Law of the Sea. (2 volumes)
Volume 1 : 1991, 900 pages.   (ISBN 978-0-7923-0924-3)
Volume 2 : 1991, 882 pages.   (ISBN 978-0-7923-1063-1)

Carreau, D., et/and M. N. Shaw (dir. publ./eds.) : La dette extérieure/The External Debt. (1995, 818 pages.)
(ISBN 978-90-411-0083-2)

Dupuy, R.-J. (dir. publ./ed.): Manuel sur les organisations internationales/A Handbook on International Organizations. (2ᵉ éd./2nd ed., 1998, 1008 pages.)
(ISBN 978-90-411-1119-7)

Eisemann, P. M., et/and M. Koskenniemi (dir. publ./eds.): La succession d'Etats : la codification à l'épreuve des faits/State Succession : Codification Tested against the Facts. (2000, 1058 pages.)

(ISBN 978-90-411-1392-4)

Caron, D. D., et/and Ch. Leben (dir. publ./eds.): Les aspects internationaux des catastrophes naturelles et industrielles/ The International Aspects of Natural and Industrial Catastrophes. (2001, 912 pages.)

(ISBN 978-90-411-1485-3)

Bothe, M., et/and P. H. Sands (dir. publ./eds.) : La politique de l'environnement. De la réglementation aux instruments économiques/Environmental Policy. From Regulation to Economic Instruments. (2002, 958 pages.)
(ISBN 978-90-411-1604-8)

Forlati Picchio, L., et/and L.-A. Sicilianos (dir. publ./eds.) : Les sanctions économiques en droit international/Economic Sanctions in International Law. (2004, 912 pages.)
(ISBN 978-90-04-13701-1)

Boisson de Chazournes, L. et/and S. M. A. Salman (dir. publ./eds.) : Les ressources en eau et le droit international/Water Resources and International Law. (2005, 848 pages.)

(ISBN 978-90-04-13702-8)

Mahiou, A., et/and F. Snyder (dir. publ.) : La sécurité alimentaire/Food Security and Food Safety. (2006, 992 pages.)
(ISBN 978-90-04-14543-6)

Kahn, Ph., et/and T. W. Wälde (dir. publ./eds.) : Les aspects nouveaux du droit des investissements internationaux/ New Aspects of International Investment Law. (2007, 1072 pages.)

(ISBN 978-90-04-15372-1)

Glennon, M. J., et/and S. Sur (dir. publ./eds.) : Terrorisme et droit international/Terrorism and International Law. (2008, 864 pages.)

(ISBN 978-90-04-16107-8)

Nafziger, J. A. R., et/and T. Scovazzi (dir. publ./eds.) : Le patrimoine culturel de l'humanité/The Cultural Heritage of Mankind. (2008, 1168 pages.)
(ISBN 978-90-04-16106-1)

Momtaz, D., et/and M. J. Matheson (dir. publ./eds.) : Les règles et institutions du droit international humanitaire à l'épreuve des conflits armés récents/Rules and Institutions of International Humanitarian Law Put to the Test of Recent Armed Conflicts. (2010, 1072 pages.)
(Relié/HB : ISBN 978-90-04-17283-8)
(Broché/PB : ISBN 978-90-04-18697-2)

Maljean-Dubois, S., et/and L. Rajamani (dir. publ./eds.) : La mise en œuvre du droit international de l'environnement/Implementation of International Environmental Law. (2011, 864 pages.)
(Relié/HB : ISBN 978-90-04-20892-6)
(Broché/PB : ISBN 978-90-04-20916-9)

POCKETBOOKS OF THE ACADEMY

(By chronological order of publication)

Gaillard, E. : Aspects philosophiques du droit de l'arbitrage international, 2008, 252 pages.
(ISBN 978-90-04-17148-0)

Schrijver, N. : The Evolution of Sustainable Development in International Law : Inception, Meaning and Status, 2008, 276 pages.
(ISBN 978-90-04-17407-8)

Moura Vicente, D. : La propriété intellectuelle en droit international privé, 2009, 516 pages.
(ISBN 978-90-04-17907-3)

Decaux, E. : Les formes contemporaines de l'esclavage, 2009, 264 pages.
(ISBN 978-90-04-17908-0)

McLachlan, C. : *Lis Pendens* in International Litigation, 2009, 492 pages.
(ISBN 978-90-04-17909-7)

Carbone, S. M. : Conflits de lois en droit maritime, 2010, 312 pages.
(ISBN 978-90-04-18688-0)

Boele-Woelki, K. : Unifying and Harmonizing Substantive Law and the Role of Conflict of Laws, 2010, 288 pages.
(ISBN 978-90-04-18683-5)

Onuma, Y. : A Transcivilizational Perspective in International Law, 2010, 492 pages.
(ISBN 978-90-04-18689-7)

Bucher, A. : La dimension sociale du droit international privé. Cours général, 2011, 552 pages.
(ISBN 978-90-04-20917-6)

Thürer, D. : International Humanitarian Law : Theory, Practice, Context, 2011, 504 pages.
(ISBN 978-90-04-17910-3)

Alvarez, J. : The Public International Law Regime Governing International Investment, 2011, 504 pages.
(ISBN 978-90-04-18682-8)

Wang, G.: Radiating Impact of WTO on Its Members' Legal System: The Chinese Perspective, 2011, 384 pages.
(ISBN 978-90-04-21854-3)

Bogdan, M.: Private International Law as Component of the Law of the Forum. General Course, 2012, 360 pages.
(ISBN 978-90-04-22634-0)

Printed in December 2011
by Triangle Bleu,
59600 Maubeuge (France)

Setting : R. Mirland,
59870 Warlaing (France)